FINISHING STRONG GOD'S WAY

KEN DOCTOR

Acknowledgements

I want to thank my wife, Donna, for being an encourager throughout the process of writing this book. She has challenged me in my content along the way. There were times when I know that she was giving up doing things with me because I was writing. She has been a real inspiration along the way.

I appreciate those who proofread my book, Sally Burger, my former secretary; Phyllis Hogerwerf, a former teacher on my staff; Angela Bacon Grimm, a former student and author; Donna Doctor; and my pastor, Merlyn Jones. Your time and efforts are much appreciated.

I am thankful for those who prayed for me while God was teaching me some lessons which resulted in the writing of this book. Seven years have passed while I worked on this book, mostly during the winter months that we spent in Arizona.

Recently, we received the report that I have cancer in between my bile duct, intestines, and pancreas, and my heart is not strong enough to have the Whipple operation, which would be the recommended cure for this cancer. Radiation and chemotherapy, which are recommended for me, will only help to prolong life maybe up to a year or more with no quality of life.

My life, as your life, is in God's hand. He is the great physician. He controls all things and we all know that God has an appointed time for each of us to die. I thank God that when absent from the body we will be present with God.

Dedication

I am dedicating my book to two special ladies in my life, my mother, Johanna, who went to Heaven at the age of ninety-seven in February 2014 and my mother-in-law, Jean Roost, who went to Heaven at the age of ninety in June 2015.

Both of them were Christians and both had a testimony of their faith with their families, their church and their community. Both were prayer warriors.

They both went through the Great Depression and they both at one time were a housewife of a farmer. Hard work was a big part of their lives.

My mother was a quiet leader. When she went forward in an evangelistic meeting to be saved, my sister and I went forward also. A couple days later my dad accepted the Lord as his personal Savior at home. She showed unconditional love to her children.

My mother-in-law (Donna's mother) was very friendly to everyone she met. She was both a Martha and a Mary. She was a Martha because she loved to cook and was always using her hands to help or make something up to the day she passed away. She was always sewing, knitting, and crocheting. She enjoyed giving things away that she had made. She was a Mary in that she was a faithful student of God's Word.

Both were a spiritual testimony to me and are missed very much. It is a joy to know that someday we will see them again in Heaven. These two women were an example of how to "Finish Strong God's Way."

Table of Contents

Introduction

"*For what is your life? It is even a vapor that appears for a little time and then vanishes away*" (James 4:14). How the years fly by, and before we know it, we only have a short time remaining. It all happened to me as I was turning seventy. It became a life-changing experience for me when I came to the realization that God had spared my life when I had just turned seventy. It has been through this almost-death experience that God has given me a desire to make sure that I am going to finish the race strong, and to help others make sure that they are finishing the race strong and doing it God's way for the purpose of bringing glory to Him.

As children, most of us put little thought into what would happen to us physically when we began to reach our senior years. When we made our wedding vows and stated, "For better or worse," we took little thought of those physical challenges that would come our way. But they do come, to some sooner and others later.

My first major physical challenge came in my fifties when I called my doctor to tell him I was having chest pains. He told me to be in his office within an hour. The left artery of my heart was 97 percent blocked. Angioplasty procedure was done, and with a change of diet and a lot of running, things went along fine with my heart. My second physical challenge in my fifties was prostate cancer. I had to have my prostate removed, and thankfully, the cancer was contained in the prostate. I sailed through my sixties without any physical situations.

My third and fourth physical challenges occurred right after I turned seventy. My wife, Donna and I had just arrived back to our home in southwest Michigan after spending the winter months in Tucson, Arizona. I came home with a bad cough and immediately went to the doctor's office. There was some concern that I might have picked up "valley fever." An x-ray and a test were ordered to find out if I had valley fever. The test came back and indicated that I did not have valley fever, but the x-ray showed a growth on the top of my right kidney.

Our Christian PA told Donna and me, "God sometimes gives us illnesses to help find diseases." And indeed we could see how true this was for me. I was immediately referred to an urologist. I can still hear the words ringing in my ears from the doctor saying, "Ken, I am sure the large tumor that is attached to your right kidney is cancerous, and the kidney will have to be removed."

Many emotions quickly flooded my mind. What if the cancer had spread to other parts of my body? Then I was told it would be six weeks before the operation would take place and I was not to play golf. The waiting gave me a lot of time to think about "what if." Waiting isn't one of my virtues.

The operation took place and the oncologist/urologist/surgeon reported to my family that the operation was successful and the cancer had not spread and in three to four days I would be out of the hospital.

On the day after surgery, I was not responding like I should have. I was unaware that a blood clot had gone into my heart because I had had an epidural to ease the pain of the kidney removal and was therefore not conscious of any chest pain. My heart monitor had been removed after the operation because it kept beeping.

Mid-morning three nurses had entered my room, ostensibly to care for my post-surgical needs. However, two of the nurses were fully engaged in quite a different situation taking place. They had turned on the television upon entering the room and with eyes fixed on it; they forgot everything except for the drama unfolding on the screen. While attempting to land, a medical helicopter had crashed onto the roof of another hospital, ten blocks away, in the city and quickly burst into flames. Emergency sirens wailed, smoke engulfed the crash site, and I was all but forgotten. Yet one nurse remained faithful to her calling, and as she worked at my bedside, she realized I was the victim of a major heart attack. After checking my heart, she ordered an EKG, and once the procedure was completed the nurse told Donna that I was being moved; someone would pack up all of our things, and she was to follow as they carted me away.

Due to the helicopter crash, all cardiologists except for one were in lockdown at the other hospital. The one cardiologist who was available to take care of the blood clot, immediately and successfully opened up the artery and inserted a stent. The doctor told my family that the heart attack had been going on for ten to twelve hours and that each hour into a heart attack, 10 percent of the heart is usually destroyed. The doctor did not give much hope for me.

I was immediately taken to ICU. By that time many family members had arrived to be with Donna. I will share more of the five day stay in ICU later.

Recovery was very slow. During one of those days in my long twenty-one-day stay in the hospital, I told Donna that I was somewhat depressed. As a Christian I was not sure that I had a right to be depressed. As I lay on my bed, I began to realize that God was trying to teach me some lessons through my circumstances. I asked Donna for some paper and during the next days I began to write down lessons that I thought God was trying to teach me. I have never felt closer to God than I did during this experience and I am sure now, that it was because there were a lot of people praying for me.

This book is the result of eleven lessons that God was teaching me. I realized that if God had taken me home at that time, I would not have finished the Christian race strong. This book is the result of looking at areas that the Holy Spirit has drawn my thoughts toward; those things that would help me strengthen my Christian walk with the purpose of finishing the race strong God's way.

Throughout the pages of this book you will read the lessons that God was teaching me. Each chapter in this book is an area that has been brought to my mind that needs to be strengthened, appreciated, and magnified in my life. May the pages of this book help you to run the Christian race a little stronger with the goal of "Finishing Strong God's Way"!

Part I

Preparing to Run the Christian Race

Chapter I

Finishing Strong

It is God's desire that we finish our Christian journey strong. If we are going to finish strong God's way, we need to make sure that the Word of God is our guide. We see this as Paul writes in Philippians 3:12-14.

> "Not that we have already attained, or am already perfected; but I press on, that I may lay hold of that for which Christ Jesus has also laid hold of me. Brethren, I do not count myself to have apprehended; but one thing I do, forgetting those things which are behind and reaching forward to those things which are ahead, I press toward the goal for the prize of the upward call of God in Christ Jesus"

Paul is using the analogy of a runner to show the Christian's spiritual growth. As believers, we have not reached the goal of Christlikeness. Paul had a clearly defined goal. (1) Paul knew what his goal was and he pursued it with all the gusto he had. He has come to the end of his race and he can say, *"I have fought the good fight, I have finished the race, I have kept the faith"* (2 Timothy 4:7). If you and I are to reach a goal, we need to know what that goal is. God has a path that He wants each of us to follow. It is a path on which He has promised to be our guide—a path that will lead us to be a testimony to a dark world and a path that will bring glory to His name.

As Christians we are like the runner in a race; the runner must continue to the finish line. We need to rely on God for strength when we become weak.

Runners who are running in a cross country race need to stay within the course that is laid out for them. A course is marked off with flags. Runners cannot choose to cut corners in order to shorten the race. They need to run the race that is marked out for them. We have a manual to follow, the Bible, which tells us how we are to run the Christian race.

"The Amazing Race," a TV show, features several pairs of racers competing against other teams as they travel throughout the world. Each week the last pair to complete the race might be disqualified from running the remainder of the race and if they are in the non-elimination portion of the race, they get another chance to compete with an additional challenge. That is the way it is for some of us who have faced challenges in our lives.

During the race there are clues and instructions to follow. When the racers don't follow instructions they have to go back and complete a task over again and do it correctly. It is the same in the Christian race. When we sin–when we don't follow the manual, the Bible–we are disqualified until the sin is confessed. Then we can get back in the race that God has marked out for us.

Think of your race (your Christian life) as a long distance marathon you are running across the United States from the East to the West Coast. Let's look at your life as a three thousand mile marathon. There can be a lot of distractions on the way. You run in all kinds of weather. Some of it is uphill and some through the valleys. It is the same in the Christian's life. You can easily get your eyes off your goal and think that another person's race is easier than your own. It should be the desire of every believer to keep his or her eyes on the goal. Heaven is the goal and you want to make sure that you finish the race strong as you cross the line into Heaven.

The success we have in our Christian life is not measured by how fast we sprint away from the starting line. Victory only comes when we have crossed the finish line. Often you will see a runner start out fast in a race and slow down going across the finish line. There are those who never cross the finish line into Heaven. *"Now the Spirit expressly says that in the latter times some shall depart from the faith, giving heed to deceiving spirits, and doctrines of demons..."* (1 Timothy 4:1).

There are those who we hear or read about who were serving the Lord but who have abandoned the faith. *"How the mighty have fallen"* (2 Samuel 1:19)! Moses faltered, not in his faith but in his conduct. (2) We need to remember, *"Let him that thinks he stands take heed lest he fall"* (1 Corinthians 10:12).

We are allowed to spend an average time on earth of 70-80 years. From the day we accept Christ as our personal Savior we are in a long-distance race, with the goal of crossing the finish line still upright and still going forward. If you have a chance to reflect back on your life on your deathbed, will you be able to say with joy and with confidence that you are finishing strong? There is a need to have a mindset that you are going to finish strong. You cannot be passive; you have to be determined. Serving the Lord is imperative. In any ministry that the Lord gives you, focus on doing your very best in that ministry and pursue it with all your energy. Put aside those things that will keep you from doing your best. Note how Paul finishes strong in 2 Timothy 4:6-8,

"For I am already being poured out as a drink offering, and the time of my departure is at hand. I have fought the good fight, I have finished the race, I have kept the faith. Finally, there is laid up for me the crown of righteousness, which the Lord, the righteous Judge, will give to me on that Day, and not to me only but also to all who have loved His appearing."

Paul is writing here shortly before the decree of Roman Emperor Nero for Paul's execution. Paul for thirty years has traveled, preached, worked and witnessed throughout the Mediterranean world. Paul was blessed and cursed, attacked and assisted, hated and helped. Paul lived an eventful life as he endured imprisonment and awaited his execution writing this passage. In verse six he uses the metaphors in telling us about the hardship of the present. (3)

Paul sees himself as a "drink offering" about to be poured out. It means that Paul's death was imminent. In the Old Testament sacrificial system, the drink offering was the final offering that was prescribed for the people of Israel. (4) Paul is saying that his life is an offering poured out for the Lord Jesus Christ. Paul has spent his life under the lordship of Christ. Paul lived his life as *"...a living sacrifice, holy, acceptable to God...,"* as he wrote in Romans 12:1. Paul is laying down his life for the One who gave His life for him. He had been a living sacrifice, serving the Lord since the day he was saved. Paul knew that the Roman authorities were taking his life, but he would die living his life for the Lord.

In verse six, Paul was looking at his present hardship, that of facing death. Then in verse seven he looks back on his life; the past thirty years of faithful service to his Lord. He compares his life and ministry to that of a long-distance runner who competed honorably in the ancient Olympic Games. *"I have fought the good fight."* The word "fight" gives a picture of an athlete coming off the field after giving it his very best. Paul is honestly saying that he gave his all for Christ. *"I have run the race."* He had given it his best; now Paul sees himself as crossing the finish line. Running a long-distance race can be easy at first, but it becomes much harder to finish a long-distance race, and even harder to finish strong. The Christian life can be compared to a long-distance race, a marathon. Paul is challenging us to run the race well, keep pace and stay focused until we cross the finish line. (5) In verse seven the apostle Paul is looking to the future, and he writes about the hope he has for the future. *"Finally, there is laid up for me the crown of righteousness, which the Lord, the righteous Judge, will give to me on that Day, and not to me only but also to all who have loved His appearing"* (II Timothy 4:8).

The winning athlete in the ancient Olympic Games was crowned, which was the greatest honor that could come to an athlete. That crown only lasted a few days before it withered. Paul knew that there is a crown for him that will never fade: a crown of righteousness, which God will be rewarding to those who are faithful and obedient to His Son.

"*I have kept the faith.*" Taking this in context of the ancient Olympic Games, Paul is telling the reader that he has run the race according to the rules. History tells us that the early Greek and Roman athletes took a solemn oath before the games, pledging that they would compete honestly and honorably. Paul is affirming that his vows have been kept. These were vows that he made to his Lord. Paul is telling us that he has kept Christ uppermost in his mind and his heart. His goal during his thirty-year marathon had been to be obedient to Christ's call. His faith was tested, but he had grown stronger. Paul's faith in the Lord Jesus was able to carry him through thick and thin. As the Lord's grace was sufficient for Paul, it also is sufficient for our every need! (6)

"*...Looking unto Jesus, the author and finisher of our faith...*" (Hebrews 12:2) You need to fix your eyes on Jesus. If you lose focus on Him, you have lost focus completely. Jesus understands what it means to finish strong. He had thirty quiet years, then three and one-half years of finishing strong. John the Baptist had about thirty years of preparation, then perhaps about one year of very fruitful ministry until his death. He finished strong!

"*...not as pleasing men, but God...*" (1 Thessalonians 2:4) Our goal should not be to be applauded by man. Let's take heed that we do not fall. We need to make sure that our eyes are on our goal, and we need to run the course that God has for us. The purpose is to please God and bring glory to Him.

"*...one thing I do...*" (Philippians 3:13) Paul simplifies the whole of sanctification to the simple and clear goal of **one thing**, and that was Christlikeness. Paul's goal was Christlikeness now and to continue to be more Christlike until he finished his course. He makes it clear that he had a definite purpose in his life. If you are going to be successful, you need to continually have wedged in your mind the goal that you are pursuing. When Donna and I travel to Tucson, Arizona, from southwest Michigan to spend the winter months, we have our MapQuest directions, directions from a friend who has traveled the same route many times, and our own atlas. More recently, we also have a GPS to help guide us. We pace ourselves so we can make the 1,900-mile trip in three days. We have a plan and a purpose.

Many fail because they do not know where they are going. Can you say as Paul did, "*This one thing I do?*" Paul knew what he was working toward. Paul's race was not easy. He was shipwrecked, spent many years in prison, was stoned, and experienced much more. His running track was rough, but he never took his eyes off his goal. Can you define clearly what that "**one thing**" is? You look at some people's lives, and they appear to be going in ten different directions at the same time. Those outside the Christian faith display confusion. Some have material goals. Evolutionists do not believe that God is the creator of everything. They have no Heaven to look forward to, which gives them little purpose in life. Many do not have any purpose in life.

The Bible does not send us such contradictory signals. God has given each of us a purpose. If we fail to fulfill the purpose God has given us, our lives will end in tragic failure. Paul makes it clear that he not only had a purpose, but a single purpose: **"this one thing I do**." We need to utilize our personality, our resources, and the faculties of our life into a single purpose. Having done some bow hunting, I know that everything has to work together in harmony if the archer is going to be successful. The bow has to work properly; the arrows, the feathers, the string, the arm and the eye of the archer focused on one purpose: to have the head of the arrow drive into the heart of the target. A basketball team has to have a single goal, which is to win the ball game. They need to work together as a team, each player carrying out his or her responsibility.

Singleness of purpose is a characteristic of many great men such as Martin Luther, John Calvin and the apostle Paul. They all directed their energy and talent into one defined direction: to love God with all their heart, soul and strength. Their goal was to serve Him with all their talents and energy.

The course that God has laid out for us may not be easy, but like Paul we must *"**press toward the mark**."* Our hearts need to be right with God. We need to be studying His Word, and we need to be asking Him each day to help us in our race. Likewise, there is a need to rely on the Lord to give us the drive and the desire to accomplish great things for Him.

There is a need for more than a single purpose; there needs to be a right purpose. Paul wrote, *"**This one thing I do**: I press on toward the high calling of God."* Paul's single purpose was to follow the call of God. He was reaching to become more Christlike. We also need to utilize all of our energy to become more Christlike. *"...**the upward call of God**..."* (Philippians 3:14) When we cross the finish line and cross over into Heaven and into His presence, it will be the moment of rejoicing–a time that we will receive a reward, which we will in return place at His feet. May God give us the grace to have an understanding of what our goal is, to put behind us everything that would keep us from obtaining that goal and to press forward with all the vigor that He has given us. When a baseball pitcher comes into a baseball game in the ninth inning for the purpose of winning the ball game, he is called a "closer." There is a spiritual lesson that we can learn from a baseball closer. God wants us to finish the ninth inning of our lives strong.

As a Christian, closing well is imperative. The Bible gives us numerous portrayals of human successes and failures. It is one of the important aspects that make the Bible unique and real. We can learn from the success and failure of biblical characters. Our churches today are in need of genuine senior Christians "finishing strong", as an example to the younger generation.

When our lives are finished on earth and we cross over the finish line into Heaven, the words that we are going to want to hear are, "Well done my good and faithful servant." It should be the desire of all Christians to seek to fulfill God's plan for their lives, with all the gusto they have, for the purpose of bringing glory to Him.

May God guide you and bless you on your journey. Keep pressing on!

Lesson One

Finding Comfort from God's Word

I was not aware of how bad things really were for me for several days after my heart attack. It was the twelfth day into my stay in the hospital when I became cognizant something serious was going on. That morning I woke up thinking that I was going to die. I had a distinct pain in my upper chest area and I had shortness of breath. Several days prior I started eating light food and the next three days had very little soft food intake. Ever since I had started eating food, I coughed up phlegm day and night and was getting very little sleep. There were a few times I lost my intake completely. It was five day later that they finally decided I was aspirating which meant that my food was going into my lungs and not into my stomach. My epiglottis was not closing properly, and then they decided that they would take all food and liquids from me. They were still giving me some liquids intravenously. However, it was not enough because my month became very dry and I thought I was going to die.

It was on the second day without any food and little food prior to that day that I thought I was going to die. First thing in the morning, they wanted me to leave the room for a test. I was able to walk the ten steps to a bed cart that took me away. When I returned to my room I could hardly make it back to my bed. I told Donna that I did not have the energy to get out of bed again until I had something to eat. My body seemed to be shutting down.

It was during the same time that I was being treated for pneumonia. I also had a blood clot go into my left arm, and they thought one had gone into my lungs. With all these complications going on, I really thought that I was going to Heaven.

All through that day a verse of Scripture kept coming to my mind. I knew the verse was from Psalm 23, but I wasn't sure which verse. It was verse 4 *"Yea, though I walk through the valley of the shadow of death, I will fear no evil: for You are with me; Your rod and Your staff, they comfort me."* I kept quoting this verse all day. This verse gave me comfort and peace throughout the day. I believe that this verse was brought to my attention and gave me peace because people were praying for me.

Somewhere back in my Christian walk I apparently had memorized this verse but had forgotten that I had memorized it. This example points out that knowing God's Word can be a great comfort to us. What a joy to know that you are child of the King of kings.

Chapter II

Knowing that you are a Bible Believing Christian

If you are going to finish strong God's way, you have to be a born again Christian first. So let's make sure that we are squared away on this issue.

The question is often asked, "Why do I need to be saved?" To answer this question we need to go back to the beginning of time when God created Adam and Eve to have intimate and sweet fellowship with them, the crown of His creation. This fellowship was lost when Adam and Eve disobeyed God's commandment in the Garden of Eden. When they sinned, they were expelled from the garden and as such denied the loving relationship that God had desired to have with them. "*And the woman said to the serpent, 'We may eat the fruit of the trees of the garden; but of the fruit of the tree which is in the midst of the garden, God has said 'You shall not eat it, nor shall you touch it, lest you die'*" (Genesis 3:2). Adam and Eve did eat the forbidden fruit. And because they ate of it, their new sinful nature made them unfit to linger in the presence of God. They were expelled from the garden and denied the loving relationship that God had desired to have with them. Because Adam and Eve sinned in the Garden, all mankind since that time is born with a sinful nature, a separation from God.

Man was created to have fellowship with God, but sin keeps God from having that fellowship with man. God is holy and cannot look at sin. God sent His Son Jesus to provide restoration for man with God. Jesus did this by giving His life, by shedding His blood. There was no other way to eradicate the effect of sin except by the blood. "*...without shedding of blood there is no remission*" (Hebrews 9:22). God knew that man would fall; therefore, he provided a means of reconciliation for man.

There is no more important question that you can ask yourself than the question, "Am I truly a Bible-believing Christian?" The terms "born again," "Christian" and "saved" are freely used today and may not mean the same thing to everybody. When we refer to being a Bible believing Christian, we are talking about one who believes in the Lord Jesus Christ as his or her Savior and Lord. It is those who know that when death takes them from this life, they will spend eternity in Heaven. To know that you are going to spend eternity in Heaven, you have to have accepted the Lord Jesus Christ as your personal Savior and Lord of your life. *"For by grace you have been saved through faith, and that not of yourselves; it is the gift of God, not of works, lest anyone should boast"* (Ephesians 2:8-9). Note that we are saved by the grace of God; it is a gift that we have to accept by faith. God's gift of salvation is something that we cannot work for, and don't deserve, but it is a love gift that we have to accept. *"For God so loved the world that He gave His only begotten Son, that whoever believes in Him should not perish but have everlasting life"* (John 3:16). God's gift of salvation is for all who will believe that God gave His Son to die on the cross for our sins, and that He rose from the dead and is now back in Heaven.

"For all have sinned and fall short of the glory of God" (Romans 3:23). It doesn't matter if it is a big sin like murder or a small sin like lying. In God's eyes, all sin is sin. Murder seems to us to be worse than hatred because of the earthy consequences of murder. All sins make us sinners, and they separate us from God. Remember, because Adam and Eve sinned, we are all born with a sinful nature.

"And as it is appointed for men to die once, but after this the judgment" (Hebrews 9:27). Because we are born sinners, we are condemned to death. It means that we are going to spend eternity in Hell if we do not accept the gift of God. *"For there is one God and one Mediator between God and men, the Man Christ Jesus, who gave Himself a ransom for all…"* (1Timothy 2:5-6). Jesus, who is both God and man, is the only one in the whole universe who can be our mediator. He can stand between God and man and bring us together again.

"For the wages of sin is death, but the gift of God is eternal life in Christ Jesus our Lord" (Romans 6:23). Jesus had to shed His blood and die on the cross for us. *"…without shedding of blood there is no remission"* (Hebrews 9:22). You might be asking, "Why does forgiveness (remission) require the shedding of blood?" Blood is a symbol of life. It is blood that keeps us alive. By Jesus shedding his blood, He gave his life for our sins so that we would not have to experience spiritual death, which would be eternal separation from God. *"But God demonstrates His own love toward us, in that while we were still sinners, Christ died for us"* (Romans 5:8). He died as our substitute: He died in our place. God laid our sins upon Jesus.

God wants us to repent. *"…now commands all men everywhere to repent"* (Acts 17:30). We need to acknowledge (believe) Him, that He is the one who bore our sin, died in our place, and was buried and whom God resurrected.

"But as many as received Him, to them He gave the right to become children of God, to those who believe in His name" (John 1:12). When you ask

Jesus Christ to be Savior of your life you are reborn spiritually, receiving new life from God.

> *"That if you confess with your mouth the Lord Jesus and believe in your heart that God has raised Him from the dead, you will be saved. For with heart one believes unto righteousness, and with the mouth confession is made unto salvation. For 'whoever calls on the name of the LORD shall be saved'"* (Romans 10:9-10, 13).

The word "confess" means more than simple acknowledgment that He is God and Lord of the universe, because even demons acknowledge that to be true (James 2:19). It is the deep personal conviction, without reservation, that Jesus is your master. It includes repenting of your sins, trusting Jesus for your salvation, and submitting to Him as your Lord. It is believing in your heart, not just in your mind, that God has raised Him from the dead. The word "confession" means basically that of being in "agreement with someone." When you "confess" Jesus as Lord, you agree with the Father's declaration that Jesus is your Savior and Lord.

If you want to spend eternity in Heaven, you have to believe that Jesus died as your substitute on the cross. You need to believe that He shed His blood for the remission of your sins, and acknowledge in your heart that He did this for you. You can have eternal life with Him by asking Him to become your personal Savior. Salvation is just a simple process of confessing and believing. By praying the following prayer you can become a born again Christian: "Father, I know that I have sinned against You, and my sins have separated me from You. Thank you for dying on the cross for me. Please forgive my sins and failures of my past. I believe that Your Son; Jesus Christ died for my sins, was resurrected from the dead, is alive in Heaven and hears my prayers. I now receive Jesus Christ as my Lord and Savior and to reign and rule in my heart from this day forward. Help me to love and serve You with all my heart. Amen." (1) *"And this is the promise that He has promised us—eternal life"* (1 John 2:25).

Can a Christian be Saved but Backslidden?

God's Word has the answer. Salvation is all of God. God always finishes what He starts. *"...being confident of this very thing, that He who has begun a good work in you will complete it until the day of Jesus Christ"* (Philippians 1:6). God's work (salvation) will be completed when we get to Heaven. We have the promise that once we are saved: *"...Neither shall anyone snatch them out of My hand"* (John 10:28). God cannot look at sin because Heaven is a holy place. These verses strongly indicate that: "Once saved always saved."

While outward appearances of salvation are helpful, they are not necessarily conclusive. Only God knows the true spiritual condition of the heart.

There are those who may act like they are Christians in their works, but they might not really be Christians.

> *"But the LORD said to Samuel, 'Do not look at his appearance or at his physical stature, because I have refused him. For the LORD does not see as man sees; for man looks at the outward appearance, but the LORD looks at the heart'"* (1 Samuel 16:7). *"The heart is deceitful above all things, and desperately wicked; who can know it? I the LORD, search the heart, I test the mind, even to give every man according to his way, according to the fruit of his doings"* (Jeremiah 17:9-10).

We then can see that God's judgment is not based on the external. God looks at the heart.

> *"Not everyone who says to Me, 'LORD, LORD', shall enter the kingdom of heaven, but he who does the will of My Father in heaven. Many will say to Me in that day, 'Lord, Lord have we not prophesied in Your name, cast out demons in Your name, and done many wonders in Your name? And then I will declare to them, I never knew you; depart from Me, you who practice lawlessness'"* (2) (Matthew 7:21-23)!

We have to realize that only God sees the heart and therefore knows if a person is saved or not.

Can a person then be saved and not act like a Christian should? The answer is yes. We need to realize that salvation is based on grace, not our works. It is not something that we do. *"For by grace you have been saved through faith, and that not of yourselves; it is the gift of God, not of works, lest anyone should boast"* (Ephesians 2:8-9). It is Christ's righteousness, not ours, on which our salvation is based. *"For we all stumble in many things. If anyone does not stumble in word, he is a perfect man, able also to bridle the whole body"* (James 3:2). It is necessary to realize that God's grace is preeminent in all aspects of salvation. Lot was righteous by faith, and God's righteousness was imputed to him by grace through faith. There was spiritual weakness in Lot's immorality and drunkenness. His heart was in Sodom, yet he did hate the sins of his culture and strongly sought ways that he could protect God's angels from harm. He obeyed the Lord by not looking back at Sodom. Christ's righteousness, not our righteousness, treats us as if we have never sinned. (3)

Provision has been made by God for the sin of His children. The provision is the blood of Christ. *"If we confess our sins, he is faithful and just to forgive us our sins and to cleanse us from all unrighteousness"* (1 John 1:9). Continual confession of sin indicates genuine salvation. When confession takes place on our part, fellowship is restored, not salvation.

As His children we have to know that God hates all sin.

> *"These six things the LORD hates, Yes, seven are an abomination to Him: A proud look, a lying tongue, hands that shed innocent blood, A heart that devises wicked plans, feet that are swift in running to evil, A false witness who speaks lies, and one who sows discord among brethren"* (Proverbs 6:16-19). *"If you love Me, keep My commandments"* (John 14:15). (4)

Because God hates sin, He disciplines His children.

> *"And you have forgotten the exhortation which speaks to you as to sons: 'My son, do not despise the chastening of the LORD, nor be discouraged when you are rebuked by Him; for whom the LORD loves He chastens, and scourges every son whom He receives'"* (Hebrews 12:5-8).

Parents discipline their children when they do wrong, so our Heavenly Father is going to discipline us when we need to be corrected in our relationship with Him.

It is Possible to Act Like One is a Born Again Christian and not be Saved?

The answer is yes. Note John 12:2-6.

> *"There they made Him a supper; and Martha served, but Lazarus was one of those who sat at the table with Him. Then Mary took a pound of very costly oil of spikenard, anointed the feet of Jesus, and wiped His feet with her hair. And the house was filled with the fragrance of the oil. But one of His disciples, Judas Iscariot, Simon's son, who would betray Him, said, 'Why was his fragrant oil not sold for three hundred denarii and given to the poor?' This he said, not that he cared for the poor, but because he was a thief, and had the money box; and he used to take what was put in it"*

Judas was one of the disciples; he was trusted with their money. He acted like one of them, but he was a thief.

There are those who arrogantly live in sin and say that they are saved. Then there are those who profess to believe and to a degree act like Christians, but they turn out to be impostors or are misinformed about true salvation. *"They* went out from us, but they were not of us; for if they had been of us, they would have continued with us; but they went out that they might be made manifest, that none of them were of us" (1 John 2:19). The true believer endures in faith and in fellowship, and in the truth. (5)

There were two brothers who gave a whole lot to their church; they were part of the church, but their lives outside of church did not back up their Sunday morning display of Christianity. Their pastor just kind of looked the other way. Then the pastor left and a new pastor came on board. The church began to grow, and soon there was a need for a new auditorium. About the same time one of the brothers died. The other brother went to the pastor and said that if he would tell the people at his brother's funeral that his brother was a saint, he would give enough money to pay for the new auditorium. The pastor agreed. So at the funeral the pastor said, "The man was dishonest in his business actions, was a liar, and cheated on his wife, but he was a saint, compared to his brother". (Source unknown)

False Christians can be identified when they abandon Christianity. (Matt. 13:38) They are called *"tares."* The Bible says in Matthew 7:22 that there will be *"Many that will say in that day 'Lord, Lord, have we not prophesied in Your name, cast out demons in Your name, and done many wonders in Your name?'"* But they still will not enter into heaven." Unfortunately, there will be pastors, deacons and faithful church people who will be very surprised to find themselves in Hell. Please, do not play games with your soul and risk eternal hellfire and damnation. Make sure that you have repented of your unbelief and turn to Christ now for forgiveness of your sins. It does not matter how you feel at this moment; it doesn't matter what faults and sins you may have in your life. What does matter is whether or not you have acknowledged to God that you are a guilty sinner and have violated His holy Law. And you have called upon Jesus Christ to forgive your sins and cleanse you with the blood of Christ. (6)

Can a Person who is Saved Choose not to Follow Christ?

We all have to make choices. Man does choose to believe. Following God in the Old Testament required making choices. This is explained in Joshua 24:15.

> *"And if it seems evil to you to serve the LORD, choose for your-selves this day whom you will serve, whether the gods which your fathers served that were on the other side of the River, or the gods of the Amorites in whose land you dwell. But as for me and my house, we will serve the LORD"*

Then in 1 Kings 18:21 we read.

> *"And Elijah came to all the people, and said 'How long will you falter between two opinions? If the LORD is God, follow Him, but if Baal, follow him…'"*

Likewise in the New Testament salvation invitation implies a choice.

> *"And the Spirit and the bride say, 'Come!' And let him who thirsts come. Whoever desires, let him take the water of life freely"* (Revelation 22:17). *"For whoever calls on the name of the LORD shall be saved"* (Romans 10:13).

Man's will, along with his intellect and emotions, make up his spiritual heart.

> *"But I say to you that whoever looks at a woman to lust for her has already committed adultery with her in his heart"* (Matthew 5:28). *"For where your treasure is, there your heart will be also"* (Matthew 6:21). *"But those things which proceed out of the mouth come from the heart, and they defile a man. For out of the heart proceed evil thoughts, murders, adulteries, fornications, thefts, false witness, blasphemies. These are the things which defile a man, but to eat with unwashed hands does not defile a man" (Matthew 15:18-19).*

It is man's heart that plays a key role in his salvation. *"For with the heart one believes unto righteousness, and with the mouth confession is made unto salvation"* (Romans 10:10). (7)

God's Perspective

From man's perspective one has to believe in God. From God's perspective God chose you long before you chose Him. He chose those who would be saved before He created the earth.

> *"Just as He chose us in Him before the foundation of the world,…"* (Ephesians 1:4). *"And He will send His angels with a great sound of a trumpet, and they will gather together His elect from the four winds, from one end of heaven to the other"* (Matthew 24:31).

We see here that only the chosen will be saved.

God's choosing you was not predicated on knowing that you would choose Him. *"…elect according to the foreknowledge of God the Father, in sanctification* of the Spirit, for obedience and sprinkling of the blood of Jesus Christ" (1 Peter 1:2). Likewise, the "sanctification of the Spirit" refers to being set apart.

> *"And we know that all things work together for good to those who love God, to those who are the called according to His purpose. For whom He foreknew, He also predestined to be conformed to the image of His Son, that He might be the first born among many brother"* (Romans 8:28-29)

God chose you because He loved you. By God choosing you, it allowed you to be able to choose God.

> *"And you He made alive, who were dead in trespasses and sins, in which you once walked according to the course of this world"* (Ephesians 2:1). *"And He said, 'Therefore I have said to you that no one can come to Me unless it has been granted to him by My Father'"* (John 6:65).

When we look at the door of salvation, it says above the door, "Whosoever will." Once we walk through the door of salvation and look back, it says above the door, "You were predestined." (8)

Once Saved Always Saved

For those who are truly saved, it is impossible to become unsaved by changing their minds about Christ. True, genuine salvation is in Christ and is protected by the fact that God chose us.

> *"And Jesus said to them, I am the bread of life. He who comes to Me shall never hunger, and he who believes in Me shall never thirst. But I said to you that you have seen Me and yet do not believe. All that the Father gives Me will come to Me, and the one who comes to Me, I will by no means cast out"* (John 6:35-37).

God promises that He will never disown those who are His. God will never lose those who belong to Him.

> *"This is the will of the Father who sent Me, that of all He has given Me I should lose nothing…"* (John 6:39). *"And He will send His angels with a great sound of a trumpet, and they will gather together His elect from the four winds, from one end of heaven to the other"* (Matthew 24:31).

He is referring here to when He will gather all the "elect" from heaven and earth to assemble them before Himself. We have the assurance that those chosen by God have to end up in a saved condition.

> *"If we say that we have no sin, we deceive ourselves, and the truth is not in us. If we confess our sins, He is faithful and just to forgive us our sins and to cleanse us from all unrighteousness. If we say that we have not sinned, we make Him a liar, and His word is not in us"* (1 John 1:8-10).

We see this truth in Hebrews 12:6-8.

> *"For whom the LORD loves He chastens, and scourges every son whom He receives. If you endure chastening, God deals with you as with sons; for what son is there whom a father does not chasten? But if you are without chastening, of which all have become partakers, then you are illegitimate and not sons"*

Knowing That You are Saved

One way we can know that we are true Bible-believing Christians is that we have the working of the Holy Spirit in our lives.

> *"If you love Me, keep My commandments. And I will pray the Father, and He will give you another Helper, that He may abide with you forever—the Spirit of truth, whom the world cannot receive, because it neither sees Him nor knows Him; but you know Him, for He dwells with you and will be in you"* (John 14:15-17). *"He who believes in the Son of God has He witness in himself; he who does not believe God has made Him a liar, because he has not believed the testimony that God has given of His Son."* (1 John 5:10)

The indwelling witness who bears testimony of Christ is the Holy Spirit. He attests to the validity of a believer's salvation.

> *"For as many that are led by the Spirit of God, these are sons of God. For you did not receive the spirit of bondage again to fear, but you received the Spirit of adoption by who we cry out, 'Abba, Father'"* (Romans 8:14-16).

Abba is an endearing term that conveys a sense of intimacy as "daddy". (9)

The book of First John is written to let us know that we have eternal life. If you doubt your salvation, you need to ask yourself if you are applying godliness. In others words, are you reading His Word; are you applying His Word to your life; and are you taking time to pray? Do you have a desire to obediently follow the leading of the Holy Spirit and to draw near to God? If your answer to these questions is yes, then you will know that you are saved because of the fruit of your salvation.

Those who are true Christian have a love for light. They have a love for truth. They believe in God because they know that He is light.

> *"This is the message which we have heard from Him and declare to you, that God is light and in Him is no darkness at all. If we say that we have fellowship with Him, and walk in darkness, we lie and do not practice the truth. But if we walk in the light as He is in the light, we have fellowship with one another and the blood of Jesus Christ His son cleanses us from all sin"* (1 John 1:5-7).

"God is light" means that God is perfectly true and holy. He alone can guide us out of the darkness of sin. A true Christian, then, has a desire to walk in the light. They choose purity in their hearts, and they choose goodness in their lives. When they sin, they freely admit it and walk in the light.

A true Christian has a desire to obey God. This is a characteristic of a saved person. It is not something you do, but something you are. You have an impulse to obey Him. If this is not true, then you probably are not a saved person.

> *"Now by this we know that we know Him, if we keep His commandments. He who says, 'I know Him,' and does not keep His commandments, is a liar, and the truth is not in him. But whoever keeps His word, truly the love of God is perfected in him. By this we know that we are in Him. He, who says he abides in Him, ought himself also to walk just as He walked"* (1 John 2:3-6).

This passage gives two ways that we can know that we belong to Christ: a Christian should live as Christ wants him to live and do what Christ tells him to do. We find the answer as to what we are to do in 1 John 3:23 *"And this is His commandment that we should believe on the name of His Son Jesus Christ and love one another, as He gave us commandment."*

A true Christian shows a genuine love for other Christians. John points out that *"He who says he is in the light, and hates his brother, is in darkness until now"* (1 John 2:9). We are all part of the family of God. A question that is often asked "Do you have to go to church to be a Christian?" The answer is no. However, if you are a Christian, it is a place where you are going to want to be as much as possible to grow and have fellowship with other Christians.

Another characteristic of true Christians is that they hate sin. They find it impossible to continually sin. We find this truth found in1 John 3:4-10.

> *"Whoever commits sin also commits lawlessness, and sin is law-lessness. And you know that He was manifested to take away our sins, and in Him there is no sin. Whoever abides in Him does not sin. Whoever commits sins has neither seen Him nor known Him. Little children, let no one deceive you. He who practices righteousness is righteous, just as He is righteous. He who sins is of the devil, for the devil has sinned from the beginning. For this purpose the Son of God was manifested, that he might destroy the works of the devil. Whoever has been born of God does not sin, for His seed remains in him; and he cannot sin, because he has been born of God. In this the children of God and the children of the devil are manifest: Whoever does not practice righteousness is not of God, nor is he who does not love his brother"*

There is a difference between committing a sin and remaining in sin. (vs. 4) The best of Christians are sometimes going to sin, but they do not desire to continue in sin. A true believer who commits a sin confesses, repents, and is forgiven. The person who remains in sin is not sorry for the sin that he is committing. This person is against God, no matter what religious claims he will make. (vss. 8-9) As Christians we are going to have areas where temptation is strong and bad habits are hard to control. John is talking about people who make a practice of sinning and justify it, not those whose victory is not yet complete.

There are steps that Christians must take if they are to find victory over prevailing sin. They must seek the power of the Word of God and the Holy Spirit. They must remove themselves from lustful desires. Likewise, they are to seek accountability to others in the body of Christ and also seek the prayers of others. (vs.9) *"Does not sin"* means the person who has been born into God's family does not make a practice of sinning. Likewise, they do not become indifferent to God's moral law. Even though Christians still sin, they are working for victory over sin in their lives. When we are born again into God's family, we have the Holy Spirit living in us. It is a rebirth, a fresh start, a new family name based on Christ's death for us. God accepts us totally and forgives us. The Holy Spirit who lives in us gives us a new mind and heart. He then helps us to become more like Christ. Our perspective changes also. Our minds are renewed each day by the Holy Spirit. Note the following passage in Romans 12:2: *"And do not be conformed to this world, but be transformed by the renewing of your mind, that you may prove what is that good and acceptable and perfect will of God."*

32

We need to renew our minds to live our lives to bring honor and obedience to Him. Because He gave His Son to make our new lives possible, and since He wants what is best for us, we should joyfully give our lives as a living sacrifice for His service. Our refusal to conform to this world's values needs to go deeper than just a level of behavior and customs; it must be founded firmly in our minds. When the Holy Spirit re-educates, redirects and renews our minds, it is then that we are truly transformed.

Are you a born-again Christian? Please don't be deceived! *"These things I have written to you who believe in the name of the Son of God, that you may know that you have eternal life, and that you may continue to believe in the name of the Son of God"* (1 John 5:13). If you are a born again Christian, rejoice that you are going to be spending eternity in Heaven.

When we know that we are saved we have the peace that can only overwhelm us with joy and contentment. It is the first step in finishing the race "strong" God's way.

Chapter III

Knowing Your True Identity

If we are going to finish strong, we need to know our true identity. We also need to understand ourselves and to know our destiny. "I am a child of God. God is my Father; heaven is my home; every day is one day nearer… every Christian is my brother too." (1)

When we accept Christ as our personal Savior we are adopted into God's family. *"Jesus said to him, 'I am the way, the truth, and the life. No one comes to the Father except through Me'"* (John 14:6).

It is when we are born again that we have this sonship. *"But as many as received Him, to them He gave the right to become children of God, to those who believe in His name; who were born, not of blood, nor the will of the flesh, nor of the will of man, but of God"* (John 1:12-13).

Our sonship is a gift of grace from God. In the Roman law when adults had no sons they adopted a male as their son so they would have an heir, someone who could carry on the family name. God so loved those whom He redeemed on the cross that He adopted them all as His heirs to share His glory. The Word tells us that

> *"God sent forth His Son…to redeem those who were under the law, that we might receive the adoption as sons"* (Galatian 4:4-5). *"…having predestined us to adoption as sons by Jesus Christ to Himself, according to the good pleasure of His will."* (Ephesians 1:5).

This is incomprehensible love that He has lavished on us when we are called children of God! When we accept Christ we are spiritually adopted into the family of God. This wonderful truth is found in 1 John 1:1-2.

> *"Behold what manner of love the Father has bestowed on us, that we should be called children of God! Therefore the world does not know us, because it did not know Him. Beloved, now we are children of God; and it has not yet been revealed what we shall be, but we know that when He is revealed, we shall be like Him, for we shall see Him as He is"* (2)

John expresses astonishment at God's love for believers in making them children of God. According to our Lord's own testimony in John's Gospel, God's fatherly relationship to Him implied four things. First, fatherhood implied authority. The Father commands His Son to exercise the initiative of resolute obedience to His Father's will. *"I have come down from heaven, not to do My will, but to do the will of Him who sent Me"* (John 6:38).

Second, fatherhood implies affection. *"'...The Father loves the Son...,' 'As the Father hath loved me . . . I have kept my Father's commands and abide in His love'"* (John 5:20; 15:9-10).

Third, fatherhood implied fellowship. *"And He who sent me is with me; the father has not left me alone, for I always do what pleases Him" (John 8:29).*

Fourth, fatherhood implied honor. God wills to exalt His Son. *"Father... Glorify your Son. The Father...has committed all judgment to the Son, that all should honor the Son just as they honor the father"* (John 17:1; 5:22-23).

All this extends to God's adopted children. In, through, and under Jesus Christ their Lord, they are ruled, loved, and honored by their heavenly Father. (3)

When a family adopts a child, that child becomes their heir. The parents love the child and meet the needs of the child. When God takes us into His family, He loves us. We are His children; we are His heirs. He displays affection and generosity. Adoption is an act of kindness to the person who is being adopted. When a couple adopts a son or daughter, they do so because they choose to. They have no duty to adopt. God chose to adopt you. We deserve to be punished for our sins, but He adopted us into his family. He redeemed us, forgave us, and took us as His sons and daughters. He gave Himself to us as our Father.

Our adoption into the family of God should be the basis of our lives. Sonship should control our thinking. Jesus' sonship relationship with God controlled His life on earth. He was obedient to God's leading in His life even to the point of dying on the cross for our sins. Christ insists that the knowledge of our adoptive sonship should control our lives too.

This is no clearer than in His Sermon on the Mount. This sermon is often called the charter of God's kingdom. It could equally be described as the "royal family code." When we become part of God's royal family, like any other member of royalty, there needs to be some preparation; there is a need for some training. We can use the British royal family as a perfect example. Observation of the upbringing of Prince William and his younger brother Prince

Harry can help us. Being sons of Prince Charles, the future King of England, and sons of the Princess Diana, these two young men have been groomed from birth for the possibility that they might someday be heirs to the throne. No age can be too young to begin learning self-identity. They were being taught their true identity before they knew they were part of the royal family.

Prince William, the older of the two, stands in line for the throne of England after his father, Prince Charles. Tutors were on hand when he was born. Their job was to teach him his true identity and to act accordingly. He was taught that there was a certain manner of speech, a certain posture, certain deportment, and a certain behavior that was expected of royalty. Prince Charles was taught to speak like a king, to sit like a king, and to walk like a king. In the same way, we need to learn to act and think and walk as the royal children of our Heavenly Father. (4)

When we are adopted into God's family, we become part of His royal family. Our code of living should be based on the instructions that our Father has given us.

Our adoption appears in the Sermon on the Mount as the basis of the Christian conduct, which are principles and ideals that should guide our Christian walk. The first principle is the principle of love. We should imitate the Father. *"But I say to you, love your enemies… that you may be sons of your Father in heaven…be perfect, just as your Father in heaven is perfect…"* (Matthew 5:44, 45, 48). Children need to show the family likeness in their conduct. Jesus is spelling it out in family-like conduct: *'"Be holy, for I am holy"'* (1 Peter 1:16).

Second is the principle of glorifying the Father. *"Let your light so shine before men, that they may see your good works and glorify your Father in heaven."* (Matthew 5:16). The love of the Father needs to shine in and through us when we are in public. People need to see in us how wonderful He is.

The third principle is pleasing the Father. We are not to be pleasers of man, but rather pleasers of God.

Adoption appears in the Sermon as the basis of Christian prayer. *"In this manner, therefore, pray: Our Father…"* (Matthew 6:9). Jesus addressed His prayer to the Father. The Father who is in heaven always answers His children. However, He often gives us what is best for us rather than what we ask for. Paul asked that God would remove his thorn in the flesh, and the Lord replied by giving Paul strength to live with it.

Adoption appears in the Sermon on the Mount as the basis of the life of faith. We trust God for our material needs as one who seeks His kingdom and righteousness. *"Therefore I say to you, do not worry about your life, what you will eat or what you will drink; nor about your body, what you will put on"* (Matthew 6:25). We are not to worry because we can trust God by faith. Is our faith too small at times? (5)

Our adoption shows us two measurements of God's love. The first one is the cross. *"But God demonstrates His own love toward us, in that while we were still sinners, Christ died for us."* (Romans 5:8). The second measurement is sonship. *"Behold what manner of love the Father has bestowed on us, that we should be called children of God"* (1 John 3:1)!

Adoption shows us the glory of the hope that the Christian has in his daily walk. In the first century adoption was specifically to have an heir to whom one could bequeath one's goods. When we accepted Christ as our personal Savior we became heirs. God adopted us into His family. We are guaranteed the inheritance that He has in store for us.

> *"The Spirit Himself bears witness with our spirit that we are children of God, and if children, then heirs – heirs of God and joint heirs with Christ…"* (Romans 8:16-17), *"Therefore you are no longer a slave but a son, and if a son, then an heir of God through Christ"* (Galatians 4:7).

Our Father owns the cattle on a thousand hills; He owns everything, and we are heirs to His whole estate. We will be co-heirs with Christ. We are promised an inheritance to share in the glory of Christ. Knowing that we have a promise to share His glory with Him is almost incomprehensible. We need to rejoice that we have such a future to look forward to.

The promise of adoption tells us that the experience of Heaven will be of a family gathering. All the redeemed will meet to have a face-to-face fellowship with their Father God and Jesus.

> *"…we shall see Him as He is"* (1 John 3:2). *"…but then face to face"* (1 Corinthians 13:12). *"Father, I desire that they also whom You gave Me may be with Me where I am, that they may behold My glory which You have given Me…"* (John 17:24). *"They shall see His face…"* (Revelation 22:4).

It will be the presence of Jesus in Heaven that will make Heaven so great.

It is through our adoption that we can better understand the ministry of the Holy Spirit.

> *"We are all aware that the Spirit teaches the mind of God and glorifies the Son of God, out of the Scriptures; also, that he is the agent of new birth, giving us an understanding so that we know God and a new heart to obey Him; also, that He indwells, sanctifies, and energizes Christians for their daily pilgrimage; also, that assurance, joy, peace and power are His special gifts…*

> *For the vital truth to be grasped here is that the Spirit is given to Christians as 'the Spirit of adoption,' and in all His ministry to Christians He acts as the Spirit of adoption. As such, His task and purpose throughout is to make Christians realize with increasing clarity the meaning of their filial relationship with God in Christ, and to lead them into an ever deeper response to God in this relationship."* (6)

Christians are to display a nature and lifestyle like their Savior and heavenly Father; their nature that is totally foreign to the unsaved. Scripture describes Christians as "pilgrims, "strangers" and "sojourners." *"...and confessed that they were strangers and pilgrims on the earth"* (Hebrews 11:13). *"Beloved, I beg you as sojourners and pilgrims abstain from fleshly lust..."* (1 Peter 2:11).

"For you did not receive the spirit of bondage again to fear, but you received the spirit of adoption by which we cry, 'Abba Father'" (Romans 8:15)! *"And because you are sons, God has sent forth the Spirit of His Son into your hearts, crying out 'Abba Father'"* (Galatians 4:6)! The unregenerate person is by nature a child of the devil. The only way he can become God's child is by spiritual adoption.

Our adoption compels us to live holy lives. We are to be true to the Father, to our Savior and to ourselves. It is a matter of being a good child, being distinct from a prodigal or black sheep of the royal family. It is the expression of our adoption in our lives. *"...just as He chose us in Him before the foundation of the world, that we should be holy and without blame before Him in love, having predestined us to adoption as sons by Jesus Christ to Himself..."* (Ephesians 1:4-5).

We can look forward to the day that we will finally realize *"...we know that when He is revealed we shall be like Him, for we shall see Him as He is"* (1 John 3:2)

> *"In this world, royal children have to undergo extra training and discipline which other children escape, in order to fit them for their high destiny. It is the same with the children of the King of kings. The clue to understanding all his dealings with them is to remember that throughout their lives he is training them for what awaits them, and chiseling them into the image of Christ. Sometimes the chiseling process is painful and the discipline irksome; but then the Scripture reminds us: 'For whom the LORD loves He chastens, and scourges every son whom He receives. If you endure chastening, God deals with you as with sons; for what son is there whom a father does not chasten' (Hebrews 12:6-7)?."* (7)

Paul confirms our assurance in Romans 8:

> *"For I am persuaded that neither death nor life, nor angels nor principalities nor powers, nor things present nor things to come, nor height nor depth, nor any other created thing, shall be able to separate us from the love of God which is in Christ Jesus our Lord"* (vss. 38-39).

Nothing will separate us from the love of God.

Paul tells us in Romans 8:16-17 that,

> "The *Spirit Himself bears witness with our spirit that we are chil-dren of God, and if children, then heirs—heirs of God and joint heirs with Christ, if indeed we suffer with Him, that we may also be glorified together.*"

In the Roman culture, for an adoption to be legally binding, reputable wit-nesses had to be present, attesting to its validity. God's Holy Spirit confirms the validity of our adoption, not by some inner, mystical voice, but by the fruit He produces in us (Gal. 5:22-23) and the power He provides for spiritual ser-vice (Acts 1:8)

If we know our true identity in Christ, then we will know our destiny. *"I am a child of God. God is my Father; heaven is my home; every day is one day nearer. ..every Christian is my brother."* (8)

We need to be thankful for our adoption and the love that God shows toward us. We need to show love back to our Father by seeking to bring glory and honor to His name. We need to thank Jesus Christ, our Savior and Lord for bringing to us not only a divine authority but also a divine human sympathy. We need to thank Him daily for how close He is to us, how completely He understands us, and how much, as our kinsman-redeemer, He cares for us. We need to hate the things that displease our Father. Lest we grieve Him, we need to strive to avoid evil things.

Do you think about and long for the day when you will meet your family which has gone before you to Heaven? Meanwhile, we need to love our Christian brothers and sisters with whom we live. Our true identity needs to be shown to others for the purpose of bringing glory to His name. We need to finish strong because we know our true identity and our destiny. Christians belong to His royal family and have all the blessings that go with sonship. It should be our daily goal to show others how to accept His sonship, by showing them the way to Christ.

Chapter IV

Learning from Bible Heroes

As we read through God's Word we encounter many different personalities from whom we can benefit by looking closely at their lives. Some of them started out strong but did not finish strong. Some stumbled along the way but got back into the race and finished strong. As we glean from those who finished strong, let's identify those characteristics in their lives that helped them do so. I trust that you will be strengthened in your Christian walk as you look at these Bible personalities who finished strong and that you will be encouraged *not* to make some of the same mistakes.

Saul

God allowed Israel to have a king at their request. Saul, Israel's first king, started out as a good king but finished as a weak king. He was a king of war. The Philistines had gathered themselves together to fight with Israel. They out-numbered Israel with their fine chariots, horsemen and people as the sand of the sea. Saul's army became afraid and some were leaving. Samuel the prophet told Saul to wait seven days. Saul became anxious and said, '*"Bring a burnt offering and peace offering here to me.'* …And he offered the burnt offering" (1 Samuel 13:9). Samuel let Saul know that what he had done was the duty of the priest only. Saul had taken things into his own hands. He did not wait for Samuel to return. Saul did not think he had done anything wrong and never repented of being disobedient. Saul reacted disobediently based upon what he saw and not by faith.

Then in another setting Saul is told by Samuel that God said

> *"I will punish Amalek for what he did to Israel…Now go and attack Amalek and utterly destroy all they have, and do not spare them. But kill man and woman, infant and nursing child, ox and sheep, camel and donkey"* (I Samuel 15:2-3).

Again, Saul does not obey the commandment of God. He spares the king's life and the best of the animals. God had given Saul an opportunity to redeem himself with obedience, but he failed.

If you look at Saul's life you see where he was jealous of David when the people sang "Saul killed thousands and David his ten thousands." He lacked faith when he did not wait until Samuel returned. When David killed Goliath the giant, Saul did not have faith that God would help them defeat the Philistines. We can learn from Saul that God wants us to be obedient to Him. He wants us to repent when we do wrong. He wants us to have faith in Him that he will never leave us; that He will guide us; and that He will meet our needs. God took Saul's kingdom away from him. We have to know that there are consequences to our disobedience; Saul lost his life in battle because of his disobedience.

David

David was tending the family's sheep when Jesse, his father, asks him to check up on his two older brothers who were fighting in Saul's army against the Philistines. When David arrives on the scene the two armies are going out to their battle positions, shouting the war cry. David greeted his brothers as found in 1 Samuel 17:23-24.

> *"Then as he talked with them, there was the champion, the Philistine of Gath, Goliath by name, coming up from the armies of the Philistines; and he spoke according to the same words. So David heard them. And all the men of Israel, when they saw the man, fled from him and were dreadfully afraid. Then David spoke to the men who stood by him, saying, 'What shall be done for the man who kills this Philistine, and takes away the reproach of Israel'".*

David then talked with King Saul,

> *"'Your servant used to keep his father's sheep, and when a lion or a bear came and took a lamb out of the flock, I went out after it and struck it, and delivered the lamb from its mouth;…and this uncircumcised Philistine will be like one of them, seeing that he has defied the armies of the living God'"* (1 Samuel 17:34-36).

41

Saul gives David permission to fight Goliath. After the giant, Goliath, mocks David, he responds:

> *"Then David said to the Philistine, 'You come to me with a sword, with a spear, and with a javelin. But I come to you in the name of the LORD of hosts, the God of the armies of Israel, whom you have defied. This day the LORD will deliver you into my hand, and I will strike you and take your head from you. And this day I will give the carcasses of the camp of the Philistines to the birds of the air and wild beasts of the earth, that all the earth may know that there is a God in Israel'"* (1 Samuel 17:45-46).

Note that when David comes on the scene his focus is on God. You do not hear anyone else talking about God but David. His concentration is on God:
"The armies of the living God" (v. 26).
"The armies of the living God" (v. 36).
"The LORD of hosts, the God of the armies of Israel" (v. 45).
"The Lord deliver you into my hand…that all the earth may know that there is a God in Israel" (v. 46).
"The LORD does not save with sword and spear; for the battle is the LORD's and He will give you into our hands" (v. 47).

David talks about God. He had faith in God and God gave him victory over the giant. God had the victory at this battle; He used a young shepherd boy to start the victory. By faith we can conquer the giants in our lives. David became a man after God's own heart. When we major on giants in our lives we stumble. When we major on God our giants tumble. (1)

God gives Saul's kingdom to David but now has sought for Himself a man after His own heart (1 Samuel 13:14). So what is the difference between Saul and David? David commits adultery with Bathsheba, she is going to have a baby, and David has her husband, Uriah, killed in battle. This was complete disobedience to God's Word. When the prophet, Nathan, confronts him, David says to Nathan, "'I have sinned against the Lord.' And Nathan says to David, *'The LORD also has put away your sin; you shall not die'"* (2 Samuel 12:13-14). The major difference between Saul and David was that David repented. When we repent from the heart, God does forgive us. However, David paid a real price for his sin. *"However because by this deed you have given great occasion to the enemies of the LORD to blaspheme, the child also who is born to you shall surely die"* (2 Samuel 12:14). We can learn that repentance which is necessary, does not always relinquish the consequences of our sins. David's sins legally demanded his death, but the Lord spared David's life through an act of grace. Then because of committing this sin and taking eight wives, David had family problems. David's son, Amnon, raped his half-sister Tamar. Absalom,

Tamar's full brother, hated Amnon for what he did to Tamar. Therefore, Absalom killed his half-brother Amnon. Absalom then fled to Geshur. After three years, he returned to Jerusalem and waited another two years before David forgave him. Then the king kissed Absalom (2 Samuel 14:33). However, Absalom was not repentant. Second Samuel 15 gives the account of how Absalom with his cleverness, and the laziness of his father, takes over David's kingdom.

David later regains his kingdom, but at the cost of Absalom's life. David speaks of his deliveries in Second Samuel 22:2-7.

> *"'The LORD is my rock and my fortress*
> *and my deliverer;*
> *The God of my strength, in whom I will trust;*
> *My shield and the horn of my salvation,*
> *My stronghold and refuge;*
> *My savior, You save me from violence,*
> *I will call upon the LORD, who is*
> *worthy to be praised;*
> *So shall I be saved from my enemies.*
> *When the waves of death surrounded me,*
> *The floods of ungodliness made me afraid.*
> *The sorrows of Sheol surrounded me;*
> *The snares of death confronted me,*
> *In my distress I called upon the LORD*
> *And cried unto my God*
> *He heard my voice from His temple*
> *And my cry entered His ears.'"*

David acknowledged that his LORD was his protector, his rock, his shield, his stronghold, his comforter in distress, and his temple. David went on to say, "The LORD delighted in me." David attempted to please God, and when he did sin against God, he repented. David paid for his sins, but he finished strong. We can learn from David that God wants us to repent of our sins and do our best to live for Him. David was a man after God's own heart. He had faith in God.

Nehemiah

Judah is exiled into Babylon. Then the Persians break the power of Babylon. Nehemiah finds himself in Susa, the capitol of Persia. He is the cupbearer of King Artaxerxes.

> *"...Hanani one of my brethren came with men from Judah; and*
> *I asked them concerning the Jews who had escaped, who had*

survived the captivity, and concerning Jerusalem. And they said to me, 'The survivors who are left from the captivity and province are there in great distress and reproach. The wall of Jerusalem is also broken down, and its gates are burned with fire.' So it was, when I heard these words, that I sat down and wept, and mourned for many days; I was fasting and praying before the God of heaven. And I said: 'I pray, LORD God of heaven, O great and awesome God, You who keep Your covenant and mercy with those who love You and observe Your commandments, please let Your ear be attentive and your eyes open, that You may hear the prayer of Your servant which I pray before You now, day and night, for the children of Israel Your servants, and confess the sins of the children of Israel which we have sinned against You. Both my father's house and I have sinned" (Nehemiah 1:2-6).

Nehemiah is convinced after much prayer and fasting that God wants him to go to Judea to rebuild the wall of Jerusalem. Nehemiah gets permission from King Artaxerxes. The king sends him, with his blessing, with troops and supplies. Nehemiah is focused with a single purpose in his life: to rebuild the wall. Under the leadership of Nehemiah, the wall was completed in fifty-two days.

There are some things that we can learn from Nehemiah's life: He was a man of prayer and spent much time praying before he was sure that God had given him a purpose—to see the wall of Jerusalem rebuilt. He was not deterred from his purpose. He refused to be shaken, discouraged or intimidated. He pressed on when others might have quit. He had complete trust in the Lord.

We see the real character of Nehemiah. We can learn that as God's children we are to work together when trials come our way. Note that Nehemiah faced sarcasm that was discouraging (4:1-6); personal attacks (4:7-23); slander (6:1-14); and disunity (5:1-19). But Nehemiah had a great attitude. He was motivated by one purpose in his life. His work for God was overwhelming. As Moses, who was called to lead the Israelite nation out of Egypt, so Nehemiah saw no other alternative but to serve God with his whole heart. We see that Nehemiah was more concerned for God than he was for himself. Note that he wasn't tempted to quit when things got difficult. He did not proceed for his own personal gain; he was not concerned for his own safety; and he did not give in to the temptation to shirk his responsibility. He left his position in Persia (the security, riches, comfort, prestige, and power) behind him. He had a great concern for God's cause, and he stayed the course until the job was completed.

We as Christians should have the same concern for the mission that He has for us. We are commissioned to tell those around us about Jesus Christ. We are to teach those who come to Christ. As you look at those around you who are on their way to Hell, are you concerned for them in the same way Nehemiah was concerned?

Nehemiah saw the need, and he developed a compassion for the mission that God placed on his heart. We are needed for the mission to whom God has called us. Nehemiah saw the need to be involved, if God's cause was to proceed. We need to be involved also.

We can learn from Nehemiah's example of confidence in God's cause. He went to the pagan king to get his permission to rebuild the Jerusalem wall. We need this confidence in the power of God within us if we are going to complete His mission.

We likewise see Nehemiah cooperating with God's cause. If we are going to complete the mission given to us we need to cooperate with God, by telling people about the Good News. There are many Christians who believe in the cause of Christ, but they do not have a cooperative spirit. We can pray for the unsaved and believe in the power of Christ to save the lost, but they will not be saved if Christians do not do their part. If Nehemiah had remained in Susa, the walls of Jerusalem would never have been completed. We need to get out of our comfort zone. We need to have the courage that Nehemiah demonstrated over and over if we are going to be effective, if we are going to see people saved.

Nehemiah was a courageous man. Even though he started out a little timid, he continued the course. He realized that he was doing what God wanted him to do. He faced discouragement, was ridiculed and mocked, and faced lies. He pressed on because he knew that when you are doing what God wants you to do the way God wants you to do it, you cannot fail. We need to learn from the courage that Nehemiah showed.

Nehemiah's courage allowed him to be uncompromising in his service (6:2-4). He would not compromise with the enemies of God who wanted him to stop building the wall and meet with them. His own people wanted him to be more flexible in his attitude (6:17-18). Again he refused to compromise when a letter writing campaign was launched against him in an effort to smear his reputation (6:19). We can learn from Nehemiah that we should not be intimidated into compromising God's will no matter the source. We should be encouraged to do what is right regardless of the circumstances.

We can learn from Nehemiah that whenever we are doing God's work, there will be troublemakers trying to discourage us. God's causes are hindered by Satan's troublemakers.

Nehemiah is an Old Testament hero after whom we can pattern our lives. We need to imitate his attitude. As we encounter great opportunities and obli-gations, let us not shirk them. We serve an awesome God and our service should be just as awesome. Nehemiah finished strong; let's learn from him so we will also finish strong. (2)

Daniel and His Three Friends

When Babylon conquered Jerusalem and exiled Daniel and his three friends, along with others, Daniel and his three friends were summoned to serve in the king's palace. They were told that they would have to eat of the king's food.

> *"But Daniel purposed in his heart that he would not defile himself*
> *with the portion of the king's delicacies, nor with the wine which*
> *he drank; therefore he requested of the chief of the eunuchs*
> *that he might not defile himself"* (Daniel 1:8).

This pagan food and drink was devoted to idols. God honored Daniel's allegiance and trust by sovereignly working favorably for him among the heathen leaders. God honors those who honor Him. (3) Because Daniel purposed in his heart to honor God, he was able to eat vegetables, and he was healthier than the others who ate the king's meat.

In chapter two of Daniel, King Nebuchadnezzar had a dream and his magicians, astrologers, the sorcerers, and the Chaldeans could not interpret the king's dream. Daniel goes before the king to ask for some time, and after that he would answer the king's dream. He goes to his house, and his three friends, Shadrach, Meshach and Abednego pray to God that He might show mercy on them. In a dream God reveals the secret of Nebuchadnezzar's dream. Daniel responds:

> *"'Blessed be the name of God forever and ever,*
> *For wisdom and might are His.*
> *And He changes the times and the seasons;*
> *He removes kings and raises up kings*
> *He gives wisdom to the wise*
> *And knowledge to those who have understanding.*
> *He reveals deep and secret things;*
> *He knows what is in the darkness,*
> *And light dwells with Him.*
> *'I thank You and praise You*
> *O God of my fathers;*
> *You have given me wisdom and might,*
> *And have now made known to me*
> *what we asked You,*
> *For You have made known to us*
> *the king's demand.'"*
> (Daniel 2:20-23)

Daniel and his friends prayed; God answered their prayer and then Daniel praised God, giving God the glory and acknowledging who He is and the wisdom He has given him.

When we come to chapter three we see King Nebuchadnezzar has made a golden image and everyone is to fall down and worship it or be cast into a burning fiery furnace. Here we find Shadrach, Meshach and Abednego have purposed in their hearts that they would not bow down to this image. In the New Testament we see that the disciples decided. *"We ought to obey God rather than men"* (Acts 5:29)! We need to obey just as the apostles did in their day. *"...Nor do I count my life dear to myself, so that I may finish my race with joy,"* said Paul (Acts 20:24). This is the spirit of Daniel, Shadrach, Meshach and Abednego. This is the spirit of those who know God. Because they knew God they had great contentment in God. They had peace of which Paul speaks in Romans 5:1 – *"Therefore, having been justified by faith, we have peace with God through our Lord Jesus Christ."*

Shadrach, Meshach, and Abednego had peace in the decision that they made. There was no panic!

> *"O Nebuchadnezzar we have no need to answer you in this matter. If that is the case, our God who we serve is able to deliver us from the burning fiery furnace, and He will deliver us from your hand, O king"* (Daniel 3:16-17).

Then in Daniel 3:25 it says, *"'Look!' He answered, 'I see four men loose, walking in the midst of the fire; and they are not hurt, and the form of the fourth is like the Son of God'."*

God rewards faithfulness. These three young men were promoted in the province of Babylon. (4)

Then we find Daniel in a situation where others of leadership wanted to put Daniel down because *"Daniel distinguished himself above the governors..."* (Daniel 6:3). These governors plotted against Daniel and got the king to sign a petition *"...that whoever petitions any god or man for thirty days, except you, O king, shall be cast into the den of lion."* (Daniel 6:7). Daniel prayed three times a day before his window so he could be seen. He does not change his habit because of this decree, and he is therefore cast into the lions' den. God sends an angel and shuts the mouths of the lions, and Daniel comes out without a scratch.

I cannot help but think of what type of training these four men had before they were taken away from their parents and/or grandparents and moved to a foreign country. Did their parents teach them how to pray? Did they tell them that they should put God first over those who ruled over them? Did they teach them to know God on a personal level? Did their parents pray for them every day even when they did not know what was taking place in their lives? We don't know the answer to these questions, but I've got to think that there were parents, grandparents and others who were praying for these men. Regardless, these men knew how to pray, and they knew they put their lives on the line by putting Him first in their lives. Daniel, Shadrach, Meshach, and Abednego are great examples for us to follow if we want to finish strong.

Esther and Mordecai

Esther wins King Ahasuerus' beauty contest and becomes queen. Ahasuerus' right hand man, Haman, wanted everyone to bow down to him. When Mordecai, a Jew, refused to bow down to him, he tricked the king to write a decree to kill all the Jews. Mordecai encouraged Esther to speak to the king. He let her know that she could be queen in such a time as this, to save her people's lives. Esther realized that if she approached the king on her own, it could cost her life. However, if she did not approach the king it would mean the lives of all the Jews and probably her own. We pick up part of the account in Esther 4:13-17.

> *"And Mordecai told them to answer Esther: 'Do not think in your heart that you will escape in the king's palace any more than all the other Jews. For if you remain completely silent at this time, relief and deliverance will arise for the Jews from another place, but you and your father's house will perish. Yet who knows whether you have come to the kingdom for such a time as this?' Then Esther told them to reply to Mordecai: 'Go gather all the Jews who are present in Shushan, and fast for me; neither eat nor drink for three days, night or day. My maids and I will fast likewise. And so I will go to the king, which is against the law; and if I perish, I perish!' So Mordecai went his way and did according to all that Esther commanded him".*

There are a number of character traits that can be seen in both Esther's life and Mordecai's life which can apply to our lives. As his adopted daughter, Esther and Mordecai have a respectable relationship with each other. Mordecai showed boldness in not bowing down to Haman. He showed obedience to God when he would not bow down to others. He was an encourager when he challenged Esther to approach the king. He fulfilled what he needed to do when Esther spoke to the king. Even after Esther became queen, Mordecai continued to have an interest in Esther's well-being. He never was very far away. He had established a healthy faith in God's sovereign power for His people.

Esther was willing to put her life on the line to do what she knew God wanted her to do. She was where God wanted her to be, at the time God wanted her to be there, in order to accomplish the purpose God had for her.

Esther was willing to do what her father wanted her to do. Likewise, we as God's adopted children should do what our heavenly Father wants us to do when He wants us to do it. This is the way to finish strong by doing God's will, in God's timing, and in God's way.

Barnabas

Barnabas had a reputation of being an encourager to those around him. His name meant *"...son of encouragement..."* (Acts 4:36). The Bible says that *"For he was a good man, full of the Holy Spirit and of faith"* (Acts 11:24).

The following are some lessons that we can learn from Barnabas:

First, our brothers and sisters in Christ are more important than our worldly possessions. Barnabas had a tract of land, but he sold it and gave it to the apostles to help needy brethren (Acts 4:36-37). Why did he give up a valuable possession? He did it out of love and a proper perspective of what is valuable. Barnabas valued his brethren more than he valued his possessions. He did not put his trust in wealth.

Second, Barnabas was willing to go where he was needed. Note Acts 11:22, 25-26.

> *"Then news of these things came to the ears of the church in Jerusalem, and they sent out Barnabas to as far as Antioch. Then Barnabas departed for Tarsus to seek Saul. And when he had found him, he brought him to Antioch."*

Then we see Barnabas and Paul being sent out by the Holy Spirit.

> *"As they ministered to the Lord and fasted, the Holy Spirit said, 'Now separate to me Barnabas and Saul for the work to which I have called them.' Then having fasted and prayed and laid hands on them, they sent them away"* (Acts 13:2-3).

We must be willing to go where we are needed. Barnabas was selected because he was the type of person who could encourage new Christians. When the gospel arrived in Syria and Antioch, many believed. When the apostles in Jerusalem heard about it, they chose Barnabas, the son of encouragement. This wasn't a week or two-week, short term mission trip. This was a lifelong commitment.

Barnabas traveled with Paul all over the known world to establish churches. He made a big sacrifice, but he was not attached to this world. He was looking forward to eternity. If we look at the life of Barnabas, we see him telling us to go where we are needed.

Third, we see Barnabas empowering others. The church of Jerusalem sent out Barnabas to go as far as Antioch. *"When he came and had seen the grace of God, he was glad, and encouraged them all that with purpose of heart they should continue with the Lord"* (Acts 11:23). Barnabas saw a need for Paul to come to Antioch. He was looking out for what was best for those with whom he was working.

Barnabas is the one who brought Saul (Paul) to the apostles (Acts 9:26-28), and he vouched for Paul. Barnabas was interested in giving others an opportunity to grow. Barnabas' initial confidence in Paul paid off as you see Paul's ministry unfold. He surpassed Barnabas in how he taught and strengthened churches. Barnabas' life encourages us to invest our time in others, giving them a chance and empowering them.

Fourth, Barnabas was patient with others. John Mark had traveled with Paul and Barnabas on their first missionary journey. Along the way John left them. When it was time to go on a second missionary journey, Barnabas wanted to take John Mark along. Paul would not hear of it; there was a disagreement. So Paul took Silas, and Barnabas took John Mark, and they went their separate ways. Barnabas' patience paid off with John Mark. Paul eventually came to see John Mark as valuable. *"Only Luke is with me. Get Mark and bring him with you, for he is useful to me for ministry"* (2 Timothy 4:11). John Mark ended up writing the Gospel of Mark.

We can learn from Barnabas that patience will always pay off in the long run. When we have patience with a brother in Christ, it will be an encouragement to that person, and the result will be seeing another believer being used of God.

Fifth, Barnabas would tell us to do what is right, even when other leaders are doing what is wrong. Note what Paul is saying in Galatians 2:12-13.

> *"For before certain men came from James, he would eat with the Gentiles; but when they came, he withdrew and separated himself, fearing those who were of the circumcision. And the rest of the Jews also played the hypocrite with him, so that even Barnabas was carried away with their hypocrisy."*

Barnabas went astray and acted with prejudice. Even though he was one of the first teachers who came to encourage the Gentile Christians, when Peter began to hold himself aloof from the Gentiles, Barnabas followed his hypocrisy. We can learn from Barnabas' experience here that we need to do what is right regardless of what others are doing.

Let us follow Barnabas' example and be faithful servants, going where God wants us to go and being encouragers to our brothers and sisters in Christ. Note that Barnabas was filled with the Holy Spirit. Let us do what is right regardless of what others are doing. We must, if we want to finish strong.

Philip

We get our first preview of Philip in Acts chapter six where he was chosen as one of the seven for the work of benevolence in the early church. *"Therefore, brethren, seek out from among you seven men of good reputation, full of the Holy Spirit and wisdom, whom we may appoint over this business."* (Acts 6:3).

When persecution came, scattering the disciples, Philip went to the city of Samaria and preached Christ. Philip was having success when God called him away to one searching soul.

> *"Now an angel of the Lord spoke to Philip, saying, 'Arise and go toward the south along the road which goes down from Jerusalem to Gaza.' This is desert. So he arose and went. And behold, a man of Ethiopia, a eunuch of great authority under Candace the queen of the Ethiopians, who had charge of all her treasury, and had come to Jerusalem to worship, was returning. And sitting in his chariot, he was reading Isaiah the prophet. Then the Spirit said to Philip, 'Go near and overtake this chariot'"* (Acts 8:26-29).

Note that Philip was obedient. His command might have seemed somewhat irrational and strange, but he knew God's way was best. If we are going to be effective workers for our Lord, we have to be submissive. We must do what He wants us to do, in His timing and at all cost. If we are going to be effective for God, the will of God must come first, not ours.

Philip was willing to give up teaching many, to travel fifty miles for one lost soul because this was the will of God for him at that moment. It takes a deep love for God for one to have that dedication. He followed the example of Jesus, willing to leave the crowds for one individual. We must let the Holy Spirit lead in our lives and have a willingness to leave the "ninety-nine" to bring a lost soul to safety.

Note in Acts 8:37 that Philip without hesitation went to the Ethiopian. The Ethiopian would be considered an outcast for a Jew; like Philip. If we are going to do personal evangelism we must be color-blind. The condition of the soul, not the color of the skin or the social status, is important. There is an urgency that exists to reach others for Christ and we need to respond to it. When the Spirit told Philip to join the Ethiopian in the chariot, Philip *"ran to him"* (Acts 8:30). Do we run when we know there is something that God wants us to do?

We can also learn from Philip the proper techniques in his dealing with the Ethiopian. He starts out by asking him a question. *"So Philip ran to him, and heard him reading the prophet Isaiah, and said, 'Do you understand what you are reading"* (Acts 8:30)? Philip showed real concern but also allowed him to talk. Questions arouse greater interest and discussion. We need to be familiar with the Word of God. When the Ethiopian asked him about a certain passage in Isaiah, Philip knew to whom the Scriptures referred. Only the Word of God can bring about salvation.

After reading Isaiah 53, Philip preached "Jesus" to the Ethiopian (Acts 8:35). "Jesus" is the only message that can save, for He alone has the words to eternal life. His word is our message and Jesus is our drawing power. We should not be satisfied leading just one person to Christ. After Philip baptized the Ethiopian, he went on his way preaching to others (Acts 8:40). He was not content to bring just one soul to Christ. Neither should we. We need to continually cast out our nets if we want to be "fishers of men."

We need to use Philip as our example in the area of soul winning. We need to be dedicated and effective servants of Jesus Christ. We need to win the lost if we want to finish strong. (5)

Those Who Walked by Faith

In Hebrews chapter 11 we have the "Hall of Fame" of those who were faithful. God wants us as Christians to walk by faith, and we are not going to finish strong in our Christian walk if we do not walk by faith. Let's take a brief look at some of those who were noted for walking by faith.

Abel

There is not a lot written about Abel. He was murdered by his brother Cain. We still can learn from Cain and Abel's lives. It is a story of what is in a man's heart having an effect on his life. Abel had a heart that was righteous and pleasing to God. We need to ask ourselves if our hearts are righteous and pleasing to God. Do we have the right motivation for doing spiritual things?

> *"By faith Abel offered to God a more excellent sacrifice than Cain, through which he obtained witness that he was righteous, God testifying of his gifts; and through it he being dead still speaks"* (Hebrews 11:4).

Abel had a more excellent sacrifice than his brother Cain. Abel's sacrifice was excellent because he did it by faith, but Cain's sacrifice was offered in disbelief. Abel left a testimony to all succeeding generations that a person comes to God by faith to receive righteousness.

Enoch

There is little written about Enoch as there was with Abel. Yet he, too, is listed in the "Faith Hall of Fame."

> *"By faith Enoch was taken away so that he did not see death, 'and was not found, because God had taken him'; for because he had a testimony, that he pleased God. But without faith it is impossible to please Him, for he who comes to God must believe that He is, and that He is a rewarder of those who diligently seek Him"* (Hebrews 11:5-6).

Enoch pleased God because he had faith. It is impossible to walk with God without faith. God is a rewarder to those who seek Him. We can learn from Enoch in that when we seek God by faith He will reward us for our faithfulness and trust in Him. Pleasing God should be a natural result of our faith. Enoch was rewarded when God took him directly to Heaven.

Noah

We read that Noah stood alone in a godless culture.

> *"By faith Noah, being divinely warned of things not yet seen, moved with godly fear, prepared an ark for the saving of his household, by which he condemned the world and became heir of the righteousness which is according to faith"* (Hebrews 11:7).

He was a man who walked with God and found favor in God's sight. It had never rained before, and God asked him to build the ark. Whether he was ridiculed or not, we do not know, we do know that he still continued to build the ark. He was obedient to God, and he faithfully completed the task.

Can we learn to stand firm for Christ, regardless of what those around us are saying? Noah built the ark with reverence and a holy fear of God. We need to make sure that we focus on the things of God and not the things of self. When we think that the things God wants us to do are hard, we need to think of Noah in the long task that he had and the perseverance and faith that it took to finish the task.

Abraham and Sarah

> *"By faith Abraham obeyed when he was called to go out to the place which he would receive as an inheritance. And he went out, not knowing where he was going. By faith he dwelt in the land of promise as in a foreign country, dwelling in tents with Isaac and Jacob, the heirs with him of the same promise; for he waited for the city which has foundations whose builder and maker is God"* (Hebrews 11:8-10).

"By faith Sarah herself also received strength to conceive seed, and she bore a child when she was past the age, because she judged Him faithful who had promised. Therefore from one man and him as good as dead, were born as many as the stars of the sky in multitude—innumerable as the sand which is by the seashore" (Hebrews 11:11-12).

God called Abraham to leave his home and family. God promised to bless him with descendants too numerous to count. Then there was the time that he and Sarah decided to "help God out" and provide a descendant through Ishmael. There was the time that they laughed at God's promise to give them a child in their old age. There are lessons that we can learn from Abraham and Sarah. We can learn that they were not perfect, but they were faithful to God. Because Abraham believed God was faithful to His promise, he was willing to step out in faith and follow God's leading. Sarah gave birth to a son past her childbearing years because she believed that God was faithful. They had faith that God would do what He said He would do. God honored them for their faithfulness even though it was not always easy. How do we respond when God tells us to step out in faith? Can we wait for God's timing in our lives? Can we continue to trust Him for what His Word promises us? Abraham and Sarah were obedient to what God asked them to do. If we follow their example, we will be obedient to what God asks us to do. May God give each of us faith and trust in Him, knowing that we will be spending eternity with Him.

"Lord, open my eyes and heart that I might learn what it means to walk with you. Help me to identify areas in my life that hinder my walk. I desire to be pleasing to you in all that I say and do."

"Faith begins where man's power ends."– George Mueller

Caleb

God told Moses to send spies into the land of Canaan which he was giving to the children of Israel. Caleb was one of the twelve who were chosen. They were to check out the land, see what it was like, see what the people were like, see if they were strong or weak, and assess how many people were there. Moses also wanted to know if the land was rich or poor; he wanted a complete report. And he wanted some fruit of the land brought back.

Ten of the spies come back with a negative report.

"It truly flows with milk and honey and this is its fruit. Nevertheless the people who dwell in the land are strong; the cities are fortified and very large" (Numbers 13:27-28). *"Then Caleb quieted the people before Moses, and said. 'Let us go up at once*

and take possession, for we are well able to overcome it'" (Numbers 13:30).

Joshua and Caleb knew that God would give them the land. However, the Israelite people believed the other ten spies. Because of their trust in God, these two were the only Israelites above the age of twenty who were able to go into the Promised Land.

Next, we pick up the account of Caleb in the book of Joshua 14:7:12.

> *"I was forty years old when Moses the servant of the LORD sent me from Kadesh Barnea to spy out the land, and I brought back word to him as it was in my heart. Nevertheless my brothers who went up with me made the heart of the people melt, but I wholly followed the LORD my God. So Moses swore on that day, saying, 'Surely the land where your foot has trodden shall be your inheritance and your children's forever, because you have wholly followed the LORD my God. And now, behold, the LORD has kept me alive, as He said, these forty-five years, ever since the LORD spoke this word to Moses while Israel wandered in the wilderness; and now, here I am this day, eighty-five years old. As yet I am as strong this day as on the day that Moses sent me; just as my strength was then, so now is my strength for war both for going out and for coming in. Now therefore, give me this mountain of which the LORD spoke in that day.'"*

We can learn from the life of Caleb that we need to trust God when there are giants to overcome in our lives. God awarded Caleb with a long healthy life. He indicated that he was as strong at eighty-five as he was at forty. God rewarded him with a land that was "flowing with milk and honey." I like the phrase, "give me this mountain" which the Lord has promised. We need to have faith that God will give us mountains that come into our lives. Likewise, we can learn that we need to put God first in our lives even when the majority is doing what is wrong. Caleb shows us that he had courage to do right when most were doing what was wrong. Can we learn from Caleb that we can do things for God when we get older? He was conquering mountains when he was eighty-five. We need to be conquering mountains until God takes us home. We need to use our talents for the Lord until he takes them away from us.

Peter

It is easy for many people to identify with Peter. My dad repeatedly told my brother and me that we always had to "learn things the hard way." That was just before we got a spanking. Peter goes through some hard "knocks" but he lived a colorful life. We meet Peter when he is called in Matthew 4:18-20:

> *"And Jesus, walking by the Sea of Galilee, saw two brothers, Simon called Peter, and Andrew his brother, casting a net into the sea; for they were fishermen. Then He said to them, 'Follow Me, and I will make you fishers of men.' They immediately left their nets and followed Him"* (Matthew 4:18-20).

Note that there is no hesitation in following Jesus. They left what they were doing and followed Him. They did not say that they had to take care of some business first; they did not say that they had to sell their home first. They did not sleep on it, or spend time praying about it. They made a decision on the spot, and they went right away. When God wants us to do something, He wants us to do it on His timetable, not ours.

The disciples had just experienced the feeding of 5,000 men along with women and children and Jesus tells them to get into a boat and go to the other side. Meanwhile Jesus sends the multitudes away. Then Jesus goes up into the mountain to pray. The disciples are out in the middle of the sea and the winds become strong. They then see Jesus walking on the water and think that He is a ghost until Jesus calls out to them not to be afraid as Matthew 14:28-30 tells us.

> *"And Peter answered Him and said, 'Lord, if it is You, command me to come to You on the water.' So He said, 'come' and when Peter had come down out of the boat, he walked on the water to go to Jesus. But when he saw that the wind was boisterous, he was afraid; and beginning to sink he cried out, saying 'Lord, save me!'"*

Peter is very spontaneous. Why was it only Peter who was willing to take steps of faith to walk on water. His faith wavered, but he had faith. Sometimes we criticize others when they waver in their faith, when we don't have any faith ourselves.

In Matthew 16:13-19, we see Peter confessing the Deity of Christ. (vs. 16) *"Simon Peter answered and said, 'You are the Christ, the Son of the living God.'"* In Matthew 17:1-8 we see Peter witnessing the transfiguration of Christ. Then we see Peter again in Matthew 26:69-75. Peter tells Jesus that he will not stumble. Peter goes on to say that even if he has to die with Jesus he will not deny Him. However, Jesus tells him that before the rooster crowed, Peter would deny Him three times. Matthew 26:69-74 tells us of the three times that Peter denies Christ. It says in verse 75, *"And Peter remembered the word of Jesus who had said to him, 'Before the rooster crows, you will deny Me three times.' So he went out and wept bitterly."*

When you read the account of Peter denying Jesus, you see him keeping an eye on what is happening to Jesus. You do not read that the other disciples were hanging around (at least not as close as Peter), except for John who was present at the crucifixion of Jesus. Peter did not live up to his promise, but he at least did not desert Jesus like the other disciples. When we see Peter weeping bitterly, we know that Peter had a repentant heart. His repentant heart drew him closer to Jesus. Peter was learning from his mistakes and was being disciplined, which helped him to become a strong Christian.

Let's pick up another scene where we find Mary Magdalene, Mary the mother of James, and Salome approaching Jesus' grave. They saw that the stone at the entrance was moved away, and they saw a young man clothed in long white robes. He told them,

> *"'Do not be alarmed. You seek Jesus of Nazareth, who was crucified. He is risen! He is not here. See the place where they laid Him. But go, tell His disciples – and Peter – that He is going before you into Galilee; there you will see Him, as He said to you'"* (Mark 16:6-7).

Peter's name is added to the disciples to let him know that he is still one of Christ's disciples, even though he had denied Him. God is in the business of giving us second chances. We live in a sinful world, and we still have a sinful nature within us. But God is willing to forgive us when we make mistakes, and He wants to pick us up and get us running again for Him.

We see Peter as a leader in Acts 1:15. *"And in those days Peter stood up in the midst of the disciples (altogether the number of names was about a hundred and twenty)…"*. In chapter two of Acts we find the disciples filled with the Holy Spirit, and Peter preaches, and three thousand are saved.

Peter continued to serve the Lord until he was martyred while serving Him. We see Peter finishing strong. Peter wrote the two epistles that are named after him. God wants us to finish strong. He wants to use our talents until He takes us home. There may be times that we fall flat on our faces like Peter, but we need to make sure that we pick ourselves up and finish the race. God never tells us that the road will be easy, but we need to continue to press forward, keeping our eyes on the author and finisher of our faith.

Who do you identify with in the Bible? God has given us accounts of many different personalities in the Bible. There are those who were faithful and those who were not faithful. There are those who started strong but failed along the way. Then there were those who stumbled along the way but picked themselves up and finished strong. Often we make mistakes, but when we learn from our mistakes we not only help ourselves, but we can also help others.

Let's learn from others as we evaluate their lives and use that knowledge to press on and make sure that we finish strong by bringing glory to God.

"Noah did a great thing for God by building the ark, but Noah was a drunk. Abraham was old, but God used him and he has had ancestors as many as the sand of the sea. Moses had a stuttering problem, but he lived close to God and God used him to lead a nation. Gideon was afraid to do what God wanted him to do. He had to rely on God to give him victory over his enemy. Samson was a womanizer, but God still used him. Jeremiah and Timothy were young, but God used them. David had an affair and tried to cover it up with murder. David became a man after God's own heart. Job lost all that he had including his children, but he was a righteous man and God blessed him for it. Peter denied Christ three times, but God still used him mightily. The disciples fell to sleep when Christ needed them the most. The Samaritan woman was divorced several times, but she brought others to Jesus. Paul started out persecuting Christians, but became an outstanding missionary and writer of several books of the Bible." (6)

Please start from where you are today and move forward in serving the Lord. Do what He wants you to do so you can cross the finish line with your head high.

PART II

Growth While Running the Christian Race

Lesson Two

Prayer

believe that I am here today because God's people prayed for me. *"...The effectual, fervent prayer of a righteous man avails much"* (James 5:16). There were people praying for me all over the country. A missionary from Florida and another one from the state of Washington told me that they had been praying for me. The first Sunday after my heart attack when my family did not know if I was going to make it or not, my Sunday school class spent the whole hour praying for me and my family. In another adult Sunday school class each person present prayed for me. My backdoor neighbor prayed for me every time they looked out their back window. Countless people have told me that they prayed for me. God is still in the business of answering prayer. It is humbling to know that there were those who were willing to pray for me, and God was so gracious to answer their prayers.

Our seven grandchildren – Luke, Lindsay, Seth, Joel holding Leah, Josiah, and Victoria–sitting in the ICU waiting room while their parents kept vigil over their grandpa.

Chapter V

Embracing the Power of Prayer

"Prayer is the Secret of Power." Evan Roberts

Prayer has a new meaning when you believe that you are alive because others have prayed for you. It has given me a desire to pray for others who are having physical difficulties in their lives. If God is in the business of answering prayer, why is there such a limited amount of prayer coming from the average Christian church today? As Christians, if we are going to finish strong God's way, we need to experience the power of prayer.

Why do so many pastors feel defeated? Why are there so many church workers so often discouraged and disheartened? Is it because there is so little prayer? What would happen if discouraged pastors, who feel defeated, had some prayer partners? I have read about pastors who are doing an outstanding job because there are those who are praying for them. One pastor's church grew from five hundred to fifteen hundred after about four dozen men began to pray for him each week.

Is prayer the greatest power on earth? Why then aren't souls being saved in our churches today? Is it because we pray so little for the unsaved? Is our success or failure in our spiritual lives contingent on our sufficient or insufficient prayer lives? Can we serve correctly when our prayer lives are not right? To answer these questions by looking at Scripture.

Let's start by looking at some of the qualifications for answers to our prayers.

1. A Clean Heart

The only prayer that an unsaved person is entitled to have answered by God is a prayer of repentance. Once a person is a born again Christian, he or she can then pray and know that God will answer his or her prayers. However, the Christian needs to have a clean heart. *"Create in me a clean heart, O God"* (Psalm 51:10). Because we are born with a sinful nature, it is our natural inclination to please ourselves rather than God. Like David we need to ask God to cleanse us from within (Psalm 51:7). God will cleanse our hearts to make room for new thoughts and desires. (1) *"Beloved, if our heart does not condemn us, we have confidence toward God. And whatever we ask we receive from Him, because we keep his commandment and do those things that are pleasing in His sight"* (1 John 3:21). When our conscience is genuinely clear, we then can come to God with no fear. (2) There is nothing the devil dreads as much as prayer. His greatest desire is to see that we do not pray. Satan trembles when we pray and has little concern about our toil or our own wisdom.

The best thing we can do for mankind is to pray. Our prayers will accomplish much more than our work.

2. A Need for Faith

> *"And when the disciples saw it, they marveled, saying, 'How did the fig tree wither away so soon?' So Jesus answered and said to them, 'Assuredly, I say to you, have faith and do not doubt, you will not only do what was done to the fig tree, but also if you say to this mountain, 'be removed and be cast into the sea', it will be done. And whatever things you ask in prayer, believing, you will receive'"* (Matthew 21:20-22*)*.

Don't these verses say that if we ask in faith and do not doubt, it will be done? Christ is speaking here figuratively about God's immeasurable power which He is willing to unleash in the lives of those with true faith. There is "limitless" power in prayer, contingent on our faith and on our praying. (3)

If we are going to pray with power, we must pray with faith. The Word of God can be very explicit and positive in its promises, but we have to confidently expect its fulfillment. James says in 1:5, *"If any of you lacks wisdom, let him ask of God, who gives to all liberally and without reproach."* This promise is as positive as it can get. Note verses 6-7*: "But let him ask in faith, with no doubting, for he who doubts is like the wave of the sea driven and tossed by the wind. For let not that man suppose that he will receive anything from the Lord;..."* There must be confident and unwavering expectation. Faith that goes beyond our expectation. It is faith that believes that our prayers are heard. You find this in Mark 11:24. *"Therefore I say to you, whatever things you ask when you pray, believe that you receive them, and you will have them."*

So how do we get this unwavering faith? We can find the answer in Romans 10:17: *"So then faith comes by hearing, and hearing by the word of God."* Real faith comes when we study God's Word and discover firsthand what is promised. Faith is simple belief in God's Word. When we find those promises in His Word, we need to rest our faith in them. (4)

3. Praying "in His Name"

Knowing how to approach the King of glory is probably the most important question that we can ask ourselves. His Word tells us to "ask anything," and it shall be done. This is true, but there are some qualifiers we need to look at. He tells us that we are to ask in His name. *"And whatever you ask in My name, that I will do, that the Father may be glorified in the Son"* (John 14:13-14). In "His name" is much more than something attached to the end of our prayers. It means that the believer's prayer should not be selfish but should be for His purposes and His kingdom. Likewise, it should be on His merits and not on ours. Then the believer's prayer should be in pursuit of His glory alone. (5) Our prayers should be to bring glory to the Lord Jesus. We are not to pray for wealth, prosperity or success, or comfort for our own enjoyment, popularity or advancement, but for His glory and for the advancement of His kingdom. When we pray in the name of our Lord Jesus we are then asking things which the blood of Christ has purchased (secured) for us. When we pray "in His name" we also need to pray so that it brings glory to God. When "In My name" or *"in His name"* is used throughout the Bible, it means about what it does in everyday language. When you write a check out of your own checking account you can withdraw up to the amount that you have put into that account. In our prayers, the Lord Jesus gives us a blank check in His name and allows us to use it. When we go to God in prayer we have nothing deposited there; we have no credit. If you go in your own name, there is nothing there. But if you go in the name of Jesus Christ you have unlimited credit in Heaven. So when you pray you are praying on His credit, not your own. When you cash a check from the bank of heaven it should be with a desire chiefly to please Him. God is going to cash your check (your prayer) if you seek to learn God's will for your life. You should not try to exceed His will. When you go in your name, you get absolutely nothing. (6)

A friend gives you a check for $1,000 and tells you to purchase something that he knows you need. When you get to the bank to cash the check you realize that the check is made out for $100,000. You know that the friend stated he was giving you $1,000. Your friend worked for a large corporation, and it was his custom to write out big checks. You also know that if your friend had given you a blank check, he would have expected you to write it out for only $1,000. You take the check back to him because you know it is the right thing to do. The point is that we cannot be sure that we are praying "in His name" unless we have learned His will for us. We need to make the blank check out for the right amount.

It is when we "abide in" Him that we can pray in Christ's name. We can only do this when our hearts are right, or our prayers will be wrong. *"If you abide in Me, and My words abide in you, you will ask what you desire, and it shall be done for you"* (John 15:7). As branches we need to be attached to the vine. (7) When we do what He desires of us, He in return does what we ask, because we are keeping His commandments. Let us ask "in Christ's name."

We must be living the victorious life if we are going to pray "in His name." We likewise need to be in "accordance to His will" if we are to pray "in His name." *"Let this mind be in you which was also in Christ Jesus"* (Philippians 2:5). Unless we intend to do God's will we cannot expect Him to reveal His will to us. It is through studying God's Word and through praying that God's will is revealed to us.

When we pray in Jesus' name, it means that we are asking something because it is in character with what Jesus would ask if He were in the same circumstances. It means then that prayer is in keeping with His nature and His character as He lives His life through us. He is our loving Father who delights in meeting our needs. However, before we add "in Jesus' name" at the end, let's make sure that everything in our prayers are in keeping with His character. (8) Remember that only when we act in His name, will He then do whatsoever we ask in His name.

4. Praying for His Will

In his book, *Quiet Talks on Prayer*, S.D. Gordon states, "The purpose of prayer is to get God's will done." Therefore, the greatest prayer that we can say is, "Thy will be done.'(9) We can act in Christ's name when we are controlled by the Holy Spirit. *"For as many as are led by the Spirit of God, these are sons of God"* (Romans 8:14).

We know that God's will is what is best for us. Therefore, we should eagerly and earnestly seek to know the "mind" of Christ, to know His will. He wants to bless us and make us a blessing.

"Now in the morning, having risen a long while before daylight, He went out and departed to a solitary place; and there He prayed" (Mark 1:35). Jesus often left His disciples and went by Himself to pray. The crowds that He drew wanted to crown Him king (John 6:15). Satan likewise tempted Him to make compromises in order to draw a following (Matt. 4:3, 6, 9). Jesus knew that His mission was to remain obedient to His Father, not to draw crowds. It was prayer that preceded His miracle (John 11:41-43); it was prayer that enabled Him to go to the cross (Luke 22:41-42); and it was prayer that allowed Him to endure excruciating pain (Luke 23:46). We need to follow our Savior's example. We need to spend time alone with God in prayer seeking His agenda for our lives. (10)

In 1 John 5:14-15 we see three promises:

"Now this is the confidence that we have in Him, that if we ask anything according to His will, He hears us. And if we know that He hears us, whatever we ask, we know that we have the petitions that we have asked of Him."

First, He promises to listen if we are praying according to His will. Second, He promises that we have already possessed what we have asked for. Then thirdly, He promises that we know that we have the petitions we desire. These two verses deal with our capacity to approach God freely, openly with confidence, and boldly and then with assurance that He will hear what we ask for now. (11)

5. We Need to Pray That God Would Teach Us to Pray

When we get to Heaven we will have to give an account to Christ for our prayer lives. If you are the average Christian today, it will be a prayerless life. We need to grasp hold of this almost unbelievable promise. On the eve of His death Jesus' message is: *"And whatever you ask in My name, that I will do, that the Father may be glorified in the Son. If you ask anything in My name, I will do it"* (John 14:13-14). This promise was given to the disciples, and it is also given to you and to me. We need to utilize this promise in our lives so that we can bring glory to God. This promise needs to become real in our lives. It needs to be fulfilled in our daily prayer lives. When we ask in His name it means that as a believer our prayer should be for His purpose and kingdom and not for our own selfish desires. Our prayers should be on His merits, not ours, and they should be in pursuit of His glory, not ours. (12)

To get his point across to His disciples and to you and me, He repeats Himself a few moments afterward. *"If you abide in Me, and My words abide in you, you will ask what you desire, and it shall be done for you. By this My Father is glorified, that you bear much fruit, so you will be My disciples"* (John 15:7-8). When we obey His commands, submit to His Word, and are devoted to doing His will, our prayer lives will be fruitful, which in return puts God's glory on display, as He answers our prayers. Christ urges His disciples and you and me to obey His command "to ask." He goes on to say (verse 14).

"You are My friends if you do whatever I command you." He then repeats His desires: *"You did not choose Me, but I chose you and appointed you that you should go and bear fruit, and that your fruit should remain, that whatever you ask the Father in My name He may give you"* (John 15:16).

Christ is making a strong case that nothing can be accomplished without prayer. Again, He comes back with the same message:

"And in that day you will ask Me nothing. Most assuredly, I say to you, whatever you ask the Father in My name He will give you. Until now you have asked nothing in My name. Ask, and you will receive, that your joy may be full.

This promise or command was given to us six times in almost the same breath, when He tells us to "ask whatsoever we will." In John 16:23 we read: *"Whatever you ask the Father in My name He will give you."* Can you think of a greater and a more outstanding promise that has ever been made to man? Why then is this promise ignored so much? Is not this promise practically being ignored by Christians today?

Do we not know that *"Now to Him who is able to do exceedingly abundantly above all that we ask or think, according to the power that works in us"* (Ephesians 3:20).

Christ is now sitting on the throne of the Father, and He is making intercession for us. He has told us that our fruitfulness is dependent upon our prayer, and our joy depends upon answered prayers. These statements should make us jump up and down with excitement.

So What Is Prayer?

Many of our prayers ask things from God, but isn't there much more that should make up our prayers? True prayer should seek God Himself, for with Him we get all we need. Prayer is turning one's soul to God. David's description is the lifting up of the living soul to the living God. *"To You, O LORD, I lift up my soul."* (Psalms 25:1). It is the lifting up of our souls to God in prayer that gives God an opportunity to do what He wills in us and also with us.

Prayer is not persuading God to do what we want. We have to understand that God is always looking out for our greatest good. Sometimes God does give us our request that is not in accordance with His will. *"And He gave them their request, But sent leanness into their soul"* (Psalm 106:15).

There are those who only pray when there are emergencies. When the Twin Trade Tower buildings were destroyed by terrorists, there were a lot of people who prayed who ordinarily do not pray. Asking God for something is a very valuable part of prayer because it reminds us of our dependence upon God. It likewise is communion with God; it is talking with and to God. When we talk with someone in person, we get to know them better. It is the same with God. However, there is much more to prayer. When we pray to God, we can sense His nearness to us. When we commune with Him as a Friend, that is prayer. When we seek God as the Giver, rather than His gifts that is prayer. Our goal should be to seek Him and Him alone. When we acknowledge who He is and that He is the King of kings that is part of prayer. We need to thank

Him for His magnificence. We need to reflect upon the exceeding great riches of His glory in Christ Jesus.

Before we lay our petitions before God, should we not dwell first in meditation upon His glory and His grace? Then because of His exceeding great glory, let us give Him adoration and praise. *"'Holy, holy, holy is the LORD of hosts; the whole earth is full of His glory'"* (Isaiah 6:3)! *"'Glory to God in the highest, and on earth peace, good will toward men'"* (Luke 2:14)!

When you look through a microscope you see His glory. When you look at the sky through a telescope you see His glory. We need to learn to approach Him in simple faith and trust because of His infinite trustworthiness and unlimited power. We need a glimpse of His glory before we can pray correctly. When we express His attributes, it helps us become sensitive to His greatness and power.

We need to acknowledge that God is most holy, that He is mighty, and that He is merciful. Because of His glory, we need to praise Him; we need to bless Him; we need to worship Him, and we need to thank Him. The following verse from a hymn sums it up for us:

> My God how wonderful Thou art!
> Thy majesty how bright.
> How beautiful Thy mercy-seat
> In depths of burning light!
> How wonderful, how beautiful
> The sight of Thee must be;
> Thine endless wisdom, and boundless power (13)

"Bless the LORD, O my soul! O LORD my God, You are very great: You are clothed with honor and majesty…" (Psalm 104:1). When we start our prayers with adoration, praise and thanksgiving, it puts us in the spirit of prayer.

Prayer is a sign of spiritual life. Our spirituality and our fruitfulness are always in proportion to the reality of our prayers. Failure comes when we see man and not God. The Great Awakening bloomed into being when Jonathan Edwards saw God. Multitudes were saved when Whitfield saw God. When George Mueller saw God, thousands of orphans were fed.

We need a new vision of God, of God in all His glory. *"Blessed are the pure in heart, for they shall see God"* (Matthew 5:8).

It is only when we intend to do God's will that He can reveal His will to us. By studying God's Word, God's will is revealed to us. It is through prayer that we align our lives with God, so He then can demonstrate His power through us. The purpose of prayer is to prepare us to be involved in God's activity, not to change our circumstances. *"When the day of Pentecost had fully come, they were all with one accord in one place"* (Acts 2:1). It wasn't the fervent prayer of His people at Pentecost that induced the Holy Spirit to come upon them.

It was prayer that brought them to a place where they were ready to partici-pate in the mighty work that God had already planned. The followers of Jesus were told to remain in Jerusalem until the Spirit came upon them (Acts 1:4-5). The disciples obeyed His command. While they waited they prayed, and unity developed among them. Prayer, therefore, had prepared His disciples for their obedient response. God's purpose in prayer is designed to adjust us to God's will, not to adjust God's will to ours. (14)

Is There a Correlation Between Asking for Much and Receiving Much?

The devil wants us to believe that we are so busy doing things for self and God, and that we do not have time to pray. If we are going to accomplish much for God, we must ask in proportionately as much in prayer from God.

God wants us to ask for much, but He tells us to ask that which will in return be used to glorify Him. So we must ask ourselves again, what keeps us from asking much from God? What is keeping our lips sealed? What is keeping us from making much of prayer? Do we not take His love seriously?

"The effective, fervent prayer of a righteous man avails much" (James 5:16). This is a promise that God has given to believers who live righteously and pray fervently. Our prayers will produce results that will be significant. The question we need to ask ourselves is, "Are we fervent in our prayers?" When we have fervent prayer, we purposely spend adequate time in intercession. There will be times when we pray fervently that we will come to God in tears with our soul and our heart. Fervent prayer comes when the Holy Spirit assists us with our praying (Romans 8:26). When God does not answer our prayers, the problem is with us. If we adhere to God's Word, we will find that it is absolutely reliable. It is when we adhere to what God requires of us that He will show us how to pray for those things that are in line with His purpose. It is then that God will answer our prayers in an abundant way. (15)

Have we forgotten His power that He has displayed for us throughout the Bible? *"All authority has been given to Me in heaven and on earth. Go there-fore...and I am with you always..."* (Matthew 28:18-20). How many souls have come to know the Lord because you have fervently and frequently prayed for them? One thing we can do beyond the years of our useful work for God is to pray. We need to appreciate the power of prayer. It should not be a duty; it should be a privilege, a pleasure, a joy, and yes, a necessity. Let's get a renewed vision of who Christ is in all His glory, and a fresh glimpse of the riches of His glory which He has placed at our disposal and the mighty power that has been given unto Him. We need to remember that God answers prayer that is prayed with faith, providing we are praying in His will.

Let us place on His throne the needs of those around us: the needs of our church, our pastors, the ministries of our church, the new converts of our church, our personal needs, our family, the needs of our city, our nation, the needy of the world and the salvation of the lost. God will share His riches with us, but we must pray. *"...for the same Lord over all is rich to all who call upon Him"* (Romans 10:12). *"And my God shall supply all your need according to His riches in glory by Christ Jesus"* (Philippians 4:19). Our Lord is rich to all those who call upon Him.

We cannot make the excuse that "I cannot pray because I don't know how to pray."

> *"Likewise the Spirit also helps in our weaknesses. For we do not know what we should pray for as we ought, but the Spirit Himself makes intercession for us with groaning which cannot be uttered. Now He who searches the hearts knows what the mind of the Spirit is, because He makes intercessions for the saints according to the will of God"* (Romans 8:26-27).

When we do not know the right words to pray, the Holy Spirit then prays with and for us. You do not need to be afraid to come before Him, because the Holy Spirit assists you. (16) It has been well said, "To be little with God in prayer is to be little for God in service." (author unknown) The more secret prayer, the more public power.

America needs a revival, but I must confess that I have not been praying wholeheartedly for a revival. Yet all revivals have been the outcome of prayer. Might the Holy Spirit convict us, His children, to confess our sin of prayerlessness. We cannot ask God to change our country if we aren't praying for our country and our leaders. "Pray without ceasing" is a biblical command. Great Christian men have been noted for their prayer lives. How would our work for Christ change if we spent an hour a day in prayer? Two, three or even four hours? Read of missionaries that God has blessed, and you will find that they spent a lot of time in prayer. If we want great things to happen in our lives, we need to spend a great deal of time with our Master in prayer. "The prayer power has never been tried to its full capacity. If we want to see mighty wonders of divine power and grace wrought in the place of weakness, failure and disappointment, let us answer God's standing challenge, 'Call unto me, and I will answer thee, and show thee great and mighty things which thou knowest not'" (J. Hudson Taylor)! "God does nothing except in response to believing prayer." (John Wesley–Famous evangelist who spent two hours daily in prayer). When asked how much time he spent in prayer, George Mueller's reply was, "Hours every day. But I live in the spirit of prayer. I pray as I walk and when I lie down and when I arise. And the answers are always coming." (Source Unknown) C.H. Spurgeon said, "Prayer can never be in excess."

When we realize that all spiritual work is dependent on prayer, we should know that God wants us to pray. We need a fresh vision of Christ in all His glory and a fresh glimpse of the "riches of His glory." It is when we understand that all the riches of His glory are at our disposal, along with all the mighty power is given unto Him, that we will then get a fresh vision of the world around us and all its needs.

What would happen in our church, through our pastors' messages, and through our labor for the Lord if we could bring home to our hearts and our conscience the true power of prayer? It is time that we act on God's promises to us about prayer. When our Lord was speaking to His disciples, He asked them to believe that He was in the Father and the Father in Him. Then He continues by saying, *"...or else believe Me for the sake of the works themselves"* (John 14:11). He was basically saying to His disciples, "If you cannot believe My Person, My sanctified life, and the wonderful words that I said; then, at least look at My works. They should be sufficient to compel belief."

He then promises them that if they do believe, they should do even greater works than these. He gives them wonderful promises in regard to prayer. It is inferred that these "greater works" are accomplished through the outcome of prayer.

It should be our goal in life to be abundantly fruitful in our Lord's service. We should not be seeking position, power or prominence. We should long to be fruitful servants. If so, then we should be spending a lot of time in prayer.

Today we have missionaries around the world who need our prayers. We have missionaries who come home to report on their work. Many in our churches do not even come to hear about their work. Are we praying for our missionaries? Do we know their needs? God may not send you to the mission field overseas, but you can pray for your missionaries who are serving overseas and at home.

When we realize that we can accomplish much through our prayers, we are then going to spend more time in prayer for the Christian ministries in which we are involved. Great things have happened on mission fields when Christians are praying back home. Great things happen at home when we pray. *"Blessed be the God and father of our Lord Jesus Christ, who has blessed us with every spiritual blessing in the heavenly places in Christ"* (Ephesians 1:3). God's storehouse is full of blessings. The keys to His storehouse are prayer and faith. Together they will open the door to which blessings can be claimed. His blessing is upon those with a pure heart, for they shall see God. When Christ is our Savior, when He is Lord and King of our whole being, it is then that He will answer our prayers.

When we can honestly and humbly say as Paul said in Philippians 1:21, *"For to me, to live is Christ..."* will He not bring forth His great power in and through us?

Let us use the power of prayer to accomplish much for God. Let us do it to bring glory to His name. Let us pray in faith knowing that His work is accomplished through prayer. Let each day see us growing closer to Jesus, and each day let us trust Jesus more, that His will may be done in and through us.

Drawing From the Bank of Heaven for His Glory

When you go to Heaven's bank in the name of our Lord Jesus, with a check that is to be drawn upon unlimited riches of Christ, God does demand that you are a worthy recipient. In other words, you need to be worthy in the sense that you are seeking the gift not for your own glory or your own self-interest, but for the glory of God. The bank of Heaven will not cash our checks if there is sin in our lives or our motives are not right. *"You ask and do not receive, because you ask amiss, that you may spend it on your pleasures"* (James 4:3). "Amiss" refers to acting in an evil manner, which is motivated by personal gratification and selfish desires. (17)

When a person charges his luxury trip to Hawaii on a credit card and then asks God to supply the means to pay for the trip, that person needs to take into account James 4:3. If this person would have asked God to supply the means for the trip, and God supplied the means that would be great. However, it is also important to pray that we are asking for something that God wants us to do.

How Does God Answer Prayer?

Those who are living in sin should not expect God to answer their prayers unless it is a prayer of repentance. But as children of God we should expect answers to prayer. "…*all things are yours"* (1 Corinthians 3:21). All things are ours because we belong to Christ.

God does answer the prayers of a righteous person. Sometimes the answer is "Yes" and sometimes it is, "No", and sometimes it is, "Wait." A husband and wife have their private devotions in the morning. The husband prays for rain because his lawn needs rain, and the wife prays that it will be a nice sunny day, because she is going on a picnic with friends and their children. You might say that God could answer both of their prayers by holding off the rain until the picnic was over. Sometimes God puts a hold on our prayers, but for a good reason. We may not be ready for the answered prayer. When God answers our prayers it is because He knows that we will give Him the glory. If we ask for something that we want for our own glory, God is not obligated to answer that prayer, at least not at that time. Often a father has to tell his children that they are going to have to wait until they are older, or bigger, or wiser, or more spiritual. We do not give our son a gun to hunt with us until he is old enough, big enough and wise enough to handle the gun.

We have to remember that sometimes God does not answer our prayers right away because it is not His will at that time. *"He is a rewarder of those who diligently seek Him"* (Hebrews 11:6). When we pray that a friend or a relative would come to Christ, we might have to pray as long as George Mueller prayed for a friend. He prayed for sixty-three years, and his friend was saved after George's death, but before his funeral. Donna and I prayed from the time we were married for three of her grandparents until each one of them were saved in their seventies. We prayed for her uncle for forty years before he became a Christian. God is not going to allow us to pray for forty or sixty-three years for someone and then say, "No.": *"...who desires all men to be saved and to come to the knowledge of the truth"* (1 Timothy 2:4). We are definitely praying in God's will when we pray for the unsaved to become born again. When we pray fervently for the unsaved by name, it is prayer that God is going to honor. It should encourage us to pray more fervently for unsaved family and friends. Each of us should have a list of unsaved people for whom we are praying every day.

When we pray we need to be reminded, *"And whatever you ask in My name, that I will do, that the Father may be glorified in the Son. If you ask anything in My name, I will do it"* (John 14:13-14). We need to pray not to change His will, but for His will to be done. There is joy, peace and satisfaction when we are in His will and we are praying in His will.

God Is in the Business of Answering Prayer

God has indwelt each believer with the Holy Spirit. *"But the Helper, the Holy Spirit, whom the Father will send in My name, He will teach you all things, and bring to your remembrance all things"* (John 14:26). It is the Holy Spirit who puts fresh ideas into the minds of praying people. God can in many ways convey His thoughts to us.

There is a story told of an old whaling captain a long time ago: "A good many years ago, I was sailing in the desolate seas of Cape Horn, hunting whales. One day we were bearing directly south in the face of a hard wind. We had been tacking this way and that all the morning, and were making very little headway. About eleven o'clock, as I stood at the wheel the idea suddenly came into my mind, why batter the ship against theses waves? There are probably as many whales to the north as to the south. Suppose we run with the wind instead of against it? In response to that sudden idea, I changed the course of the ship, and began to sail north instead of south. One hour later, at noon, the lookout at the masthead shouted. 'Boats ahead!' Presently we overtook four lifeboats, in which were fourteen sailors, the only survivors of the crew of a ship which had burned to the water's line ten days before. Those men had been adrift in their boats ever since, praying frantically to God for rescue; and we arrived just in time to save them. They could not have survived another day." Then the old whaler added, "I don't know whether you believe in religion or not, but I happen to be a Christian. I have begun every day of my life with prayer that God would use me to help someone else, and I am convinced that God, that day; put the idea into my mind to change the course of my ship. That idea saved fourteen lives." (Source Unknown)

Is it possible that at times we are so busy doing things for God or for ourselves that we don't allow God to put thoughts into our minds? When we read

God's Word and when we pray, we need to allow God to speak to us, to put thoughts into our minds of what He wants us to do. How often have you heard it said that a missionary had a special need for prayer and there was a specific time that their prayer was answered, only later to find out that God had laid on the heart of someone back home to pray for that missionary at that very moment? When we are filled with the Spirit of God, we cannot help but influence others toward God. God is in the business of answering prayer. Are we in the business of praying? God has placed this marvelous power at our disposal! Let us use this power to bring glory to Him.

Prayer Hindrances

God wants Christians to pray, so what keeps a Christian from praying? As much as God wants us to pray, the devil does not want us to pray, and he does everything he can to keep us from praying. The devil knows that through our prayers we can accomplish much for God, which is a whole lot more than we can accomplish through our own efforts. Satan and his host of evil angels will do anything to keep us from praying. We must remember that God's holy angels are stronger than the fallen angels.

Many times we are our worst enemy when it comes to praying. We need to look at our own hearts to see if there are sins in our lives that will hinder our prayers. *"If I regard iniquity in my heart, the Lord will not hear"* (Psalm 66:18). Let's make sure that there is confession in our prayer, because even a little sin can hinder our prayers. Our unconfessed sin causes God to turn off His ear to our prayers, and He refuses to listen. Unless we confess our sins He is not going to listen to us.

Unbelief can also be a big hindrance to our prayers being answered. "But let him ask in faith, with no doubting, for he who doubts is like a wave of the sea driven and tossed by the wind" (James 1:6). How often does God not answer our prayers because we do not believe? Abraham was an outstanding example for us. "He did not waver at the promise of God through unbelief, but was strengthened in faith, giving glory to God, and being fully convinced that what He had promised He was also able to perform" (Romans 4:20-21).

Prayer is a humbling thing, and pride prevents prayer. Jealousy also can ruin our prayer lives. When we criticize others, our prayers are hindered. As we become more Christlike, we will become less judgmental of others. We need to remember, "Love suffers long and is kind"(1 Corinthians 13:4).

Our goal should be solely to bring glory to God. It is then that God can answer our prayers. (Psalm 37:4) We should not seek His gifts but Christ Himself "Beloved, if our heart does not condemn us, we have confidence toward God. And whatever we ask we receive from Him, because we keep His commandments and do those things that are pleasing in His sight" (1 John 3:21-22). Selfishness hinders our prayers. "You ask and do not receive, because you ask amiss, so you may spend it on your pleasures" (James 4:3). When our prayers have a selfish purpose, it robs them of power. We might pray things in the will of God, but if our motive is wrong, then there is no power in the prayer. When we ask for something for our own gratification, we "ask amiss," and we should not expect the prayer to be answered. (18)

Then there is the lack of love in our hearts which is a hindrance to our prayer. When we have a loving spirit we have a condition of believing in prayer. We cannot wrong a fellow man and be right with God. When our spirit of prayer is essentially the spirit of love, our prayer is an intercession of love.

> Can we hate those whom God loves? *"But I say to you, love your enemies, bless those who curse you, do good to those who hate you, and pray for those who spitefully use you and persecute you, that you may be sons of your Father in heaven "* (Matthew 5:44-45).

It is a waste of time to pray if we harbor an unforgiving spirit toward someone.

We need to remove those hindrances that keep us from having powerful prayers. We need to have a love for God and a love for those around us. We need to be involved in doing what God wants us to do in our lives. When we pray for something and refuse to do our part, it may hinder God from answering our prayers. Love compels us to have compassion and service in our lives. We cannot be sincere in our prayers for the conversion of the lost unless we are willing to speak a word or make some attempt to bring someone under the hearing of the gospel.

Is the spiritual life in many churches today weak because there is inefficient prayer? Should our weekly prayer meeting not be a live gathering where prayer is a living force, and testimony of answered prayer is the norm? If we grasp the power of prayer, I think our weekly prayer time in our churches should be exciting, moving and encouraging.

Giving Thanks and Rejoicing

> *"Be anxious for nothing, but in everything by prayer and sup- plication, with thanksgiving, let your requests be made known to God; and the peace of God, which surpasses all under- standing, will guard your hearts and minds through Christ Jesus"* (Philippians 4:6-7).

When someone does something special for you, you in return thank them for what they did for you. If a friend pays off a five-hundred-dollar payment for you, you are delighted and you, in return, give him a great big "thank you." When we bring a petition to God in prayer we need to thank Him for all the things that He is presently doing for us. We need to stop and think about all the prayers that God has answered and how seldom we have thanked Him. We need to be just as faithful in our thanking Him as we are in asking Him. One reason that our prayers are not answered is because we have neglected to thank God for blessings that we have already received from Him. (19)*"Delight yourself also in the LORD, and He shall give you the desires of your heart"* (Psalm 37:4). God is pleased when we praise Him. When we praise Him, we are then in return blessed.

It is from the ignorance of or disobedience to God's Holy Word that all hindrance to prayer arises. When we can truthfully say to the Father, "All that I am and have is Yours," then He in return can say to us, "All that belongs to Me is yours."

God has given us much power in prayer, but we have to pray. Our hearts need to be right with Him. We need to obey His Word and follow His will for our lives, and then He will ANSWER OUR PRAYERS! Let's finish strong by asking much from Him to bring glory to God. Let's pray! Remember when you become too old to work within the church; you can be a prayer warrior for those who do work in the church, and for the missionaries that your church supports. Again, let's pray! Let's expect answers! Let's give God the thanks, praise, honor and glory when He answers our prayers. Remember, God is in the business of answering prayer!

Lesson Three

The Need and Value of Advocates

After getting out of the hospital we asked the hospital for the records of my twenty-one day stay. I started reading an inch thick booklet of material and after reading "a 70 year old Caucasian unable to make decisions for himself", I put it down and never did read the remainder. My wife, Donna and our three children had to make decisions for me. Donna and I had made out a Living Will prior to my hospitalization which allowed her to make decisions on my behalf.

The first days after the heart attack they were not giving much hope that I would make it. One of the many decisions she had to make was when she and my children were called to a conference four days after the heart attack. At the conference, the doctor let my family know that he was called off the golf course to talk with them. The decision that Donna had to make was whether to have a pacemaker or a defibrillator/pacemaker implanted. This was the last hope to regulate my heart, but was also considered to be serious in view that I was still not responding to anything and my body was weak and my heart badly damaged. The doctor said the pacemaker was the Ford and the combo was the Cadillac. The boys said "let's get Dad a Cadillac," and the decision was made to install the defibrillator/pacemaker. Peace came with the decision as the family waited. Later we would know the power of prayer.

Another time that Donna became my advocate was when a doctor wanted to use a test using dye to determine if a blood clot had gone into my lung. My oncologist did not want dye used because it could easily do damage to the one good kidney that I had left. She literally had to "fire" that doctor as he refused to listen. Then there was the time that a nurse came in and listed the five medications she was going to give me. At this point, I was so out of it that I did not know what she was saying or what meds she was going to give me. But Donna said to her, "Does he get those pills every hour?" After confirming with her that I had been given the same five pills one hour prior, she left the room, and we never saw her again.

Donna or one of our three children was with me continually day and night. They were my advocates in many different ways. Just knowing that they were there was a comfort and a blessing.

Likewise, Donna was an advocate for me by e-mailing a large number of friends and family the details of how to pray for me. Then there were those that got Donna's almost daily up-dates that sent the e-mail to others that know us or were part of their church's prayer chain. I have become over whelmed with all the people that have said that they had prayed for us during this time. Those who prayed for me were also an advocate for me through their prayers. God was answering their prayers on my behalf.

Jesus Christ is our superior advocate. When people prayed on my behalf, He interceded to God for them. *"...we have an advocate with the Father Jesus Christ the righteous"* (1 John 2:1).

Chapter VI

Allowing the Holy Spirit to Control Your Life

If we are going to finish strong in our Christian walk, we need to understand the working of the Holy Spirit in our lives. We need to yield to the Holy Spirit in our daily walk. We need to be filled with the Holy Spirit. We need to walk in the Spirit. We need to allow the Spirit of God to lead us and guide us in our everyday walk.

We are born with a sinful nature, but when we became "born again" we are indwelt by the Holy Spirit. John explains this in John 3:5-7.

> *"Jesus answered, 'Most assuredly, I say to you, unless one is born of water and the Spirit, he cannot enter the kingdom of God. That which is born of the flesh is flesh, and that which is born of the Spirit is spirit.' Do not marvel that I said to you, 'You must be born again'. The wind blows where it wishes, and you hear the sound of it, but cannot tell where it comes from and where it goes. So is everyone who is born of the Spirit"*

When we accept Jesus Christ as our personal Savior we are born again. The Holy Spirit becomes the new ruling force in our lives. "And He said, *'Therefore I have said to you that no one can come to Me unless it has been granted to him by My Father'"* (John 6:65). It is the work of the Holy Spirit that allows us to have the new life in Christ. The Holy Spirit speaks to you, which prompted you to accept Christ as your personal savior. Therefore, we cannot boast. It is a gift! It is the grace of God working in our lives.

So How Do We Walk By the Spirit?

Our first step after salvation is given to us in Galatians 5:25: *"If we live in the Spirit, let us also walk in the Spirit."* As a new born in the faith, our steps need to be made in the help and guidance of the Spirit. We are born into this world as sinners and with an old nature. But when we become born again we have a new nature within us. The Spirit causes us to die to sin and live for God. Note Galatians 5:16 *"I say then: Walk in the Spirit, and you shall not fulfill the lust of the flesh."* Here we see that the opposite of walking in the Spirit is to walk in the flesh or what is referred to as our old nature. We have a choice to either walk in the Spirit or to walk in the flesh. The flesh is our old nature before we were born again. The old nature doesn't leave us, but through the power of the Holy Spirit in our lives we can overcome the flesh, the old nature. We have the flesh pulling us to sin and our new nature with the help of the Holy Spirit prompting us to live a holy life, doing that which pleases God. We are given the power that we need to do those things that are pleasing to God through the Holy Spirit. Without the Holy Spirit indwelling us none of our desires would be holy and just. *"Because the carnal mind is enmity against God; for it is not subject to the law of God, nor indeed can be"* (Romans 8:7). When the Holy Spirit comes into our lives he implants within us a desire to do that which is right in the eyes of God. When these desires are stronger than those of the flesh we are "walking by the Spirit". Our stronger desires dictate our actions. *"I will put My Spirit within you and cause you to walk in My statutes, and you will keep My judgments and do them"* (Ezekial 36:27). (1)

Paul says, "walk in the Spirit"." Walking here refers to a continuous action, or habitual lifestyle. As the believer submits to the Spirit's control he is walking according to God's Word. Galatians 5:18–*"But if you are led by the Spirit, you are not under the law."* He leads us. He gives us a stronger desire to walk with Him. "Being led by the Spirit" is the Spirit's enablement and initiative in our lives. When we "walk in the Spirit" it stresses the result of our behavior. The desire is to obey God is the leading of the Spirit, and our walk fulfills those actions and desires.

Contrasting the work of the flesh and the fruit of the Spirit we need to look at Galatians 5:19-24.

> *"Now the works of the flesh are evident, which are: adultery, fornication, uncleanness, lewdness, idolatry, sorcery, hatred, contentions, jealousies, outbursts of wrath, selfish ambitions, dissensions, heresies, envy, murders, drunkenness, revelries, and the like; of which I tell you beforehand, just as I also told you in time past, that those who practice such things will not inherit the kingdom of God. But the fruit of the Spirit is love, joy, peace, longsuffering, kindness, goodness, faithfulness, gentleness,*

self-control. Against such there is no law. And those who are Christ's have crucified the flesh with its passions and desires."

We have here a contrast between the "working of the flesh' (19-21) and the walking by the Spirit" (22-23). We have the natural evil desires which cannot be ignored. We need to crucify desires including not only the "big ones" like sexual immorality, but less obvious sins such as ambition, anger, and envy. When we gratify the "desires of the flesh" we are doing the "work of the flesh". We have a contrast between the work of the flesh (19-21) and the work of the spirit (22-23). (2)

The "fruit of the Spirit" is the Holy Spirit spontaneous work in us. It is the Spirit that produces these character traits, which are found in the nature of Christ. When Christ controls our lives they are by-products of our life. If we want the fruit of the Spirit to grow in our lives, we need to know Him, love him, remember Him, and imitate Him. We need to love God and man. We need to ask ourselves which of these qualities do we desire the Spirit to produce in us. It is His fruit, not our works. (3) It is important that we are cognizant that it is His fruit that He displays through us when we yield to His Spirit.

Love is the first thing mentioned in the fruit of the Spirit. If we go back to verses 14 it tells us to love our neighbors. Verse 14 says, *"You shall love your neighbor as yourself."* The whole law is completed in this statement. Love becomes the whole life style of those that bear the fruit of the Spirit, and are led and walk by the Spirit. Verse 18, *"But if you are led by the Spirit, you are not under the law."* God is pleased when we walk by the Spirit, live by the Spirit and bear fruit by the Spirit. We need to go beyond knowing what love looks like to actually loving by the Spirit.

If we are going to walk in the Spirit we need to be praying. We need to ask for forgiveness, confess our sins so the Holy Spirit can control our lives. When we sin the Holy Spirit losses control of our lives, and the old nature kicks in gear. We have to realize that we need help in living above the radar of sin. It is the Holy Spirit that gives us the desire to overcome sin in our lives and live a life that is pleasing to God. Let us pray as Paul did in 1 Thessalonians 3:12, *"And may the Lord make you increase and abound in love to one another and to all, just as we do to you."* We need to pray as the Psalmist prayed in Psalm 51:10 *"Create in me a clean heart, O God, and renew a steadfast spirit within me."* After we pray, we need to trust that we walk by faith in the Spirit. *"For sin shall not have dominion over you, for you are not under law but under grace."* (Romans 6:14) If we believe that the Spirit of God is in control of our lives, then we have to trust. *"Likewise you also, reckon yourselves to be dead indeed to sin, but alive to God in Christ Jesus our Lord"* (Romans 6:11).

As a new born Christian we have to realize that in and of ourselves we are helpless to do well apart from the Holy Spirit within us.

> *"For I know that in me (that is, in my flesh) nothing good dwells; for to will is present with me, but how to perform what is good I do not find"* (Romans 7:18). *"I am the vine, you are the branches. He who abides in Me, and I in him, bears much fruit; for without Me you can do nothing"* (John 15:5).

We cannot do anything that is good; however, we can sin and we do. It may affect our egos, but we can only do what is good through the power of the Spirit within us.

After we have acknowledged that we cannot do it in our own strength, and we have prayed for His help and trusted in Him, we will do what is pleasing to Him. Let us let the Holy Spirit bear fruit in our lives.

> *"If anyone speaks, let him speak as the oracles of God. If anyone ministers, let him do it as with the ability which God supplies, that in all things God may be glorified through Jesus Christ, to whom belong the glory and the dominion forever and ever. Amen"* (Peter 4:11).

When we are walking in the Spirit we need to be thanking God for what he is doing in and through us. We need to go beyond asking Him for enablement, we need to be thankful when He does enable, us to do what is right. *"But thanks be to God who puts the same earnest care for you into the heart of Titus"* (2 Corinthians 8:16). (4)

The Meaning of Being filled with the Spirit & How to Be Filled with the Spirit

"And do not be drunk with wine, in which is dissipation; but be filled with the Spirit…" (Ephesians 5:18). Paul is not speaking of the Holy Spirit indwelling here, because Christians are indwelt and they are baptized by the Spirit at the time of their salvation. Paul is commanding the believers to live under the influence and control of the Spirit by letting God's Word control them, confessing all their known sin, dying to themselves, seeking God's will for their lives, and depending on His strength and power for everything. When we are filled with the Spirit it brings joy. *"Do not sorrow, for the joy of the LORD is your strength"* (Nehemiah 8:10). There is joy in overcoming sins that beset us and being led by the Spirit. There is joy when we are seeking to live as Christ lived, serving Him and bring glory to God.

When we are filled with the Holy Spirit we are continually under the influence of the Spirit by letting the Bible control us. By seeking pure lives, confessing our known sins, dying to self-daily, seeking and surrendering to the will of God, and being dependent on His power in our lives we are filled with the Spirit. When we are filled with the Spirit we are consciously living in the presence of the Lord Jesus Christ. When we are filled with the Holy Spirit we are not filled with the world that surrounds us.

We are commanded to be filled with the Spirit. So what formula do we need to be filled with the Spirit? Let's look at Barnabas in Act 11:23:

> *"When he came and had seen the grace of God, he was glad, and encouraged them all that with purpose of heart they should continue with the Lord"* And Acts 6:5: *"And they chose Stephen, a man full of faith and the Holy Spirit."*

Both of these men were confident in God. They did not depend on their own strength, but the strength of God. We likewise need to be dependent on the strength of God; He has to do it through us. When we are filled with faith, we are filled with the Spirit. (5)

There is joy, hope and peace when we are filled with the Spirit. *"Now may the God of hope fill you with all joy and peace in believing, that you may abound in hope by the power of the Holy Spirit* (Romans 15:13). Hope comes from the power of the Holy Spirit in our lives. The joy and peace of the believer arises chiefly from their hope. The more hope (faith) a believer has the more joy and peace he or she will have. As Christians we should desire and labor for abundance of hope. Hope will not make us ashamed. Our hope (faith) comes through the power of the Holy Spirit. When our hope is abounding in our lives, the Holy Spirit must have all the glory. (6)

If we are going to finish our course strong we need to be filled with the Holy Spirit so the fruit of the Spirit will flow through us. Let's confess our sins, let's let the Holy Spirit control our lives to the finish line. When we are filled with the Spirit, He will accomplish His will in and through us. There will be joy, hope and peace in our lives when we are guided by the Spirit of God.

Lesson Four

God and You Only

There are only three things that I remembered from my time in ICU with a ventilator down my throat and my arms tied to the railing of the bed. First, there was the frustration of not being able to communicate. My son, Mark, also became frustrated and went to get some paper for me to write on. He untied one of my hands and put a pencil in it. He put the paper up above my head (I was laying on my back) I tried to write something. When I looked at it, I could not read it and neither could he. Seeing that it was not going to work he retied my arm to keep me from pulling out the tubes.

Another thing that I remember was staring at a clock on the wall. It was the only thing to look at during the long evenings. I would look at the clock, and then shut my eyes expecting forty-five minutes to have gone by, and then when I would look again, the clock would have only moved about five minutes. This happened numerous times.

Then there was the short talk that I had with God. "God, I am suffering a lot and if you are going to take me home, do it now for I don't want to suffer any more. However, if you are not going to take me home, I would still like to be a husband to Donna, a parent to my children and a grandparent to my grandchildren. Also, I think there are still some things that I can accomplish for You." As I completed that little talk with God, He reminded me quickly that His Son suffered for me very much on the cross. I then had to change my prayer to, "God, if you want me to suffer so I know what your Son went through, then I am willing to suffer."

I have to conclude that He is still working on me, in conforming me to His image. Likewise, looking back, I can see that God still wants me to be an example and leader to my family.

Chapter VII

Living by Faith

"**F**aith" according to Webster's dictionary is "an unquestioning belief that does not require proof or evidence." However, the Christian does have evidence for his faith. The Bible consists of 66 books with 40 authors. It was written over 1600 years in three different languages. It includes prophecy, and spiritual and moral truth. We have evidence of God's truth in our lives. We have the confidence of His words; and we have the resurrection of Jesus. The best definition of faith is found in Hebrews 11:1. To get a deeper understanding of this verse, let's look at several translations. *"Now faith is the substance of things hoped for, the evidence of things not seen"* (KJV & NKJV). The NIV says, *"Now faith is being sure of what we hope for and certain of what we do not see."* The RSV, NRSV and NASB each say, **"Now faith is the assurance of things hoped for, the conviction of things not seen."**

To His redeemed, faith is where the promises and work of God are made real. Ephesians 2:8-10 states that we are saved by faith.

> *"For by grace you are saved, through faith, and not of your-*
> *selves; it is the gift of God, not of works, lest anyone should*
> *boast. For we are His workmanship, created in Christ Jesus for*
> *good works, which God prepared beforehand that we should*
> *walk in them."* (1)

The Christian lives by faith. *"For in it the righteousness of God is revealed from faith to faith; as it is written, 'The just shall live by faith'"* (Romans 1:17). *"From faith to faith"* means that from start to finish, God declares us to be righteous by our faith. God justifies the sinner by grace, on the basis of faith alone.

Paul's intention is to prove that it has always been God's way to justify sinners by grace on the basis of faith alone. (2)

God's children receive the righteousness of God by faith. *"For the promise that He would be the heir of the world was not to Abraham or to his seed through the law, but through the righteousness of faith"* (Romans 4:13).

Likewise, we are justified in Christ by faith. *"Therefore, having been justified by faith, we have peace with God through our Lord Jesus Christ"* (Romans 5:1). Through faith we have peace with God. When we have peace with God, it means that we have been reconciled with Him.

There is access to God's grace by our faith. *"Through whom also we have access by faith into this grace in which we stand, and rejoice in hope of the glory of God"* (Romans 5:2). It is by our faith in Jesus Christ, and by His grace, that we are declared not guilty, and not His enemies. We are His friends and His children. We receive the promise of the Spirit by our faith as we read in Galatians.

> *"That the blessing of Abraham might come upon the Gentiles in Jesus Christ, that we might receive the promise of the Spirit through faith"* (Galatians 3:14). *"For we through the Spirit eagerly wait for the hope of righteousness by faith"* (Galatians 5:5)

As God's children we already possess the imputed righteousness of Christ, but we still are waiting for the completed and perfected righteousness which will come at glorification. Glorification is the final work of God upon the Christian which takes place when we get our new spiritual bodies in Heaven. God's ultimate purpose for Christians is that they will be conformed to the character of Christ, which is glorification. We wait for the return of Christ by faith. (3)

We also do God's work by faith. *"Nor give heed to fables and endless genealogies, which cause disputes rather than godly edification which is in faith"* (1 Timothy 1:4).

We as Christians need to make sure that our faith is placed in the right things. If you put your faith in government to solve all of your problems, then you have misplaced your faith.

If you think about it, we put our faith in a lot of things. When you sit down in a chair, you have faith that the chair is going to hold you up. When you get in your automobile, you have to have faith that the car is going to hold together. You have to have some faith that the person driving the car coming at you is going to stay on his side of the road. You have faith in the doctor who is going to operate on you. You have faith that the food you eat is not going to poison you. Some people have difficulty flying, but those who do fly have to have faith in the pilot and the flight plan. Without some faith in others around us, we would have a lot of difficulty in daily living. (4)

Looking back at Hebrews chapter eleven, let's glean how faith affected the people of God. Verse 4 says, *"By faith Abel offered to God a more excellent sacrifice than Cain, through which he obtained witness that he was righteous, God testifying of his gifts; and through it he being dead still speaks."* Both Abel and Cain knew what was required. Abel obeyed by acting in faith, but Cain acted in unbelief. It was natural for Abel to worship God. When a Christian does not want to worship God, there is something wrong. Cain had a wrong attitude, a lack of faith. It is our faith that causes us to look for opportunities to worship. Hebrews 11:5 says,

> *"By faith Enoch was taken away so that he did not see death, 'and was not found, because God had taken him'; for before he was taken he had this testimony, that he pleased God"*. Genesis 5:22-24 says, *"After he begot Methuselah, Enoch walked with God three hundred years, and had sons and daughters. So all the days of Enoch were three hundred and sixty-five years. And Enoch walked with God; and he was not for God took him"*.

God took Enoch away to Heaven because he walked with God. When you trust in Christ, your walk will change. Second Corinthians 5:17 says, *"Therefore, if anyone is in Christ, he is a new creation; old things have passed away; behold all things have become new"*. We are new creations, living in vital union with Christ. We are not the same anymore. We are now living a new life under a new Master.

Is God pleased with you as He was pleased with Enoch? Is God pleased with your recreation, what you watch on T.V., and the words and conversation you have? Is He pleased with your future plans?

Enoch was delivered from death because he walked with God by faith. Because you walked by faith when you accepted Jesus Christ as your personal Savior, you have been delivered from death-the death of damnation. (5)

In Genesis chapter six we read the tragic account of the decline of mankind into sin. God was sorry that He had made man because mankind's hearts were only evil continually. But God, a God of grace, saved Noah. We see this in the following verse:

"By faith Noah being divinely warned of things not yet seen, moved with godly fear, prepared an ark for the saving of his household, by which he condemned the world and became heir of the righteousness which is according to faith." (Hebrews 11:7).

Noah's faith was expressed in his obedience to God's calling. Can you imagine spending 120 years building a large boat in a land where it had never rained? Noah had great respect and awe for the command given him. Not only did Noah build the boat, but he warned the people of his time of the judgment that was coming. (6) Noah received rejection from his neighbors because he was different. Noah's obedience made him appear strange to his neighbors. When we obey God we should not be surprised that others will consider us different. The Christian's obedience makes others' disobedience stand out. From Noah's example, we need to know that when God asks us to do something, He will give the necessary strength to carry the task out.

Verses 8-10 of Hebrews 11 continue:

> *"By faith Abraham obeyed when he was called to go out to the place which he would receive as an inheritance. And he went out, not knowing where he was going. By faith he dwelt in the land of promise as in a foreign country, dwelling in tents with Isaac and Jacob, the heirs with him of the same promise; for he waited for the city which has foundations, whose builder and maker is God."*

Abraham had faith when he left his home, at God's command and went to an unknown land. He was obeying without question. He believed in the covenant that God had made with him (note Genesis 12). Abraham had faith when he was obedient to God by being willing to sacrifice his son Isaac. (Note Genesis 22:1-19) We should not be surprised when God asks us to give up secure, familiar surroundings to carry out His will. I can remember at the age of 37, when a college friend-then a missionary to Chile-asked if we would be willing to be missionaries in his invitation. God spoke to Donna and me and we went forward in the conference indicating that we would be willing to be missionaries. Because we were both certified teachers in the state of Michigan, we wrote missionary boards asking if they had a need for short-term missionary teachers. This was in the winter of 1974. The reply came back from Baptist Mid-Missions that they needed teachers that coming fall in both of our fields. I had a good paying job working for the State of Michigan and in order to go, I had to give up my job.

By the beginning of August 1975, we were in Fortaleza, Brazil teaching missionary children. We went for one year, but stayed two years. God was directing us into a new field of ministry, that of Christian education. I spent twenty-six years in teaching and administration in Christian education, and Donna spent eight years teaching in Christian schools. We went by faith to the mission field, and God supplied our needs while on the field and ever since. I had completed ten years of working for the State of Michigan when we went to the mission field and when I turned sixty I knew that I would receive a pension that would probably pay my house taxes, which it has been doing. However, I did not realize that I would have health, dental and vision insurance through the state also. God is faithful!

Faith is more than trusting Jesus for our salvation; it is trusting Him for everything. It means to trust Him when things are difficult. It means that every day you continue to trust Him, and you continue to manifest the fruit of your faith. *"But without faith it is impossible to please Him, for he who comes to God must believe that He is, and that He is a rewarder of those who diligently seek Him"* (Hebrews 11:6).

It is faith that connects you to God; it's you admitting that you are dependent upon Him. Your hope is in Him. God is pleased when you are trusting in Him.

In the life of the Christian, faith is vitally important. It is by faith Christians are saved, justified, and cleansed. It is by faith that the Christian looks forward to the return of Jesus Christ.

Living by Faith

Jesus said to his disciples, "Follow me and I will make you fishers of men" (Matthew 4:19). The disciples had to step out by faith and follow Jesus. They had to step out of their comfort zone to follow Jesus. When Christ died on the cross and then left the disciples, they had to step out in faith, a faith that turned the world upside down. As his disciples, when we live by faith, we "live in motion with God". God created us to be in motion for Him. God sets up divine appointments for us when He opens up doors for us to walk through. By faith God wants us to open those doors and fulfill the assignments that He places before us, as He did with Philip as recorded in Acts 8:26-27.

Chapter VIII

Putting on the Whole Armor of God

In Ephesians 6:10-20, Paul is describing the armor of God that the Christian needs to wear. In chapters one through three, he talks about the true believer who lives a Spirit-controlled life. Then in chapter four through chapter six, verse nine, he states that the Spirit-controlled Christian is going to be involved in a Spiritual war. Therefore, the spirit-controlled Christian needs to make sure that he has on the whole armor of God.

If we are going to finish our race strong we need to be filled with the Spirit and we need to have on the whole armor of God. *"Finally, my brethren, be strong in the Lord and in the power of His might" (v*s. 10). Ultimately, we know that Satan's power over the Christian is already broken. The war is won through Christ's crucifixion and resurrection, which has forever conquered the power of sin and death. But, in this life here on earth, there are battles of temptation that are going on regularly. If there is going to be victory, the Lord's power, the force of biblical truth, and the strength of His Spirit are required. (1)

The apostle Paul is giving forth the first words of encouragement for battle: Be strong in the Lord and in His mighty power. A Christian soldier needs resolution and a daring courage. The soldier needs to rely on the strength of the Lord and not on himself.

The strength of the Lord comes from putting on the whole armor of God. This is done by putting on the shield of faith, the breastplate of righteousness, the sword of the Spirit, and the rest of the armor.

The devil is our chief enemy and we have to combat him with Christian warfare. It is when the armor is worn all the time that we can withstand the wiles of the devil. (2) *"Put on the whole armor of God, that you may be able to stand against the wiles of the devil"* (vs. 11).

"For we do not wrestle against flesh and blood, but against principalities, against powers, against the rulers of the darkness of this age, against spiritual hosts of wickedness in heavenly places" (vs. 12). When the apostle Paul speaks of "not against flesh and blood," he does not mean to say that Christians have no enemies among men that oppose them, but that the main controversy is with the invisible spirits of wickedness that seek to destroy them. (3)

Our enemy is powerful; he has principalities and powers, and rulers. He has thousands of ways of beguiling the unstable Christian. Our enemies are great because they are unseen, and they assault us as we are unaware of them. Our enemies strive to keep us from Heaven. They assault us in the things that belong to our souls. The Christian needs faith in the Christian warfare because we have these spiritual enemies to contend with. Because we know what our danger is, it is our duty to put on the whole armor of God, to stand our ground, and withstand our enemies. (4)

"Therefore take up the whole armor of God, that you may be able to withstand in the evil day, and having done all, to stand" (vs. 13). Paul is emphasizing the necessity for Christians to appropriate God's full spiritual armor by putting it on in obedience. The girdle, the breastplate, and shoes/boots were worn all the time on the battlefield; and the shield, helmet, and sword were kept nearby to be used when actual fighting took place "the evil day". The goal is to stand firm against the enemy without wavering or falling. (5) We have to stand our ground for when we stand against Satan, we strive against sin. Because he stands against us, we must stand against him. When we resist him, he will flee!

The Girdle

"Stand therefore, having girded your waist with truth, having put on the breastplate of righteousness" (vs. 14). When we stand we need to stand armed, armed with the armor of God. (6)

As Christian soldiers we need to be able to resist every attack, as a soldier does in battle. Paul therefore uses a description of the ancient armor of a soldier in his day. The girdle, or sash, was an important part of the soldier's dress, both in war and in peace. (7) The soldiers wore tunics of loose-fitting cloth. A belt, therefore, was necessary to draw up the loose-fitting cloth, which was a potential hindrance and danger. A girdle was necessary to cinch up the loosely hanging material. As the ancient soldier girded up, he was pulling in those loose ends in preparation for battle. The Christian's belt pulls in all the spiritual loose ends, and is "truth," or better stated, "truthfulness." Truth makes the soul sincere, firm, consistent, and always on its guard. When a man has no consistent view of truth, he is the man who the adversary can successfully assail. (8)

Everything that hinders the Christian is to be tucked away. The idea is for a sincere commitment to fight and win without hypocrisy, but with self-discipline and with a devotion to victory. (9)

When our "loins are girded with truth" it is more than just reading the Word; we must understand our position in Christ and also His position in us. We have to realize that the real struggle is between God and Satan. When we have holes in our theology, it is then that Satan builds his stronghold. With our loins girded about with the knowledge of truth, it is then that we are truly prepared for battle. (10)

The Breastplate of Righteousness

The breastplate was usually a sleeveless piece of tough leather or other heavy material, often with animal horns or hoof pieces that were sewn on, which covered a soldier's full torso and protected his heart and other vital organs. (11) It covered the body from the neck to the thighs. It consisted of two parts, one which covered the front and the other covering the back. It was made of rings or in the form of scales or of plates. They were fastened together so that they would be flexible, and at the same time guard the body from spear, arrow, or sword. It is also referred to in other passages as a coat of mail.

> *"He had a bronze helmet on his head, and he was armed with a coat of mail, and the weight of the coat was five thousand shields of bronze (about 125 lbs.)"* (1 Samuel 17:5). *"So it was, from that time on, that half of my servants worked at construction, while the other half held the spears, the shields, the bows, and wore armor, and the leaders were behind all the house of Judah."*(Nehemiah 4:16).

When Christ's righteousness is over our hearts, we are unlikely to suffer harm.

As the breastplate defended the vital parts of the body, so the breastplate of righteousness defends the Christian's integrity, holiness, and purity of life against the assaults of Satan. As the coat of mail preserved the heart of the soldier from the arrows of an enemy, so the breastplate of righteousness protects the Christian from the arrows of Satan. (12) When there is a lack of holiness, it leaves the Christian vulnerable to the great enemy of his soul.

If we are to be prepared for battle we need to accept the gift of righteousness. As Christians we already have the righteousness of God. It is hard for us to think of ourselves as righteous. In His sight we are righteous, a gift we need to accept (Rom 5:17). To go into battle we need this truth, lest we allow Satan to make us feel unworthy in God's presence. When we realize that we already have His righteousness, we can enter into spiritual warfare and be victorious. (13)

Shod with the Gospel of Peace

"...and having shod your feet with the preparation of the gospel of peace" (vs. 15). The Roman soldiers wore boots that had nails in them for the purpose of gripping the ground in combat. (14) The boots (1 Sam. 17:6) were made of brass and were almost universally used by both the Greeks and Romans. (15) They were to protect the feet against gall-traps and sharp sticks, which were laid to obstruct the marching of the enemy. (16)

In the heat of battle the Roman soldier had to do a lot of fancy footwork to insure that he did not get killed. The Roman soldier's battle was mostly hand-to-hand with the enemy within close range. Historians tell us that successes of both Julius Caesar and Alexander the Great were due to their footwear. The feet of their armies were shod with footwear which allowed them to travel great distances in a short time and also to navigate rough terrain with ease. Today's equivalent would be a football or baseball player wearing cleats. They allow the player to dig into the turf and to make a quick start or stop without slipping.

There are lessons from this passage which are applicable. One would be preparedness. As Christians we are to be ready to go out at a moment's notice to present the gospel of peace, the Word of God. We need to know His Word well to be prepared.

> *"Be diligent to present yourself approved to God, a worker who does not need to be ashamed, rightly dividing the word of truth"* (2 Timothy 2:15). *"But sanctify the Lord God in your hearts, and always be ready to give a defense to everyone who asks you a reason for the hope that is in you, with meekness and fear"* (1 Peter 3:15).

A second lesson is that as believers we have a sure foundation because the believer is already reconciled to God through the gospel of peace, which gives him a sure foothold in battle.

> *"Therefore whoever hears these sayings of Mine, and does them, I will liken him to a wise man who built his house on the rock: and the rain descended, the floods came, and the winds blew and beat the house; and it did not fall, for it was founded on the rock"* (Matthew 7:24).

Jesus uses the rock to describe Himself. The Roman soldier's shoes gave him sure footing and grip; our spiritual shoes shod tightly to our feet will keep our feet firm, not to be moved by the schemes of Satan. We also can move quickly to avoid enemy strikes. When rough times come we have the adequate footwear to maneuver through those times unharmed. When Jesus was ready to send his disciples out to evangelize, He empowered them with the Holy Spirit and instructed them: "*Behold, I give you the authority to trample on serpents and scorpions, and over all the power of the enemy, and nothing shall by any means hurt you*" (Luke 10:19).

In retrospect Jesus was dressing His disciples in armor before he sent them out. The disciples were to trample over the serpents and scorpions of Satan. In the same way, when Christians put on the spiritual armor footwear, the Christian soldier can trample on the wiles and works of Satan. (17)

The Shield of Faith

The Roman soldier's shield was rectangular and about as tall as the soldier. It protected every part of his body, and it could be turned in every direction. It covered all other parts of the armor, just as faith is similar in importance in the Christian life. The shield was made of either light wood or a rim of brass, covered with several thicknesses of stout hide and preserved by frequent anointing (oiling). The outer surface of the shield was somewhat rounded from the center to the edge, and it was polished smooth or treated with oil, which would make the darts glance off. As the shield is an important protection for the soldier, so faith protects the Christian from the fiery darts of the wicked one. As long as the soldier has the shield, he has a sense of security, and as long as the Christian keeps his faith, he is safe. Faith comes to his aid when attacks are made on him. A faith that never doubts is the best of all defenses that the Christian can have against Satan. (18)

The fiery darts used in war were small, slender pieces of cane that were filled with combustible materials and would be set on fire, or contained combustible materials which set the target on fire. By the "fiery darts of the wicked," Paul probably is referring to the temptations of our adversary. His temptations come from unexpected quarters, like arrows that are shot suddenly from an enemy in ambush. They pierce and penetrate, as an arrow would that is on fire. The only way that the Christian can meet them is by the "shield of faith," by having confidence in God and relying on Him. We cannot do it with our own strength; we have to have faith in God because we are wholly defenseless. The Christian's "shield of faith" is a faith that can turn in any direction at any time to put out the fiery darts. (19)

We are told to take up our shield of faith, which is the knowledge that God has our lives in His full view, and He controls every situation and circumstance that comes our way. Faith encompasses believing that Jesus is the Messiah, believing Jesus for His promises, for His love, for His grace and for His return. It believes that every circumstance that comes our way is in His hand. Faith, then, is the shield which allows us to quench the fiery darts that are sent our way; they may hit us, but they will not harm us. (20) Our faith is our protecting shield.

Helmet of Salvation

"And take the helmet of salvation..." (Hebrews 6: 17). In battle, a major target was the head, and the helmet protected it. Paul is not speaking here about attaining salvation, but is speaking to those who have already been saved. (21) If a person is not born again, then he is not saved by God's grace and cannot put on the "helmet of salvation." Our new life, our salvation, was procured by the precious blood of Jesus, which cleanses us and initiates us into the kingdom of God.

Satan does everything he can to convince every Christian sometime during his or her Christian walk that the last sin that was committed was the last straw, and it exceeded the limit of God's grace. It is a lie, because God's grace has no bounds and is limitless. When Christians are convinced that they have exceeded God's grace limit, they have in essence removed the helmet of salvation and the rest of the armor.

Because of the weapons that were used, the Roman helmet was somewhat different from today's military helmets. In Paul's day the Roman army wore a helmet that not only protected the brain, but had a sloping edge down the back which protected the neck and flaps that draped down between the ears and the eyes. Because swords were used, the soldier's neck was protected from a sword. If approached from the back, the enemy could not take his head off. Soldiers without heads are not good fighters. The metal flaps between the ears and eyes also were for protection from the blow of a sword from the side. Through many military campaigns the Romans knew the enemy liked to strike at the most effective place, and they therefore guarded their soldiers against that harm.

Paul knew, from his wisdom from God, that the mind of the Christian is where Satan first wants to attack. Thoughts, ideas in action, come through the eyes, ears, nose, tongue and sensory nerves of the skin, and they are first processed in the brain. Once processed in the brain, the information goes to the heart and is either good or evil. If it is good or even something that is holy, it brings joy, and that joy is manifested in the person, and in return spreads to others. When the information is evil or lustful and not dealt with while in the brain, it goes to the heart, and there evil grows and is manifested by words and action. This is why Paul says, *"And do not be conformed to this world, but be transformed by the renewing of your mind, that you may prove what is that good and acceptable and perfect will of God"* (Romans 12:2).

When a person is born again he has his mind renewed. At the beginning of each day the Christian needs to confirm his salvation through the blood of Jesus. That confirmation is putting on the helmet of salvation, which causes us to realize that we are born again, that we have faith, that we are righteous and we know the truth. Likewise, we know that the Holy Spirit, who is called the sword, indwells us. He is in the believer to help fight the good fight. What a comfort to know that the Holy Spirit is walking with us in the battles that we fight. (22) "We need to live within the power and the direction of the Holy Spirit. It is imperative that we submit our minds, our wills and our emotions to the authority of the Spirit of God." (23) The Word of God is also called a sword, which makes it imperative that we read His Word and meditate on it so our brains and our hearts will be filled with good things, not the garbage the world offers.

The "helmet of salvation" is the basis upon which all the other pieces of armor work so effectively. By putting on the "helmet of salvation," the Christian is recognizing each and every moment of every day that he or she is saved through the precious blood of Jesus Christ. So keep the "helmet of salvation" on! (24)

The Sword of the Spirit

"...the sword of the Spirit, which is the word of God" (vs. 17). The sword was the soldier's only weapon. All the other parts of his armor were for protection. The Word of God is the only needed weapon for the Christian, which is infinitely much more powerful than any of Satan's weapons. (25) *"For the Word of God is living and powerful, and sharper than any two-edged sword, piercing even to the division of soul and spirit, and of joints and marrow, and is a discerner of the thoughts and intents of the heart"* (Hebrews 4:12).

All the other armor was only defensive; the sword was for defense and offense. We are to attack Satan, as well as secure ourselves, with the shield in one hand and the sword in the other hand. When we fight the powers of Satan we need both. The whole armor and the sword show us how great it is to be a Christian. If we miss even one part of the armor of God, it makes us incomplete. (26)

The Word of God is called the "sword of the Spirit" because it comes from the Holy Spirit and receives its fulfillment in the soul through the operation of the Holy Spirit. When the Christian can bring to mind a passage of Scripture in times of temptation and trials, it has a wonderful tendency to cut in pieces the snares of the adversary. The Christian, through God's Word, can have unlimited confidence. (27)

The Roman's sword was short and double-edged and made of superior metals. The Romans armed their soldiers with the best, knowing that the soldier was all that stood between the barbarian and their lifestyle. The Roman sword was not cumbersome, and the shortness was not a disadvantage to the Roman soldier. It was an effective weapon for the Romans because of the skill of their soldiers. They were outstanding swordsmen who were put through rigorous training. Their mastery of the sword made their enemies tremble in fear. They used their swords as both a defensive weapon for the purpose of glancing off strikes of their enemies and as an offensive weapon to strike blows at their enemies. Likewise, the best offensive and defensive weapon the Christian has is the Word of God, which is our sword of the Spirit. The Bible is our sword, and when the Christian quotes God's Word in the time of battle, it is really Jesus saying those words to the enemy. In reality, the Christian is quoting Jesus' words and knows that He is the commander, which causes the enemy to shudder and flee. *"Therefore submit to God. Resist the devil and he will flee from you" (James 4:7)*. Resist means "to take a stand against." When we take allegiance to God and His Word, which is our sword, the devil will flee from us.

When Jesus was led into the wilderness and was tempted by Satan, He used the Word of God to rebuke Satan. Jesus chose to use the sword of The Spirit not only because it was ordained for Him to do so, but to be a lesson to His people. The Christian is to be an imitator of Christ Jesus. Therefore, if Jesus used the Scripture to rebuke Satan, should not the Christian also use his "sword"? (28)

With Much Prayer and Supplication

"...praying always with all prayer and supplication in the Spirit, being watchful to this end with all perseverance and supplication for all the saints..." (vs. 18). In our battle as a Christian soldier we need to pray for victory. For a Christian soldier, prayer is indispensable. No matter how complete our armor might be, no matter how skilled we might be in the art of war, no matter how courageous we are, we can be certain that without prayer we will be defeated. It is God who gives victory. As a Christian soldier goes forth with the full armor of God in spiritual conflict, and if he has looked to God through prayer, he will surely be successful. This prayer needs to be continuous in every temptation and spiritual conflict we encounter. Prayer makes the Christian armor shine, and Satan trembles when a saint is upon his knees. (29) We cannot see the battles that are taking place in the spiritual realm, but we can pray that there will be victory. We also need to pray before our spiritual battle so that we turn the glory away from us and give it to the One who gives us the victory, not only for present and past battles, but also the future ones. (30)It is imperative that Christians clothe themselves each day with the full *"armor of God."* It begins with the knowledge of our salvation, which is through the precious blood of Jesus our Savior. With salvation we have righteousness through faith. Righteousness which is imparted by God must therefore be maintained through acts of faith. When the Christian is righteous, he wears the belt of truth and must be truthful even though he lives in a world of deception and lies. The Christian's daily walk is a walk of truth as he walks with the "Master of Truth" and reads the Book of truth that He left for him. Our footing is firm when the shoes that are on our feet stand on the truth of God's Word. It gives us that foundation that

allows us to fight our enemy. We are allowed to ward off the flaming arrows of Satan with our "shield of faith," dipped in the spring of living water. Likewise, we have His Word, our "Sword," to fight off the enemy. With prayer we receive help from Heaven in our battles. We are also to pray for others, because they face the same battles we face. All Christians are in a spiritual warfare, *and it is imperative that they wear the full "armor of God".* We must fight together in a unified effort to win for our Lord and Savior, winning the race that is set before us, finishing strong for the purpose of bringing glory to Him. With God's armor we can win over our enemy and finish strong God's way.

Lesson Five

Patience

"My brethren, count it all joy when you fall into various trials, knowing that the testing of our faith produces patience. But let patience have its perfect work, that you may be perfect and complete, lacking nothing" (James 1:2-4).

The first testing of my patience came when I was told that I would have to wait six weeks before I could have my right kidney removed. People would ask me how I was doing, and I would reply that I was "hanging in there." I was hanging in there, but I was having a rough time waiting. Even though my cancer/urologist/surgeon doctor said that the cancer was contained on the right kidney, in my mind waiting six weeks meant that it could spread to other parts of the body. Waiting wasn't fun for me. God was definitely testing my patience.

Then I was told that I would be in the hospital for up to four days, and when those days stretched out to twenty-one days, my patience was again tested. It seemed that at times I would take one step forward and two steps backward.

When I finally got out of the hospital, I thought that my patience-testing had ended. But as the days went by and my recovery was very slow, I could see that my patience was still being tested.

I have to be reminded again and again that God is still working on me. *"But let patience have its perfect work, that you may be perfect and complete, lacking nothing"* (James 1:4). And we need to remember to count it for joy when God is working on us in the area of patience.

Chapter IX

Living a Life of Christian Joy

J oy is the opposite of sorrow and unbelief. The theme of the book of Philippians is joy. Paul was in a prison in Rome when he wrote this book. Some would look at Paul's circumstances and feel sorry for him. His life was in danger, yet he rejoiced. He had opposition and persecution, yet he rejoiced. The situation that he found himself in would appear to an unsaved person as a pitiful situation at best. Yet we find Paul rejoicing. Why can he say, *"Rejoice in the Lord always. Again I will say rejoice!"* (Philippians 4:4)? Paul is not rejoicing because he is in prison and things are not going well. He is rejoicing for what he has in Christ. He knows that Jesus Christ died for him on the cross. He knows that because he believes that Jesus Christ died for him on the cross as his substitute that he will spend eternity in Heaven. That brings not only joy but contentment. How can he or you and I who are born-again believers not rejoice in what we have in Christ?

Paul instructs Christians to rejoice in all things. *"Rejoice always, pray without ceasing, in everything give thanks; for this is the will of God in Christ Jesus for you"* (1 Thessalonians 5:16). Paul commended the Macedonians for having joy even when they encountered severe trials in their lives. *"...that in a great trial of affliction the abundance of their joy and their deep poverty abounded in the riches of their liberality"* (2 Corinthians 8:2). This church had difficulties, but joy rose above their pain because they had devotion to the Lord and to the cause of His kingdom. James tells us to rejoice in our trials. *"My brethren, count it all joy when you fall into various trials, knowing that the testing of your faith produces patience"* (James 1:2-3). James writes about having joy in our trials because he knew that *"all things work together for the good."* He could say to have joy because he knew that trials can benefit us by strengthening us. These churches, in spite of their very difficult circumstances, had joy that rose higher than their pain. It was because of their complete devotion to the Lord. When trials hit us, we can have joy by trusting God that He will work things out for what is best. When difficult circumstances come our way, we can have joy because we have hope. *"...Rejoicing in hope..."* (Romans 12:12). We have the hope and the assurance of our redemption, which is a promise. (1)

There are consequences in not living for Christ with a joyful heart.

> *"Because you did not serve the LORD your God with joy and gladness of heart, for the abundance of everything, therefore you shall serve your enemies, whom the LORD will send against you, in hunger, in thirst, in nakedness, and in need of everything; and He will put a yoke of iron on your neck until He has destroyed you"* (Deuteronomy 28:47-48).

This is a curse that God put on the nation of Israel for their disobedience. When there is sin in our lives, we cannot rejoice in the Lord.

Jesus presents an example of hope filled with joy. We find this in John 16:20-24.

> *"Most assuredly, I say to you that you will weep and lament, but the world will rejoice; and you will rejoice; and you will be sorrowful, but your sorrow will be turned into joy. A woman, when she is in labor, has sorrow because her hour has come; but as soon as she has given birth to the child, she no longer remembers the anguish, for joy that a human being has been born into the world. Therefore you now have sorrow; but I will see you again and your heart will rejoice, and your joy no one will take from you."*

There is a big contrast between the disciples and the world. The world rejoiced as the disciples wept, but they would see Jesus again in three days and then rejoice. The world's values are, many times, opposite of God's values. Jesus knew He was about to die, but in the drama of the event He spoke of joy. Even though life may be difficult now, one day the Christian will rejoice. We need to keep our eyes on God; we need to keep our eyes on the finish line. (2)

The true source of joy for the Christian is Christ. *"But there is a friend who sticks to us closer than a brother"* (Proverbs 18:24). *"Rejoice in the Lord, always"* (Philippians 4:4).

Jesus is our example. He persevered on the cross, carrying through to complete perfection.

> *"Looking unto Jesus, the author and finisher of our faith, who for the joy that was set before Him endured the cross despising*

the shame, and has sat down at the right hand of God. For consider Him who endured such hostility from sinners against Himself, lest you become weary and discouraged in your souls" (Hebrews 12:2-3).

It was His joy which allowed Him to endure the cross. When we keep our eyes focused on Jesus as the object of our faith and salvation, we can endure our trials and tribulation with joy. (3)

"Blessed are you when men hate you, and when they exclude you, and revile you, and cast out your name as evil, for the Son of Man's sake. Rejoice in that day and leap for joy! For indeed your reward is great in heaven" (Luke 6:22-23).

Persecution is not something we should desire. But when a Christian has evil spoken against him falsely for Christ's sake, that persecution carries God's blessing with it. (4)

The joy of the Christian is given by the power of the Holy Spirit. We cannot muster it up, but it is the outcome of a life given over to the Holy Spirit. *"But the fruit of the Spirit is love, joy, peace..."* (Galatians 5:22). We see a biblical connection between being filled with the Holy Spirit and having joy. *"And the disciples were filled with joy and with the Holy Spirit"* (Acts 13:52). At Antioch the disciples were filled with joy. This was a happy event in the midst of persecution, a time that the gospel was able to fill the soul with joy, even when there were severe trials. (5)

"For the kingdom of God is not eating and drinking, but righteousness and peace and joy in the Holy Spirit" (Romans 14:17). The kingdom of God is not meat and drink, which represent outward and indifferent things. The kingdom of God is righteousness, pardon from sin, and holiness of the heart. It is peace in the soul from a sense of God's mercy. It is peace regulating, ruling, and harmonizing the heart. It is joy in the Holy Spirit. It is a solid spiritual happiness; it is a joy which springs from a clear sense of God's mercy; it is the love of God being shed abroad in the heart by the Holy Spirit. It is happiness brought into the soul by the Holy Spirit, and then being maintained there by the Holy Spirit. It is righteousness without sin, and it is peace without inward disturbance. (6)

Jesus also received joy through the Holy Spirit. *"In that hour Jesus rejoiced in the Spirit and said, 'I thank You, Father, Lord of heaven and earth, that You have hidden these things from the wise and prudent and revealed them to babes'"* (Luke 10:21). This joy of Jesus was directly due to the Holy Spirit. It is joy in the work of His followers and their victories over Satan and is also akin to what Jesus felt in John 4:2-38. (7)

Joy is found in the presence of God.

"In the multitude of my anxieties within me, Your comforts delight my soul" (Psalm 94:19). *"You will show me the path of life; in Your presence is fullness of joy; at Your right hand are pleasures forevermore"* (Psalm 16:11).

Peter quoted this verse on the day of Pentecost when there was an outpouring of the Holy Spirit. (8)

Do others see the joy of your salvation in your lifestyle? Is joy the theme of your life? Do you have joy when things do not seem to be going your way? Do you let circumstances steal from you the joy that you have in your salvation? Can you rejoice in all things? We need to remember that true joy comes from Christ. It comes from serving Him, following His example in our lives and rejoicing in what He has done for us. Let us finish the race of our life strong by having joy in our hearts. Let's allow that joy to show forth in our actions, in our outward appearance and in our daily duties of life. Let us rejoice in what we have in Christ. Remember that joy is internal and is based on Christ. (9)

Joy comes when we are content with what we have in Christ, not our circumstances. The devil does everything that he can to steal our joy from us. New Christians have a great joy, a joy that God has forgiven them when He took away their sins, a joy that they are going to Heaven. Then the devil brings circumstances into our lives which we allow to take our joy away from us. Yes, our taxes may go up, gas prices may go up, our medical care cost may go up and there may be physical difficulties that we face, none of which we may be happy about; but we need to look beyond the circumstances that we find ourselves in and look at the hope that we have within us. Our salvation and all that it means to us should continue to give us joy. Thank God each day for what you have in Christ, and don't let the devil steal joy from you. Let's make sure that we cross that finish line with joy in our lives regardless of our circumstances!

Lesson Six

Heart Right with God

When we face life-threating encounters, God can use these valleys in our lives to help us grow closer to Him. God gave me twenty-one days in the hospital, which allowed me time to think about my relationship with Him.

"Blessed are the pure in heart, for they shall see God" (Matthew 5:8). When we face death, our relationship with God is the only thing that is important. Knowing that we are going to spend eternity in Heaven brings real peace to the heart. How much we have put away in our 401(k) doesn't matter. The material things we have do not have any value. The size of home we have and the year and model of car we drive don't mean anything. When we come face to face with God at death, nothing matters other than our relationship with Him. There will be no Brink's truck following the hearse that takes us to the cemetery. If our hearts are right with God, that is the only thing that is important. It is when our hearts are right with God that we will then become more like Him.

It was the circumstances that God allowed me to go through during those twenty-one days in the hospital, that made me realize that my relationship with God was paramount.

Chapter X

Becoming More Christ Like

The hymn, "Just a Closer Walk with Thee," comes to my mind when I think of becoming more Christ-like. You need to have a "closer walk with Him" if you are to become like Him.

Colossians 3:1-3 shows us the pathway to be more like Christ in our Christian walk.

> *"If then you were raised with Christ, seek those things which are above, where Christ is, sitting at the right hand of God. Set our mind on things above, not on things on the earth. For you died, and your life is hidden with Christ in God."*

Verse 2 says, *"Set your mind on things above."* When we accepted Christ as our personal Savior, we died to earthly things. We now have lives that are hidden with Him in God. Just as a compass always points north, so should our desires and actions point to Christ and the things of Heaven. We have within us as Christians the old and the new natures.

In our garden, Donna and I plant vegetables, but weeds keep growing up among the vegetables. If we don't keep the weeds out of our garden, they soon will take over. Those weed seeds are in the soil of our garden, just like our old nature is within us. I hate weeds in my garden. I work hard to pull them out when they are small. Large weeds in my garden take the moisture and the minerals out of the soil. They weaken my plants. The same thing happens with sin in our lives; we need to hate sin in our lives. It drains us spiritually, and it weakens our Christian testimony. Verse 5 of Colossians 3 tells us, *"Therefore put to death your members which are on the earth: fornication, uncleanness, passion, evil desire, and covetousness, which is idolatry."* We should put to death these sins just as we pull the weeds out of a garden.

Donna likes to put fertilizer around our tomato plants. The fertilizer that we give to our plants helps them grow. We need to feed on God's Word if we want to become more like Christ. Do you get up on Sunday morning and eat enough breakfast to last you the whole week? No, you eat breakfast each day, and that gets you going for that day. It is the same with God's Word; we need to feast on it each day. The more we read God's Word and apply it to our lives, the more we become like Him.

We have a mandate in the Word of God to become more Christlike. *"For whom He foreknew, He also predestined to be conformed to the image of His Son, that He might be the firstborn among many brethren"* (Romans 8:29). God's purpose for those who have been predestined is for them to become like Jesus. To become conformed to the image of God, means to become like Jesus. *"I press toward the goal for the prize of the upward call of God in Christ Jesus"* (Philippians 3:14). Here on earth it should be our goal to become more Christlike.

But we all, with unveiled face, beholding as in a mirror the glory of the Lord, are being transformed into the same image from glory to glory, just as by the Spirit of the Lord" (2 Corinthians 3:18). The indwelling of the Holy Spirit helps us to be changed from glory to glory. We move from God's eternal predestination to His present transformation of us by the Holy Spirit. It is the work of the Holy Spirit that transforms us into the image of Jesus. (1) *"And do not be drunk with wine in which is dissipation; but be filled with the Spirit."* (Ephesians 5:18). We are filled with the Holy Spirit when sin is not controlling our lives. We are to be continually under the influence of the Holy Spirit, and we do this by letting God's Word control us. The Holy Spirit controls us when we pursue a pure life, confessing all our known sins, dying to self, surrendering to God's will in our lives and depending on His strength in all things. When we live with a conscious presence of the Lord Jesus Christ, we are filled with the Spirit. We need to let His mind, through His Word, control everything we do. When we are filled with the Spirit we are walking in the Spirit. (2)

"Beloved now we are children of God; and it has not yet been revealed what we shall be, but we know that when He is revealed, we shall be like Him; for we shall see Him as He is" (1 John 3:40). The details are not given to us, but we know that we will be like Christ. We can be very content with the glorious truth that we will be with Christ and we will be like Him forever. We need to be thankful that we have been predestined, that we are being changed and transformed by the Holy Spirit, and that we will be like Him when we get to Heaven. The biblical basis for us becoming Christlike is because it is His purpose for the people of God. (3)

"He who says he abides in Him ought himself also to walk just as He walked" (1 John 2:6). Jesus' walk on earth was a walk of obedience, which is a pattern

for the Christian to follow. Those of us, who claim to be Christians, should therefore live as He lived because we possess His Spirit's presence and His power. (4)

"For there shall raise false christs and false prophets and show great signs and wonders; to deceive, if possible, even the elect" (Matthew 24:24). We need to be well-grounded in God's Word so we will not be drawn away from the truths of His Word. By consistently studying His Word we will not easily be deceived by others.

When we look at Jesus' life here on earth, we see a life of service. We find Jesus with His disciples in the upper room and afterward, *"Jesus" poured water into a basin and began to wash the disciples' feet, and to wipe them with the towel with which He was girded"* (John 13:5). We need to be like Christ in His service. We should not regard any task as too menial or degrading to bring glory to our Lord. Washing feet in their culture was reserved for the lowliest of menial servants. Peers didn't wash each other's feet, except on rare occasions as a mark of great love. The disciples were shocked when Jesus washed their feet; it is a model of Christian humility for us to follow. This action, coupled with His death on the cross, supremely exemplified selfless service. (5)

We need to be followers of Christ. He was a servant when He washed the feet of His disciples. When we follow Jesus' example throughout His lifetime and when we duplicate His walk, we will become more Christlike, we will have a more fruitful ministry for Him.

Ephesians 5:2 provides another example that Christ gives us to follow: *"And walk in love, as Christ also has loved us and given Himself for us, an offering and a sacrifice to God for a sweet-smelling aroma"*. As we see children imitate their parents, we need to imitate Christ. God's love for us was so great that He sacrificed Himself so that we might live. Our love for others should go beyond affection to self-sacrificing service. (6)

If we are going to be like Christ we need to have patient endurance. We see this in Peter 2:18-21.

> *"Servants, be submissive to your masters with all fear, not only to the good and gentle, but also to the harsh. For this is commendable, if because of conscience toward God one endures grief, suffering wrongfully. For what credit is it if, when you are beaten for your faults, you take it patiently? But when you do good and suffer, if you take it patiently, this is commendable before God. For to this you were called, because Christ also suffered for us, leaving us an example, that you should follow His steps."*

There were many Christians who were household servants. It was easy to submit to their masters when kindness was shown to them, but when their masters were unjust to them, it was hard. Peter encouraged these servants to be loyal and persistent when they faced unjust treatment. We should do likewise and submit to our employers whether they are kind or harsh. Our goal is to win them to Christ. (7) Christ suffered a great deal for us; we should be willing to do likewise for Him.

We are to be like Christ in mission. *"So Jesus said to them again, 'Peace to you! As my Father hath sent Me, I also send you'"* (John 20:21). Christ is our example. He was sent here by God. Christ finished His mission by shedding His blood on the cross; He took our place. He took on sin, that we might have eternal life. He then told His disciples that He was sending them. And because His words were also for us, He is now sending us. We have been commissioned by Him to be His witnesses to a dying world. To be like Christ means to be a witness to our neighbors and to those who are watching us or who come into contact with us that we do not even know. Christ gave His all. Are we giving our all to see others come to Christ? We cannot all go to the entire world, but we can support those who do by financially supporting missionaries, praying for them and encouraging them.

God has given us promises in His Word that we need to take hold of and not let go. *"Behold, I am coming quickly! Hold fast what you have, that no one may take your crown"* (Revelation 3:11). We live in a world of temptation, where the enemies of truth abound; we need to be obedient to God's Word so we will not be robbed of the crown that awaits those who are faithful to the end. (8)

When the Christian takes his or her eyes off Jesus and places them on man, there is a possibility of losing crowns. When our eyes are on Jesus and we stay close to Him, we will finish strong with rewards awaiting us. As the songwriter has written: "Turn your eyes upon Jesus. Look full in His wonderful face. And the things of earth will grow strangely dim, in the light of His glory and grace." (9) Let's keep our eyes on the finish line.

Chapter XI

Building Christian Character

"When I was a child, I spoke as a child, I understood as a child, I thought as a child; but when I became as a man, I put away childish things"* (1 Corinthians 13:11). Once you are born again, into God's family, you need to change your character to feed on the meat of God's Word. When a Christian does not feed on the meat of God's Word, they act childishly, and they do things to please themselves when they should be doing things to please God. There needs to be growth in the Christian's walk, because others are watching. The unsaved are watching, and the Christian needs to be a witness. *(1)*

"But Jesus said to him, 'no one having put his hand to the plow, and looking back, is fit for the kingdom of God'" (Luke 9:62). Christ wants total dedication from His children, not half-hearted commitment. Some Christians selectively choose what the Bible has to say. As Christians we should focus on Jesus; we should not let things of this world distract us from living and walking according to God's Word.

There are some Christians who get off to a good start, but they lose their first love. They are just quitting on God. Then there are those who keep on growing in Christ. They show credibility in their walk. (2) *"Then said Jesus to those Jews who believed Him, 'If you abide in my Word, you are My disciples indeed. And you shall know the truth, and the truth shall make you free'"* (John 8:31-32). If you are going to grow in Christ toward becoming a true disciple, you need to be obedient to God's Word. The word "abide" means to habitually live by Jesus' Word. If we feed on the meat of God's Word, we will then hold to those truths, obeying and practicing the teaching of Jesus. (3)

"Let us hold fast the confession of our hope without wavering…" (Hebrews 10:23). "Hold fast" is evidence of salvation. "Confession of our hope" is affirmation of our salvation. When we have confidence in God's promises, we will

walk the Christian walk without wavering. (4) If we say we are saved, then it is our obligation to act like we are saved. If we profess to be Christians, we should act like Christians and not waver.

There is a need for credibility in our Christian walk. When a farmer is planting and looks back while he is planting he will end up with a crooked row. When the Christian looks back (backslides), his walk becomes crooked and difficult for others to follow.

By some Christians' conduct you would not know that they are really Christians. There are those who act like Christians on Sunday morning when they are in church, but during the remainder of the week you would not know that they were a Christian by their lifestyle. *"But if I am delayed, I write so that you may know how you ought to conduct yourself in the house of God, which is the church of the living God, the pillar and ground of the truth"* (1 Timothy 3:15). (5)

Our conduct should be to bring glory to God. Is God blessed with the conduct of a lot of Christians today? I don't think so. It is sad to say that many Christians by their conduct are no different from those who are not saved. If we are saved we should act like we are a "child of the King." As Christians we are part of God's Royal Family. And being part of that family, there are principles that we are to live by given to us in His manual, the Bible.

> *"That the older men be sober, reverent, temperate, sound in faith, in love, in patience; the older women likewise, that they be reverent in behavior, not slanderers, not given to much wine, teachers of good things"* (1 Titus 2:2-3).

Those older men who are more mature in the faith should be showing the younger men that their conduct is pleasing to God. They are to be honorable and dignified. Likewise, they are to be sensible and spiritually healthy for the younger man to observe. (6) Younger women are to learn how to have harmony in the home from the older, mature women in the faith. The mature Christian women need to show forth a conduct that is an example to the young women. (7)

"...being filled with the fruits of righteousness which are by Jesus Christ, to the glory and praise of God" (Philippians 1:11). Donna and I have two apple trees and a couple cherry trees in our backyard in Michigan. There are years that I get too busy and don't spray them as I should, and then the fruit has worms. When the trees are sprayed properly there are no worms, and we can eat the fruit. As Christians we either bear good fruit or bad fruit. When we bear good fruit, others will want what we have. As Christians our conduct, our fruit, should draw others to Christ. It is imperative that Christians have their lives under control. It is when the Christian wants to control his or her own life that it often gets out of control. We want to be the pilot and let God be the co-pilot.

If we are going to have good Christian character, our lives need to be under the control of the Holy Spirit. *"That each of you should know how to possess his own vessel in sanctification and honor"* (1 Thessalonians 4:4).

Lesson Seven

Witnessing Takes Time

"I planted, Apollos watered, but God gave the increase" (1 Corinthians 3:6). When I went to the hospital to have my right kidney taken out, I took four *Gospels of John* with me. These *Gospels of John* have the plan of salvation in the front page of the booklet. I told Donna that I wanted to give out these booklets during my three or four day stay in the hospital. I was reminded as my hospital time extended to twenty-one days that it had been said to me that witnessing takes time. Once I was feeling somewhat better, I asked Donna how we should give out the *Gospels of John*. She suggested that we have our son bring an assortment of Hershey candy bars from his convenience store and give them out to the nurses who worked with us. The nurses worked three twelve-hour shifts. When they were completing their three-day shift, we would offer them a Hershey candy bar, which none of them refused, and a *Gospel of John*, along with a thank you note. We were able to give out fourteen *Gospel of John* booklets during the twenty-one days. Most all of the nurses came back to thank us for the note of thanks. We had the opportunity to sow the seed, even though it did take some time.

Chapter XII

Developing a Compassion for the Lost

As I look back over the last several years, I can see how God has been working on me to give me a compassion for the hearts of the lost. I have had an interest for the lost throughout the years of my Christian life and have had the opportunity to lead a few people to Christ. Since I spent twenty-six years in Christian Education, my contact with the unsaved was limited. However, it has only been in the last few years that God has given me a deeper compassion for the lost.

This desire to see the lost come to the Lord came after reading a book entitled; *One Thing You Cannot Do When You Get to Heaven Is Tell Someone How They Can Get into Heaven.* (1) This book had a profound impact on my life. Through this book I became burdened for the lost as I never was before. How can I not tell others about Christ when I have the opportunity and responsibility to tell them? I realized after reading this book that now is the day to be a witness to the lost. I was then challenged in my readings to establish a purpose for the rest of my life. The purpose of my life is to put God first, my wife and family second. It is my goal to be the best husband, parent and grandparent that I can be with God's help. Likewise, I want to establish in my heart to be a soul winner and strive to serve God in any way that He wants me to serve Him, to bring glory to His name.

I then began to read every book and material that I could get my hands on about evangelism. I had two books given to me that also had an impact on my life. The first book was, 90 *Minutes in Heaven* by Don Piper. This book was given to me, by my daughter & son-in-law, while I was in the hospital. It was during the time when they did not give me much of a chance of living. This book gave me a desire to be in Heaven. However, I believe that the Lord still has some things that He wants me to do. One of those things is to be a witness for Him. As the apostle Paul said in Philippians 1:21, *"For to me, to live is Christ, and to die is gain."* As long as Christ keeps me going, I want to be a witness for Him.

The second book which I read shortly after my hospital stay was *Twenty Three Minutes in Hell* by Bill Wiese. He also has a newer book out called *Hell. His* book also had a really profound effect on my life. The author describes what Hell is like from his "personal experience" and from what the Bible has to say about Hell. Hell is a horrible place!

Bill Wiese, in his book, *Hell* lists forty-six verses in which Jesus talks about Hell and destruction. He also lists all the verses on Hell and destruction found in the Bible. Hell is not just a New Testament term.

> *"Then I shall bring thee down with them that descend into the pit, with the people of old time, and shall set thee in the low parts of the earth, in places desolate of old, with them that go down to the pit…"* (Ezekiel 26:20). (KJV) *"But those who seek my soul, to destroy it, shall go into the lower parts of the earth"* (Psalm 63:9). The New Testament also describes the location of Hell. *"…shalt be thrust down to hell,…"*(Luke 10:15). (KJV) *"…but cast them down to hell."* (2 Peter 2:4). *"To him was given the key to the bottomless pit. And he opened the bottomless pit, and smoke arose out of the pit like the smoke of a great furnace"* (Revelation 9:1-2).

Hell is also a place of fire and burning.

> *"Let burning coals fall upon them; let them be cast into the fire; into deep pits that they rise not up again"* (Psalm 140:10). *"For a fire is kindled in mine anger, and shall burn unto the lowest hell"* (Deuteronomy 32:22). (KJV) *"…he shall be tormented with fire and brimstone…"* (Revelation 14:10). (KJV) *"…cast into the lake of fire and brimstone…and shall be tormented day and night forever and ever"* (Revelation 20:10). (KJV) *"…shall have their part in the lake which burns with fire and brimstone"* (Revelation 21:8). *"And shall cast them into a furnace of fire, there shall be wailing and gnashing of teeth."* (Matthew 13:42). (KJV) *"…cast into hell fire"* (Mark 9:44). *"…where 'their worm does not die, and the fire is not quenched'"* (Matthew 18:9). (KJV)

Hell is a Place. *"But I will show you whom you should fear: Fear Him who, after He has killed, has power to cast into hell; yes, I say to you, fear Him!"* (Luke 12:5) *"How can ye escape the damnation of hell"* (Matthew 23:33)?

There is Torment in Hell. "*...There shall be weeping and gnashing of teeth.*" (*Matthew 24:51*) *"For the dark places of the earth are full of the habitations of cruelty"* (Psalm 74:20). (KJV)

There is Darkness in Hell. "*...into outer darkness...*" (Matthew 25:30). "*... delivered them into chains of darkness...*" (II Peter 2:4). "*...cast him into outer darkness; there shall be weeping and gnashing of teeth"* (*Matthew 22:13*).

Contrast of Heaven and Hell

If we are going to be witnesses for Christ, we need to have a realistic picture of Hell implanted in our minds. Read the above verses over and over until you get a picture of Hell that grips your heart. Look in your Bible commentary and read all the verses on Hell. We need to see people as saved and unsaved people. We need to see people as those who are headed for Hell and those who are going to have the enjoyment of Heaven. We need to have an urgency mindset that if we don't tell the unsaved about Christ, they may not have another opportunity to hear God's Word and accept Christ as their personal Savior.

How can we look an unsaved person in the eye and not tell them that there is a way to Heaven? Unless they accept Christ as their personal Savior, they will spend eternity in Hell. God has commissioned Christians to tell the unsaved about His Son, who died for their sins and to tell them that they can have eternal life by believing that He died for them as found in Matthew 28:18-20.

> *"And Jesus came and spoke to them, saying. 'All authority has been given to Me in heaven and on earth. Go therefore and make disciples of all the nations, baptizing them in the name of the Father and of the Son and of the Holy Spirit, teaching them to observe all things that I have commanded you; and lo, I am with you always, even to the end of the age.' 'Amen.'"*

"But you shall receive power when the Holy Spirit has come upon you; and you shall be witnesses to Me in Jerusalem, and in all Judea and Samaria, and the end of the earth" (Acts 1:8). These verses have commissioned us as Christians to tell others the good news of the Bible.

Imagine you are driving along on a rainy night and suddenly you see that the bridge in front of you has been washed out. You are able to stop just in time! You back your car up before another car comes; you turn on your emergency lights. Then you get out of your car and you do everything to flag down the next car or truck that is coming. Why? It is because you do not want anyone to face death. That is the same urgency that we need to have when it comes to telling people who are unsaved, that they are on their way to Hell.

You can have an occupation, and the responsibility of raising a family, but as a Christian your commission is to tell others about Jesus Christ. When you become a Christian you are accepting Him as your Lord and Savior. The Savior part means that we are going to Heaven. By believing by faith that Christ died for our sins we have eternal life. However, accepting Him as Lord of our lives is a commitment to Him that we will give our lives back to Him. Our desire should be to bring glory to His name. When we really understand and appreciate what Christ did for us by saving us from Hell and adopting us as His children, we will want to bring glory to His name. We can do this by being verbal witnesses for Him.

You do not witness to the unsaved to earn your salvation. *"For by grace you have been saved through faith, and that not of yourselves; it is the gift of God, not of works, lest anyone should boast"* (Ephesians 2:8). When you accept Christ by faith you have eternal life in Heaven. It is by His grace that you have eternal life; it is not by works, otherwise you could brag about what you have accomplished. God so loved you that He gave His only begotten Son for you. It is because of our love toward Him for what He has done for us that compels us to serve Him and to be obedient to His commandments.

When you witness to an unsaved person, it is because you want to show your love to Him by obeying His commandments. We are commissioned to witness to the unsaved. It is an obligation that each Christian needs to take seriously. Talking to an unsaved person should become common to us. It should be as easy as talking to someone about the weather. We need to develop a heartbeat for the lost. It needs to become an intentional urgency to witness to the lost. It should become a life and death urgency.

Why is the average Christian not a verbal witness to the unsaved? Could it be because they do not see any need to witness? Is it because they are too busy to witness? Is it because they are self-centered and don't care that others are lost? The question that you need to ask yourself is, "Why am I not a verbal witness (if you are not)?" If someone had not shared the gospel with you, you would be on your way to Hell.

Some people say that they are witnesses through their lifestyle and that is good, but we are commissioned to be verbal witnesses. No one will become a Christian just by watching your lifestyle. People need to be told how to be saved.

1. Ways to Be a Verbal Witness

An easy way to be a witness is to share your testimony by explaining how you were saved. You have heard of those who were deep in sin and then accepted Christ. They may have an exciting story to share; but you do not have to have a spectacular salvation experience to share how you were saved. Their testimony can make a great compelling story. Your testimony is to tell people what Christ did for you and how His Word has strengthened you to be a better person. God can use your testimony just as well as someone else's. Start by telling them what your life was like before you accepted Christ. You were lost and on your way to Hell. Then tell them about your salvation experience. Close with how your life has changed since you were saved. Give God the credit for your change of life.

As an example, I would like to share my salvation experience with you. My testimony is unique, but it is not dramatic. I grew up in an unchristian home. My parents as children were brought up in church by my grandparents. My father went to a Pilgrim Holiness church (Wesleyan today), and my mother went to a Christian Reformed church. When my parents got married they did not go to church at all. Finally my mother started taking my older brother, Bob, and me to her church sporadically. We often laugh about the times that she spanked us two guys before we went to church so that we would be good during church. You have to understand that we were "boys" and in the Christian Reformed church, at that time, you walked into the church and you did not say anything until you left. You also had to sit still for a very long time. Anyway, we found that to be quiet during the service and to sit still was difficult for us. It was when we were about seven and eight years old that my mother told my dad that we boys and now two sisters needed to be in church regularly. My dad said he would go to church if she would go to his church, the one he had grown up in. My dad regretted many times that he had said those words, until he was saved. However, my dad was a man of his word and every Sunday morning we went as a family to Sunday school and church unless one of us kids was sick, and then he was more than happy to stay home with us.

It was during the time from about age seven to almost sixteen that I had the opportunity to hear God's Word every Sunday morning. Twice a year we had evangelistic services. The Holy Spirit started working in my life when I was about fourteen, and I realized that I needed to become a Christian. On Sunday, April 25, 1954, at age fifteen, our church was having an evangelistic meeting and the Holy Spirit was tugging on my heart.

It was a bright, sunny morning. It was my habit to sit in the back of our church with my friends. That Sunday morning, however, I sat with my mother, and when my dad came upstairs from his men's Sunday school class, he sat in the seat behind my mother and me. I don't remember my dad ever not sitting with my mother before that day or after that day. The evangelist in his invitation that morning started walking down the outside aisle across the auditorium from us to talk to a couple people and then walked across the back of the church and up our side. My mother was sitting on the outside, and the evangelist tapped her on the shoulder and told her she needed to accept Christ. My mother went forward, and at that time I was crying and I went forward also. My oldest sister, Fay, went forward, also to be saved. My best friend, Chuck, who had been sitting in the back of the church, came forward and knelt down beside me and was saved that day likewise. It was that Sunday morning that I accepted Jesus Christ as my personal Savior, a day that I will never forget.

Two days later my dad accepted Christ as his personal Savior at home. Nine days after I accepted Christ as my personal Savior, I turned sixteen. I often have said that I was saved at a crossroad time in my life. I was turning sixteen and able to drive and was looking forward to doing things that other unsaved guys were doing.

After my salvation experience, I was soon baptized in Lake Michigan. I had not had the opportunity to hear all the familiar Bible stories as a child. A little over two years after my salvation experience, when I was still a little green behind the ears, I was on my way to Cedarville, a Christian college. There I had to have a Bible minor, and I started gaining a deeper understanding and trust of God's Word.

This is much more detailed than you have to make your testimony. But by sharing your testimony you can also use Scripture verses that were used to show you how to be saved. You can continue to explain how you have been growing in the Lord, since you became a Christian.

2. Bringing Small Talk to Spiritual Talk

Donna and I were out in Tucson for the winter months, and I needed a haircut. I have a regular barber back in Otsego, Michigan, but had not found one out in Tucson. So I went to this place where they cut hair and a young lady of about 25 brought me to her station. I started with some small talk by asking her how long she had been cutting hair. "Do you like to cut ladies' hair or men's hair?" Her response was ladies' longer hair, but she didn't enjoy hearing about all their problems. Then I asked her if she had a boyfriend, and she answered that she had had one for six years. (Here I am getting a little more personal.)

"However," she continued, "I think that I need to be looking for a new one." My next question was, "Where do you go to church?" She said, "I go to a Catholic church." I then asked her how Catholics believe they get to Heaven.

She said, "By going to church, and getting married in the church." I was then able to share with her from the Bible the plan of salvation. Six weeks later when I needed another haircut, I gave her a *Gospel of John* with the plan of salvation in the front pages.

I like to get to the point of asking people where they go to church. If they don't go to church, then I try to find out if they have in the past. If they have no church background, then you can ask them if they believe in God. You can continue to ask questions until you get to the point where you can tell them how they can get to Heaven.

Every person is going to have a little different background. You want to bring your conversation to where you can give them the plan of salvation. Some like to ask the person they are talking to if they mind being asked a spiritual question. That question can be: "If you died today, would you go to Heaven?" In a short conversation with a gentleman in his eighties, he indicated that he had Parkinson's disease and something else wrong with him. I exchanged a few comments about my cancer operation and heart attack. Then I told him, "It is not all that bad to have physical challenges if you know where you are going after you die." Then I asked him if he was going to Heaven. He indicated that he hoped so, but stated that he was not sure. I then had the opportunity to tell him that he could know for sure.

Whenever we are talking to unsaved people in general we need to be able to seize those split-second opportunities that come our way. The only way that we are going to walk through those open doors is to be ready. When we have a mindset that it is our responsibility to witness to the unsaved, we will be looking for those opportunities. We will attempt to direct the conversation so we can witness to them. Those split-second opportunities then come not as a surprise, and you will be ready for them.

3. A Direct Approach

You can say to people, "Would you mind if I asked you a personal question?" If they give you permission, then you can ask them several different personal questions. Questions that you can ask include the following: "If you were to die today, do you know for sure that you will be going to Heaven?" If the answer is "no," or "I am not," then you can give them the plan of salvation. If the answer is "yes," then you can ask them how they know that they are going to Heaven. If they have the right answer, you can assure them that they are on their way to Heaven. However, if they give you the wrong answer, then you can tell them how the Bible says that you can get to Heaven. You may ask, "Has anyone ever shown you from the Bible how you can know that you are going to Heaven? Do you ever wonder what happens to you when you die? If you'd ever like to know the difference between religion and Christianity, I would like to show you."

4. People are Open to the Gospel

"Behold, I say to you, lift up your eyes and look at the fields, for they are already white for harvest" (John 4:35)! The Bible tells us that people around us are ready to receive the message of Jesus Christ. Gallup Polls indicates that nine out of ten Americans believe in God. Seventy-five percent believe that Jesus is the Son of God and two-thirds believe the Bible is God's Word. *"...The harvest truly is plentiful, but the laborers are few"* (Matthew 9:37). (1)

"For I am not ashamed of the gospel of Christ, for it is the power of God to salvation for everyone who believes ..." (Romans 1:16). We often act like we are ashamed to tell others about Christ. This verse tells us that we are not to be ashamed. We also have fear that keeps us from talking to others about

Christ. We have to realize that we are only the messengers; it is only the power of God that is able to overcome man's sinful nature and give him new life. We often think that the power is in the messenger. The power is the message. Because we think the power is in the messenger, we think only professional evangelists and ministers can proclaim the message. It is not about you or me, it is about the message.

We need to pray that God will help us with our fear. If God is for us, who can be against us? God will never leave us or forsake us when we are witnessing for Him. We don't like to be rejected. The worst thing that can happen to us is to get the response, "I am not interested," or "No, thank you."

We have to let people know that we care. Usually when we let people know that we care about them, they will let us share with them. When we really care, then God will give us the boldness that we need.

The word "compel" refers to pressure which causes action. Because Paul realized the truth of Christ's substitutionary death, Paul was motivated to offer his life to the Lord. Because Christ gave His life for us, we are compelled to serve Him.

> *"For the love of Christ compels us, because we judge thus: that if One died for all, then all died; and He died for all, that those who live should live no longer for themselves, but for Him who died for them and rose again"* (2 Corinthians 5:14-15).

"He died for all," which compels us to tell the unsaved about what Christ did for them. Paul is an example that we need to follow.

> *"And He said to them, 'Go into all of the world and preach the gospel to every creature'"* (Mark 16:15). *"For this is good and acceptable in the sight of God our Savior, who desires all men to be saved and to come to the knowledge of truth"* (I Timothy 2:3-4).

The disciples were given power, and you have also been given power.

Preparing to Bring Someone to Christ

1. Being Filled with the Spirit

We need to be filled with the Holy Spirit if we are going to be effective witnesses. There cannot be sin in our lives. We need to ask that the Spirit of God guide us when we are witnessing. *"But you shall receive power when the Holy Spirit has come upon you; and you shall be witnesses to Me in Jerusalem, and in all Judea and Samaria, and the end of the earth"* (Acts 1:8). We have the power of the Holy Spirit within us. The Holy Spirit guides us as to what to say and how to say it.

2. Prayer

We need to be praying for the lost. *"Praying always with all prayer and supplication in the Spirit…"* (Ephesians 6:18). We need to continually be praying for the unsaved.

We need to pray for boldness, that we will open our mouths when the opportunity comes. We need to pray for opportunities to share the Gospel. We need to pray that we will be protected from the evil one. He does not want us to be witnesses.

Pray for the unsaved by name. Pray for your loved ones, friends, neighbors and those whom you are seeking to reach for Christ. Make a prayer list of those whom God has laid on your heart that you want to see saved. God does not want anyone to go to Hell, so when we are praying for the unsaved we are praying according to His will. We need to pray that the seed that we plant will fall on good ground. Praying is something that every Christian can do.

3. Having a Plan

Each fall my family takes a fishing trip up to the Upper Peninsula of Michigan. Our goal is to catch walleye fish. My sons try to determine which week of September is the best week. They buy the best lures they can find. We try several different colored lures to see which one is going to work the best. Once on the lake, we use our fish finder to help us locate where the fish are. A lot of planning goes in to our trip. In Mark 2:1-5, we see a man brought to Jesus. The man was paralyzed and his friends wanted to bring him to Jesus, but because of a crowd in the home, they could not get him to Jesus. So they took him up on the house top and lowered him down into the room before Jesus. These men had a plan. Note that they had determination. If you are going to give out a tract, you have to have a tract with you. If we are going to witness, we need a plan. We also need to memorize some Scripture so we can share the gospel.

Jesus told his disciples to put their net down on the other side of their boat. We need to be obedient to where and to whom God wants us to be a witness. He may be prompting us to walk across the street and talk with a neighbor.

4. We Need to Care for the Lost

We need to be open to God's leading in our lives. Remember that our commission is to tell others about Christ. We need to ask God each day to direct our walk for that day. We need to ask Him to show us who we are to speak to about Christ.

We need to develop a compassion for the lost, those who are on their way to Hell. If you do not have compassion for the lost, you need to ask God to give you compassion for those who are lost and without Jesus Christ in their lives. When we really become concerned for the lost, when we see people as unsaved, as lost, as on their way to Hell, then we will have the compassion that we need. We need to purpose in our hearts that we will do everything we can to be a testimony to those with whom God gives us an opportunity to come into contact. Every opportunity that we get we need to be a verbal witness. We need to be faithful in sowing the seed; knowing that God gives the increase.

We need to have faith that people will be saved. We cannot save our neighbor; God does the saving.

We need to visualize the consequences of the lost going to Hell. Get a vision in your mind as to what Hell is like. Think of the torment, the loneliness, and the eternity of Hell.

We need to develop a heartbeat for the lost. Our hearts beat for the lost when we have compassion for their souls and when they are on our minds on a daily basis. It is our responsibility to do everything we can to see that the lost come to Christ.

We need to answer the following question: Do we want people to come to Christ? If so, we need to let our nets down on the other side–the side of prayer, the side of faith and the side of compassion.

May you have the joy of rescuing someone from spending eternity in Hell– the joy of knowing that someone is going to spend eternity in Heaven with you because you told them about Jesus and they accepted Him as their personal Savior! There is no greater joy!

Paul Little in his book *How to Give Away Your Faith* provides a definition for "witnessing." "*Witnessing is that deep-seated conviction that the greatest favor I can do for others is to introduce them to Jesus Christ.*"

Lesson Eight

Lesson from Lazarus and the Rich Man

W hen I was going without food and with a limited amount of liquids coming into my body intravenously, my mouth became very dry. I was given a beverage cup with a lid on top. In the cup was a little water with lots of ice. Then I was given a stick with a small sponge on the end. I would stick the sponge in the ice water and pull it out through the straw hole, which took the water off the sponge. Then I would place the cool sponge in my month. The coldness would make my month feel good and would take the dryness away for a short time.

This experience reminded me of Lazarus and the rich man found in Luke 16:19-26.

> *"There was a certain rich man, who was clothed in purple and fine linen, and fared sumptuously every day. But there was a certain beggar named Lazarus, full of sores, who was laid at his gate, desiring to be fed with the crumbs which fell from the rich man's table. Moreover the dogs came and licked his sores. So it was that the beggar died, and was carried by the angels to Abraham's bosom. The rich man also died and was buried. And being in torments in Hades, he lifted up his eyes and saw Abraham afar off and Lazarus in his bosom. 'Then he cried and said, 'Father Abraham, have mercy on me, and send Lazarus that he may dip the tip of his fingers in water and cool my tongue; for I am tormented in this flame.' But Abraham said, 'Son, remember that in your lifetime you received your good things, and likewise Lazarus evil things; but now he is comforted and you are tormented. And besides all this, between us and you there is a great gulf fixed, so that those who want to pass from here to you cannot, nor can those from there pass to us.'"*

The dryness of my mouth made me think about the rich man wanting Lazarus to come and dip his finger in water to cool his tongue. This account of God's Word gives us a contrast between Heaven and Hell. I could only thank the Lord that I am one of His children, and my destination is Heaven.

Hell is an unbearable place. When a loved one or someone we know well passes away without Christ, there should be great sorrow. Let's make sure that we do our part to see that others come to know Jesus Christ as their personal Savior.

Part III

Running the Race to Fulfill God's Purpose for Your Life

Chapter XIII

Giving God's Way

"The earth is the Lord's, and all its fullness, the world and those who dwell therein" (Psalm 24:1). God owns the universe and everything that is in it. He made mankind. *"Or do you not know that your body is the temple of the Holy Spirit who is in you, who you have from God, and you are not your own"* (1 Corinthians 6:19)? The body of a Christian belongs to the Lord and is the Holy Spirit's temple. You are His child, and those who have accepted Him as their Lord and Savior are His children. He created mankind to bring glory to Himself. So the question that needs to be answered is, "How do we bring glory to God through our finances?"

First, we need to establish who really owns the money and possessions that we have. If God owns everything, including you and me, then are the monies that we have in our possession His or ours? We need to develop the mindset that what we have is not our own. All the material things that we have are a gift from God to us. If everything we have is God's, then we are managers of His estate that He has entrusted to us. We should never forget this truth when we are giving.

We need to make sure that we ask Him how to manage His estate that He has allowed us to oversee. You might be saying that you don't have much of anything in material things or monies to manage; God wants us to show Him that we are faithful in little things before He gives us bigger things to manage.

Ask God for Wisdom

We need to ask God for wisdom, praying to Him to direct in the decisions that need to be made with the wealth He has given to us. There are daily essentials that we need for living. However, when we eat out all the time, we spend a lot more money than if we were to fix meals at home. Donna and I have some friends who have a very large home, but in the evening they only turn lights on in the rooms that they are in. You can say that is a little thing, but when we compound many little things, they become big. In other words, do not waste monies that God has entrusted to you. When a person has money to daily purchase coffee at a specialty shop, but can't give when a special offering is taken to help the needy, that person needs to question where his or her priorities are.

Be Obedient to His Word

Likewise, be obedient to His Word. In the Old Testament the people were to give a tithe, which was ten percent. We find this being stated in Leviticus 27:30, *"And all the tithe of the land, whether of the seed of the land or of the fruit of the tree, is the LORD's. It is holy to the LORD."* In the New Testament, the Christian is to give according to how God has blessed him. Many Bible scholars believe that this should be at least ten percent.

> *"That in a great trial of affliction the abundance of their joy and*
> *their deep poverty abounded in the riches of their liberality. For*
> *I bear witness that according to their ability, yes, and beyond*
> *their ability, they were freely willing"* (2 Corinthians 8:2-3).

"Abundance" means surplus. They gave abundantly with joy in their deep poverty. "Riches of their liberality" can be translated "generosity" or "sincerity." The Macedonian believers were rich in their selfless generosity to God and to others. They gave according to their ability. Giving is proportionate. God sets no fixed amount or percentage and expects His people to give based on what they have. Giving beyond their ability would be sacrificial giving. (1)

Then we need to develop a steward's mentality toward the assets that He has entrusted to us. As His steward, you manage His assets to His benefit. (2) That requires a new mindset for many Christians.

Paul's desire was to get the church in Corinth to be givers. He didn't order them to give, but he encouraged them to prove that their love was sincere. If you love someone, you want to give her or him your time and attention and to provide for that person's needs. If you don't help, it may mean that there is not genuine love.

God is expecting us to give financially so His work can be completed. When we give to our church we are helping pay the pastor's salary; we also give to our church to provide for different programs, and outreach ministries, and to help pay the utilities, etc. Likewise, our giving helps provide for support for missionaries who are spreading God's Word to those throughout the world.

God's Word challenges us to surrender everything we have to God, including ourselves. God owns everything that we have. It is then that we can realize that everything we possess is on loan from God so that we can use His resources to bring Him glory and expand His kingdom. God has given us the ability to make a living. *"Then you say in your heart, 'My power and the might of my hand have gained me this wealth. And you shall remember the LORD your God, for it is He who gives you power to get wealth...'"* (Deuteronomy 8:17-18). Thanking God for providing for our needs is important.

"Honor the Lord with your possessions and with the first fruits of all your increase; so your barns will be filled with plenty" (Proverbs 3:9-10). God expects and deserves that we give to Him our first fruits before anything else.

When we get paid, the first thing we should do is take out what we are going to give to God; and whatever we have left, we live on that amount. When this principle is not followed, God is cheated. Likewise, we miss out on a blessing.

A Personal Testimony

When Donna and I were first married, we started giving ten percent of our income to our church. We were married on December 28th and when the next Christmas came along, our pastor challenged us to give an extra gift to Jesus, equal to what we were spending on Christmas gifts. In faith, we gave. We were planning on spending Christmas with Donna's parents, but we did not have the money to pay for gas to visit them. I was only working part-time and going to college full-time to get my student teaching done in order to get my credentials to become a teacher in Michigan. Donna was working full-time, but our income was quite limited. When we received our electric bill that month, it stated that we did not owe any money because they had overestimated the bill the previous month. That meant we had gas money to go home. God is faithful.

As a personal testimony, God has always supplied our needs. When Donna and I along with our three small children left Michigan to be short-term missionaries in Fortaleza, Brazil, I left a good paying job working for the State of Michigan. I had just finished ten years working for the State, which meant that at age sixty I would be able to draw a small retirement from the State. But when I reached sixty, I not only got my small retirement fund, but I also received full health, dental and vision insurance from the State retirement program. When our friends told us that they are paying $12,000 a year for their insurance, we knew that the Lord had blessed us for our faithfulness in following His leading in our lives. After spending two years as short-term missionaries teaching missionary children, Donna and I both taught in small Christian schools for several years. We always gave to the Lord of our first fruits even though we lived on very little, and God always supplied our needs. Friends of ours would purchase a side of beef and tell us that they only liked the hamburger and give us everything else. We found out many years later that they liked the hamburger the best, but also liked other parts of the beef. Two bags of groceries were left at our door just when we needed them most. When I quit my job working for the

State of Michigan so we could be short-term missionaries, we had three small children. It was a big step of faith for us. As we look back, God has always supplied our needs.

Give with a Cheerful Heart

God wants the believer to give cheerfully as is seen in 1 Corinthians 16:1-2.

> *"Now concerning the collection for the saints, as I have given orders to the churches of Galatia, so you must do also: On the first day of the week let each one of you lay something aside, storing up as he may prosper, that there be no collections when I come."*

Paul tells the Church at Corinth to set aside a sum of money out of their income. Paul did not give any legislated amount for these Christians to give. The New Testament does not give any specific monetary figures or percentages.

The question then is how much money should be given to the church? When we give financially to God, He will enrich us in every way.

> *"Now may He who supplies seed to the sower, and bread for food, supply and multiply the seed you have sown and increase the fruits of your righteousness, while you are enriched in everything for all liberality, which causes thanksgiving through us to God"* (2 Corinthians 9:10-11).

God promises to replenish with generosity. God gives temporal and eternal blessings to the cheerful giver. If we give to God, He promises that we will be rich in every way. We will be rich spiritually, and He will supply our needs and give us eternal rewards. No blessing is more important than spiritual riches.

If we give to God, He is saying that He will bless us financially. However, if we have a desire to be wealthy so that we can spend these resources on ourselves, don't expect to claim this reward.

> *"But those who desire to be rich fall into temptations and a snare, and into many foolish and harmful lusts which drown men in destruction and perdition. For the love of money is a root of all kinds of evil, for which some have strayed from the faith in their greediness, and pierced themselves through with many sorrows"* (1 Timothy 6:9-10).

There are those who teach that you give to get back. God says we should give to give again.

There is a joy in giving to God. I like the saying, "You can't out-give God." It is true and has been proven over and over in people's lives when they give generously. When Donna and I were in Fortaleza, Brazil, as short-term missionaries, there was a couple who told us that they would give us a thousand dollars in financial support each year (a lot of money in the 70's) that we were on the mission field as they had wanted to be missionaries but due to health reasons they could not go. They actually gave us two thousand each year because God had blessed their business beyond their expectations.

Penalty of Not Giving

> "Will a man rob God? Yet you have robbed Me! But you say, 'in what way have we robbed You?' In tithes and offerings. You are cursed with a curse, for you have robbed Me, even this whole nation" (Malachi 3:8-9).

This passage teaches that when we refuse to honor God with our wealth, He accuses us of stealing from Him. The passage also teaches us that we will be under a curse and that He will punish us for stealing from Him. (3)

I like this statement that I have heard lots of times, "You cannot take it with you, but you can send it on ahead." That statement gives us the principle of giving.

> "Do not lay up for yourselves treasures on earth, where moth and rust destroy and where thieves break in and steal; but lay up for yourselves treasures in heaven, where neither moth nor rust destroys and where thieves do not break in and steal. For where your treasure is, there your heart will be also" (Matthew 6:19-21).

Do our treasures on earth last? When an expensive automobile is purchased, does it last? Did that new car you bought thirty years ago end up in the junk-yard or is it still new-looking and still in your driveway? In Luke chapter twelve Jesus speaks about a rich man who spent his wealth on himself. He decided to tear down his barns and build larger ones, storing up for himself so he could take it easy and retire. But God called the man a fool, saying, "This night your soul will be required of you; then whose will those things be which you have provided" (Luke 12:20)?

Jesus tells us where we need to invest our money. He does not want us to store up treasures for ourselves, but He wants us to store them up in Heaven. What we store up in Heaven we are not going to lose, as you can in the stock market or some other investment. The difficulty that many of us have is that we do not like delayed gratification. Our society has programmed us for instant gratification. Many get into credit card debt because of this push to have it now and pay later. Young couples today want right away what took their parents years of hard work to accomplish. Consequently, many get into debt over their heads. I know of young couples who are not tithing because they are credit card poor.

When we store up treasures in Heaven, they will last forever.

> *"Do not be afraid when one becomes rich, When the glory of his house is increased. For when he dies he shall carry nothing aways; His glory shall not descend after him." (Psalm 49:16-17)*

The man who builds up riches on earth leaves it all here. None of it goes with him. After John D. Rockefeller, one of the world's most wealthy men, died, his accountant was asked as to how much he left. The reply was "He left…all of it." (4)

Giving to God draws us closer to God. Spending and accumulating money for ourselves draws us away from God. When we buy things for ourselves, they take up our time. When a family buys a luxury boat, they then think they need to spend time using it to get their money's worth. Therefore, they may also decide to spend most of their summer weekends at the lake and forget about going to church.

Giving to God Gives Us Joy

We find this with the Macedonian Christians who understood the joy of giving: *"…that in a great trial of affliction the abundance of their joy and their deep poverty abounded in the riches of their liberality"* (2 Corinthians 8:2). In spite of their difficult circumstances, the church's joy rose above their pain because of their devotion to the Lord and the causes of His kingdom. Giving is not just for the rich but is also a privilege of the poor. *"For they all put in out of their abundance, but she out of her poverty put in all that she had, her whole livelihood"* (Mark 12:44). Jesus praised her for her sacrificial giving. That brings "goose bumps" to think that when we give sacrificially, God will praise us for doing so.

How many accounts have you heard about lottery winners who receive no joy from their newfound wealth? Many are more miserable a few years after winning than they were before. Having material wealth does not make a person joyful. In many cases it is just the opposite. Here is what some of the wealthiest people of their day said:

- "The care of $200 million is enough to kill anyone. There is no pleasure in it." W.H. Vanderbilt
- "I am the most miserable man on earth." John Jacob Astor

- "I have made many millions, but they have brought me no happiness." John D. Rockefeller
- "Millionaires seldom smile." Andrew Carnegie
- "I was happier when doing a mechanic's job," said Henry Ford. (5)

Many people become enslaved by their possessions. Their possessions often take up their time, leaving little time to enjoy life or do things for their church or other ministries that bring glory to God. Solomon, who was the wealthiest man on earth, learned that affluence didn't satisfy.

> *"Whatever my eyes desired I did not keep from them. I did not withhold my heart from any pleasure. For my heart rejoiced in all my labor; and this was my reward from all my labor. Then I looked on all the works that my hands had done and on the labor in which I had toiled; and indeed all was vanity and grasping for the wind. There was no profit under the sun"* (Ecclesiastes 2:10-11).

Being wealthy is not the answer to joyful living. If wealth is not the answer to joyful living, what is? It is giving! (6)

In Luke 19:11-27 we have the parable of the minas. A man of noble birth went to a distant country to have himself appointed king (Jesus is speaking of Himself) and then to return (a reference to His Second Coming). He called together his servants and gave them ten minas. *"Do business till I come"* (verse 13). He is a wealthy landowner who is going on an extended trip to a distant land. He is expecting to be gone for a long time, but he eventually will return. He calls together ten of his trusted servants and gives each one a mina, a month's salary, and tells them to invest it in business until he returns.

They were to use their money to make more money. They were to put their money to work. In our day it could apply to stocks and bonds, gold coins, rental properties, and even baseball cards. If we have money, we should invest. Use it to make more money. This is biblical advice.

The master leaves on his journey. His caravan disappears over the horizon. Time goes by quickly. Weeks turn into months, and months into years. Some are not sure he will ever return. Other servants wait patiently for his return. Finally he returns. His first order of business is to send for his servants to whom he had given the money. He wants to find out what their gains were. He wants to know how well they did with the money he had asked them to invest.

He is trusting that they have invested wisely, so he can reward them and not have to punish them for not investing wisely. The master is trusting that they were not lazy and just goofing off in unbelief. His hope is that they have done things right so he can reward them. If they had obeyed their master, they did not have to fear his return.

The master questions the first man to whom he gave a mina. The first man said he now had ten minas. His master told him because of his faithfulness in a small matter, he was putting him in charge of ten cities. The second man said he had gained five more and the master told him to take charge of five cities. They both had invested their money wisely and made a good profit for their master. Their reward was according to the work they had done.

God is going to reward us as we use our abilities to earn money to give to Him. Remember that He owns everything, and everything we make belongs to Him. He wants us to manage what He has given to us so He can reward us accordingly.

The third man then gave his report, which was considerably different (verses 20-21).

> *"Then another came, saying, Master, here is your mina, which I have kept put away in a handkerchief. For I feared you, because you are an austere man. You collect what you did not deposit, and reap what you did not sow." (7)*

This man did not even put his money in the bank to draw interest on it. He did not believe his master's word.

This man is called a wicked servant (verses 22-23):

> *"And he said to him. 'Out of your own mouth I will judge you, you wicked servant. You know that I was an austere man, collecting what I did not deposit and reaping what I did not sow. Why then did you not put my money in the bank, that at my coming I might have collected it with interest?'"*

The master is not angry because he did not make ten minas. He was angry because his servant didn't even try to use his money for the master's advantage.

Do we realize that our rewards are in Heaven? When we invest for the future by giving back to God what He has entrusted us with, He is going to reward us greatly. We are on a journey through this life on earth to collect rewards for when we get to Heaven. God wants us to invest our monies, our time, and our talents for Him on earth. This is for the purpose of bringing glory to His name.

Should I Give Now or Later?

The answer is both. You should never forget that you cannot "out-give God." God will bless you for giving. You may ask, "How do I know if I am going to have enough to live on when I retire?" Should a retired person who has more than enough to retire on give the surplus to God, or should they hang on to it and invest the profits? We need to remember that we are God's children. He is going to meet our needs, but He does not promise to meet our wants.

We in America are so blessed with material things that we think we can't live without them. Christians need to ask God to direct them in the decisions that they are required to make. We know that God is going to bless us for giving to Him. He may bless us here on earth, and we know that He will bless us when we get to Heaven. If we give now, we know that we will be rewarded for it. If we wait, we have no assurance that we will still have that money to give in the future. God could take us home unexpectedly, or we could lose that money in a declining market.

I highly recommend leaving money to your church or other Christian ministries in your will or your trust. You may want to give ten percent or more. I would recommend at least ten percent, regardless of how much money you have. You may want to decide how much you want to leave with your children and make sure the remainder goes to Christian ministries.

Your Children's Inheritance

Yes, we may want to and be able to, to leave an inheritance to our children. However, leaving a large inheritance to our children is not necessarily the best way to go. First, it takes away from the opportunity that we can have to invest in the kingdom of God. Second, if we leave too much to our children, it could do harm to them. Looking at the lives of those who have inherited a significantly large amount of money, you will find that for the majority of them, it has made them more unhappy, greedy and cynical. Often a large estate divides siblings. They have more time on their hands to find new temptations, which sometimes includes addictions.

If you have a disabled child, you should help that child if you can. Let God direct you in your decisions. He wants what is best for you and your children. (8)

Having a Will or a Trust

You need to have a will or a trust. If you do not, the state decides who gets what. If you do not have either one, make it a high priority to have one or the other. You probably can find out how to write your own will on the Internet, but you really need to have a lawyer draw up a will or a trust. In most cases, a will costs less than a trust.

However, a will probably will cost more when your estate is settled. A will has to go through probate court, and usually a lawyer is involved. It is going to take longer to settle an estate if you use a will.

In a trust, everything is spelled out as to where, and to whom, your estate goes. The downside of a trust is that you have to have everything listed in your trust. If you make changes in investments, they need to be recorded. Anything that is not listed may have to go through probate court.

You will find that many lawyers are opinionated when it comes to trusts and wills. Do your homework and find which is best for you. Giving to God brings us eternal rewards and a promise that He will supply our present needs. When we give to God, we are obeying His Word. If you are in debt and cannot give to God, then work hard in get out of debt. Seek financial counseling if direction is needed. Make sure that you pray and ask God what He wants you to give. Remember that you cannot out-give God. If you are going to finish the race strong, give generously.

Have you ever seen a hearse pulling a U-Haul trailer behind it? We know that when we leave this world we cannot take anything with us. However, we can send a great deal ahead of us. *"In my Father's house there are many mansions; if it were not so, I would have told you. I go to prepare a place for you"* (John 14:2). Based on what you are sending ahead both monetarily and through service, God will bless you. The short time that we spend here on earth does not compare to even a second of time spent in eternity. When we establish a mindset that we are going to do all we can each day with the talents that God has given us, then we will bring glory to His name and at the same time build dividends for Heaven, our eternal home. May God bless you as you give back to Him what He has given to you. Let's work hard to finish strong in giving back to Him.

Chapter XIV

Being There for the Elderly

Visiting

The local church needs to have a calling program set up for the elderly. I don't know how many times I have heard that those who are in nursing homes in particular, say that they are lonely. If you stop to think about it, we too could very likely be spending our last days in a nursing home.

Let's find out who in the church is willing to call on those we will call shut-ins. Shut-ins are those who cannot get out to any church services. Then set up a schedule so they are called on regularly. If possible, call on them at least once a week. You may have to ask some who have not volunteered. There are always those in the church who will get involved if they are asked.

Gifts

Next, have a program where those shut-ins are given something special on holidays. On Easter, a small box of candy would be nice. These special gifts could be something that is homemade. Senior classes or a women's ministry could be involved in seeing that the shut-ins are given something special for holidays and their birthdays. Having each Sunday school class adopt a shut-in would be a way to spread the opportunity to serve more in your church without making it overwhelming for a smaller group.

Special Activities

Sometimes there are those who are elderly who do not see themselves driving much out of town or any distance. If your church has a bus, it can be used for taking trips out of town for a senior group. Taking a color tour in the fall would be appropriate. Going to hear a special music group could be another possibility. Talk to your seniors and see what they would like to do.

Our home church started what was called "dinners for eight." This would be four couples or three couples and two singles (both male or female so that there was no matchmaking attempt) getting together for a meal once a month. Every four months the groups change so you get to know more couples on a personal basis. Those who were involved really enjoyed them, and they got to know people from different age groups. You might want to start the dinners of eight by having two couples of seniors and two younger couples.

When Donna and I were in Tucson, Arizona, we were involved in an Adult Bible Fellowship class of a megachurch. This class consisted of about seventy to eighty senior adults. From that class we were assigned to a small group. These small groups meet once a month in different homes or a restaurant. We liked the small groups of our age bracket, but there are advantages of having them mixed with older and younger adults too.

Donna and I go to a "game fellowship" of a small church when we are in Arizona. They play table games. It meets twice a month in the morning and ends with a potluck lunch. Once a quarter they go out to eat. Each week they collect two dollars to go toward the outing. Setting up a game day activity or evening activity twice a month could work for your church. It is an opportunity to have fellowship and an outing for the retirement-aged adults in the church.

Our home church has had a midweek prayer time in the morning for those seniors who do not want to drive at night. We do not have a large group that comes out to this meeting, but it is set up to meet a need for some.

Years ago, our home church built an addition to our church just for the seniors of the church. The addition has a divider that makes it into two rooms. These rooms are accessible for disabled people. Seniors use these rooms for their Sunday school classes, prayer meetings, and special events that they have going on. Others in the church can use this area, but the seniors have priority.

Making the Elderly Feel Needed

How often do you hear from the elderly that they do not feel needed or that there is nothing in the church that they can do? Since I am one who believes that God has something for everyone to do until God takes them home, I believe it is the church's responsibility to make sure that we utilize the elderly of our church.

Every Christian can pray. Every church has needs within it that can use prayer. Every ministry of the church needs prayer. The pastor needs prayer; the Sunday school teachers need prayer; the deacons need prayer, those who serve on committees and in every ministry need prayer. I think if we want the elderly to be praying for our church, we need to keep them up-to-date on what they can pray for. Also, when they pray, they need to know when that prayer has been answered. People like to know what to pray for. When I pray for a missionary, I like to know specific prayer requests. If they are witnessing to someone, it is helpful to have the names of those persons. In the past, in our home church, I was able to start a senior men's Sunday school class. We had a senior women's class, but for the last few years there had been no class for men. Thinking that I would probably get four to five men who would attend the class, I invited several men who did not attend Sunday school at all, and we soon averaged ten men in the class. We spent several weeks talking about prayer and our need to be praying for our church. I asked our two pastors if they would e-mail me some special prayer requests once a month so that our senior men's class could pray for them intelligently. The pastors indicated that they would be glad to do this, and once a month they sent special prayer requests. They were also asked to send any answers to the prayer requests. This is a way that seniors can get involved.

A monthly newsletter can let them know what to pray for and what requests have been answered. Letting your seniors know that they are needed to pray for their church and letting them know when their prayers are answered is important. They also can be part of a prayer chain. In our home church the senior ladies are the ones who call others when there is a special need in the church. Today much of this is done by e-mail. However, many seniors do not e-mail but need to be included.

Donna and I are subs in a large senior church bowling league when we are out in Tucson for the winter months. Each week we get to bowl on different teams. This year I bowled with a ninety-three-year-old man. Three days a week during tax season he visits different churches where he does tax returns for the poor. Wow! Bowling at ninety-three and doing tax returns free is outstanding. He bowled one game this year over two-hundred, and his average is over one hundred and fifty.

Seniors can be helpful to each other by making a phone call to one another or making a visit. They can send birthday cards to each other. We have a senior lady in our church that sends a birthday card to everyone in the church on behalf of the church, which is a ministry that you can use a senior in your church to fulfill.

A senior couple can adopt a younger couple in your church. Sometimes young couples join a church and do not have family in the area. You can make a point to get to know them well enough so you can adopt them as their parents while they are away from home. If they are away from their family's home during the holidays, invite them to spend those days with you.

Ask your pastor or a church board member what you can do in your church. If your church is sending out a newsletter, ask seniors to come in and stuff envelopes, stamp and seal them.

Finding out what each senior likes to do and what they are capable of doing will get you a long way in getting them involved in your church and making them feel they are useful.

Assisting the Elderly with Physical Needs

All churches should have a work team that helps the elderly. Our church gets together a work team to replace roofs for those in need in our church. This is especially helpful and needful for the senior citizens of our church. Fixing a faucet that leaks is something that many different men can do. Seniors who cannot do yard work or need repair work to be done, should have a contact person they can talk to when they have a need. In other words, you need someone to coordinate this ministry. There are usually men in most churches who have recently retired and still have the need to be useful. Getting them involved in helping the older people in your church can be a blessing to them.

Traditional vs. Contemporary Music

We have seen a big change in music in many churches from traditional to contemporary music. Many seniors like the traditional music. This is the music that they have grown up with. Many of them will say that the traditional hymns speak to them, and in the same breath they will say that contemporary music does nothing for them. As an elderly person you need to realize that when you speak to young people, they may likely say that contemporary music speaks to them. My point is that many churches have not taken into consideration those who like a different kind of music than they do. God wants unity in the church, and we need to consider the likes and dislikes of others when it comes to traditional and contemporary music.

Some churches that are large enough have two morning services; one service with traditional music and the other contemporary. Other churches have a blend of both contemporary and traditional. The point is that we need to take into consideration our seniors. They should never be told to go to a nursing home if they don't like the contemporary music. At the same time those who only like traditional hymns should be considerate to what the younger generation likes. I recently read that when church music changed from singing the Psalms to hymns that many thought it was wrong. Change is never easy.

Recognition of Our Seniors

Donna and I have been members of our home church for over twenty-nine years. We are still learning about seniors and their previous involvements within our church. Having a special banquet in the church to honor seniors who have put forth a lot of service could be a way to learn about the elderly. If your church has a newsletter, a senior person could be featured in each issue. Letting those in the church know about previous accomplishments of seniors can help the seniors' self-esteem and also can let the younger generation get to know these seniors better.

It is important that we do not forget those who are elderly in our church. When they can no longer attend our church because of physical or mental situations in their lives, we need to continue to treat them as members of our church. We need to let them know that they are still members. When they are visited each week, they need to receive a bulletin and a prayer bulletin, if the church has one. The person who visits shut-ins needs to let them know what is going on in the church and how they can pray for their church. They need to know that they are still part of the church. Also, the person who visits the shut-ins needs to ask them if there are things they can pray for on their behalf. Have a word of prayer with them before you leave. Bring prayer requests back to your church to pray for on their behalf.

Keeping the elderly doing ministry in the church is important. They want to feel useful. We may need to become creative to get them involved, but keeping them involved is a must. Let's help them finish strong.

Chapter XV

Being There for the Younger Generation

P aul was a good example to us by coming alongside of Timothy and discipling him to become a mature Christian and to become all that God wanted him to be. As parents help their children in their growing-up process, it is imperative that this takes place in our churches, where the mature Christian comes alongside the younger Christian.

We often speak of a generation gap between the older and the younger generations. Our culture keeps changing and often we, of the older generation, fall behind the younger generation. I was talking with my eleven-year-old grandson this afternoon on the phone and asked him what he was doing. He replied, "I have been talking with my friend on Facebook." Some of the senior generation have never even become involved with the Internet.

Even though the younger generation may be growing up in a newer world of technology, God's Word is always the same and it does not change. We as the mature generation need to help the younger generation with spiritual challenges that come their way. Young Christians need mature Christians to come alongside them and help them in their Christian walk. They are facing many challenges that we did not have to face. One way to help the younger generation is through mentoring them.

Mentoring is a process of learning from others who have traveled the road before you. Someone comes alongside you and encourages you. Mentors are passing on to you things that they have learned through their life experiences, helping you to have wonderful fulfillment in your Christian walk.

Mentoring simply put is "follow me." Christ asked His disciples to follow Him. They followed Jesus for three years and were mentored along the way. After Jesus returned to Heaven, they turned the world upside down.

Mentoring involves people. Often there can be a number of people that God brings into a person's life at different times for various purposes. These are people whom God is using to help you grow in your Christian walk. *"But grow in the grace and knowledge of our Lord and Savior Jesus Christ"* (2 Peter 2:18). Peter summarizes his letter as he began it, by telling his readers to pursue Christian maturity and a deeper knowledge of the Lord Jesus Christ, which will lead to doctrinal stability and will help prevent a Christian from going astray. He is telling us that as long as we are living, we need to be growing in Christ. When we stop growing, we stop being an example to those who are watching us.

How do the younger-generation Christians become mature Christians? They can do this by learning from the example of mature Christians. Younger Christians are watching older Christians to see how they act, how they worship God, and how they live their lives at church and outside of church.

I remember as a junior high student that there was a high school guy, and I wanted to be just like him. He was my hero. You might say that I idolized him. He was an outstanding athlete, and he came from a well-to-do family. He drove a nice car and was good-looking. I watched him play basketball and baseball, and I wanted to play like he did. I continued to watch his life after high school. He married a good-looking cheerleader from another school; he went into the army and went into business with his father. He was the type of person who I wanted to follow. Once I left home after college, I had little contact with him. I met him at a coffee shop in the area where I grew up a year or so before he passed away and had my first one-on-one conversation with him. I found out that he was a Christian, which I was excited to know. My mother had told me, when my father was in his last days with cancer, that my childhood hero had made some visits to see my dad. I was able to thank him for making those calls.

Tradesmen use the concept of mentoring. Plumbers and electricians use mentoring for a young man or woman to learn the trade. He or she works as an apprentice for several years before he or she is licensed to be a tradesman in his field. Michelangelo, the great artist, is known by most, but few know about his teacher, Bertoldo.

A Christian mentor is a person who has a spiritual commitment. Mentors are seriously committed to life change. Their priority is lasting development of excellence in their protégé. They dislike mediocrity, the attitude that anything is okay for God. Mentoring is the process of helping another to develop to his maximum potential for Jesus Christ. *"Him we preach, warning every man and teaching every man in all wisdom. (Why?) That we may present every man perfect in Christ Jesus"* (Colossians 1:28). Then Paul adds (vs. 29), *"To this end I also labor, striving according to His works in me mightily."*

Paul's desire was that believers would not remain spiritual babies.

> *"And I, brethren, could not speak to you as to spiritual people*
> *but as to carnal, as to babes in Christ. I fed you with milk and*
> *not with solid food; for until now you were not able to receive it,*
> *and even now you are still not able"* (1 Corinthians 3:1-2).

Paul's desire was that new Christians would become spiritually mature. Spiritual immaturity makes it impossible to grasp rich truths.

Paul was committed to mentoring because his objective was clear. Your outcome is determined by your objective. If you don't have a goal, you never achieve it. Paul saw the importance of building the present generation to help the next generation.

Paul is an example for us. Paul took Timothy on his second missionary trip, and Timothy probably was a convert from his first missionary journey. Paul was a coach (mentor) to Timothy. Timothy's name means "one who honors God." Timothy was in his late teens or early twenties when he went with Paul. Timothy was Paul's disciple, friend, and co-laborer for the rest of Paul's life. Paul lived an example for Timothy to follow. Timothy was willing to learn from Paul.

We all need a Paul in our lives. We need a more mature person who is willing to invest into our lives. This person needs to be someone who is willing to share with you, not just his strengths, but also to share with you his weaknesses. This mentor needs to be one whose life experiences can help you. This person doesn't need to be more gifted than you or smarter but does need to be one who has overcome his or her weaknesses and learned from them and has grown from them. *"And the things that you have heard from me among many witnesses, commit these to faithful men who will be able to teach others also"* (2 Timothy 2:2). Paul believed in multiplying himself in others.

I have had the privilege when we are in Michigan to go calling with my pastor. I have learned a lot about making calls. While out in Arizona I have been able to put some of my learning into practice. Pastor Jones is very skilled in making fruitful calls. He has been a mentor to me, not because of his age (for I am older than he), but because of his experience. Calling is something that he has a passion for; he is a soul-winner. His enthusiasm for calling and soul-winning is contagious.

We also need a Barnabas (son of encouragement). This person could be a peer and someone who knows you well. This person could be your spouse. It is someone who you need to be accountable to, someone who can speak with you in trust. This is someone who tells you the truth about yourself; a person who will give you a kick in the pants when you need it—a person whom you can consider your accountability partner. Usually the role is reversible, where you hold your friend accountable also. *"As iron sharpens iron, so man sharpens the countenance of his friend"* (Proverbs 27:17).

There is a need for mature Christians to have a Timothy in their lives so that they can pass the baton on to the next generation. A mature Christian has the responsibility to pass the baton on to the younger generation. That responsibility is to help the younger Christian become all that God wants him or her to be. Ideally, every church should have a mentoring program where new Christians are mentored by mature Christians. If every church would assign a new convert to a mature Christian, we could have a stronger church. How often do we see a new Christian start out great in their newfound faith and then fall away. (1)

I know of a church that decided to have a couple of young Christians on their church board for the purpose of learning from the older men. Usually there were one or two young men on the board. This did two things. It gave the younger generation representation on the board, and it became a learning experience for them. I had the opportunity to be part of a deacon board with an older gentleman, whom I watched carefully. There was a great deal to learn from him. He did not know it, but he was a mentor to me. I watched him carefully and learned how he approached the challenges that a board faced. He usually let others give their opinions first. Then when he had gained insight from others, he would express his opinion, and usually with a very logical solution. He did not say a lot, but he had thought through the situation carefully before giving his opinion or solution to a situation.

I remember as a young Christian (in my early thirties) being on the deacon board of my church. Our pastor was having marital problems. His wife had left him and there was a rumor, not proof, that he had been seeing another woman. I wanted the pastor fired on the spot. But a mature deacon said, "No." The board offered to pay for some counseling for the pastor and his wife. Counseling did not work, and the pastor stepped down. The whole thing was handled in Christian love. The pastor left the ministry, divorced his wife and in time married another lady. As an immature deacon, I was mentored to show Christian love to others in a responsible and biblical way.

We need a mature Christian like Paul to guide us. We all can use an accountability partner, an encourager to keep us accountable. If you are an older, mature Christian you need to come alongside younger Christians and help build Christian principles into their lives.

Donna and I do some volunteer financial counseling. It is not our policy to give those we counsel money or necessarily direct them to where they can get money. Our goal is to teach them to use what they have. We give them an assignment during our first meeting. After giving them a small notebook, we ask them to keep track of every penny that they spend each week. The next step is to work on a "spending plan." The saying, "If you give a man a fish he will need one tomorrow, but if you show him how to fish he can meet his own needs." As a "mentor/coach," we are directing those we counsel in the right direction; they have to take the responsibility to make the proper changes. We become accountability partners with them. We also become encouragers.

There are many Christians who could use financial counseling. Financial difficulty in a marriage is one of the major reasons for divorce. Every church can benefit from having financial counselors (coaches) to help those who are struggling financially.

So what are the responsibilities of the older generation to the younger generation? As Christian leaders in the church, how do we come alongside to model, to encourage, to be an example and to teach the younger generation? We need to think in terms of mature Christians. It is a seasoned Christian helping an unseasoned Christian. Jesus used this method. The twelve disciples were not put in a classroom for three years and given lessons in theology. They learned as they walked by His side; they learned by sharing His ministry. Our goal is to come alongside a younger Christian and help that person to reach their God-given potential. Our protégé needs a brain to pick, a shoulder that he or she can cry on and a gentle reprimand when needed.

Mentoring can be used in the church to develop leadership in younger adults. It is often easier to do something ourselves than to teach someone else to do the job. However, it is imperative that younger Christians learn to take over responsibilities. For example a children's ministry director who has had years of experience needs to mentor an inexperienced person. Once the trainee is properly trained they can take over the responsibly as director of children's ministry. When I told my school board that I was going to retire in two to three years, I asked them to hire someone whom I could mentor for a couple of years. This did not happen, and the school had a big drop in enrollment that might have been prevented if the person who took over my responsibilities had been mentored.

Donna and I have headed up a ministry in our church called Friendship Festival, where we have our church parking lot full of games, with several inflatables, including a thirty-five foot slide. We have a free lunch for everyone and much more. This takes place when our city has a Creative Arts Festival, and we have over a thousand people visit us. We have a tent where the Gospel is given out. When we decided that we should give up this responsibility, we asked a younger couple to take this leadership over. We spent the first year still being in charge, but they worked with us. Then the next year they were in charge, and we helped them as needed. Now they are able to carry out the responsibility on their own.

In Titus 2:1-2 we find some qualifications for mentoring: *"But as for you, speak the things which are proper for sound doctrine: that the older men be sober, reverent, temperate, sound in faith, in love, in patience."* If an older man is to be a mentor to a younger man he needs these character qualities displayed in his Christian walk. We also find the following in Ephesians 5:18: *"And do not be drunk with wine, in which is dissipation; but be filled with the Spirit."* The older man is to be sober-minded and steady. (2) Temperate or self-controlled literally means to "act with a saved mind." A disciplined man is a self-controlled man. Matthew Henry says, "That this man governs well his passions and affections, so as not to be hurried away by them to anything that is evil or indecent."

Mentors need to be sound in their faith. "Sound" means to be healthy. The mature man is one who is grounded in God's Word. He has put his trust in God and the teaching of His Word.

He is to be sound in love. He is healthy in his love relationship with God and the love he shows to others. Agape love is a choice and not a feeling. He is willing to help with the burdens of others. He is not to be, what we would call, a "grumpy old person"; he is not to let bitterness control his life. (3)

As a mature Christian you need to find a younger Christian in the faith to mentor. If you need help in finding a person to mentor, talk with your pastor and ask him to direct you to that person. Maybe you can ask your pastor if you could help start a mentoring program for new Christians within your church.

If you need a Paul in your life, one who can help mentor you, then ask your pastor to direct you to that person. You may need mentoring in a certain area (such as your finances), and he can direct you to a person who can help you in that area. If we are going to finish strong, we need others to come alongside us. Likewise, we need to come alongside others.

I have a great concern for the younger generation today who lack commitment to God, and therefore, to their church. Many are in debt over their heads; therefore, they think that they cannot tithe to their church. Many young couples today both work out of the home and don't seem to have time for church. They need a Paul in their lives, and you may be the person whom they need to come alongside them as a mentor.

Let's come alongside others as accountability partners and mentors, and let's help each other to become all that God wants us to be. We must not let the younger generation down. The growth of our churches and spiritual well-being of our churches are dependent on the older generation coming alongside the younger generation to help them grow as mature, spiritual Christians. Let's keep the younger generation on the right track so they will finish strong too.

Chapter XVI

Retiring Is Optional?

The answer is yes-or-no. "I retired from my job, and I am going to just sit in my rocking chair until I die." That may be the goal of some people, but it sure isn't the right goal. Because of modern medical care and the fact that many Americans are eating better diets and exercising, they are living longer. Does that mean they should work longer or not?

Some might say that since you are going to live longer, you need to work longer. Someone might say I have worked all my life, and now I am going to take it easy. Others might say that life is too short, and I want to enjoy myself for a few years. So as a Christian, what should determine if you work longer or retire as soon as you are able?

Factors to Consider When Retiring

Age Is One Factor

Many people are living longer and are healthier longer and therefore have the ability to work longer. Some people enjoy their work and would not mind working longer, but sometimes their employers are encouraging them to retire to make room for younger workers. Others only keep working until they get full retirement, and then they are out the door. If a person has a job that requires a lot of physical strength, and it is getting difficult for him or her to do, it may be time to retire from that job. Others might have a lot of stress in their positions, and they need to get away from that stress. Sometimes there needs to be a change in the type of work that a person does. So, if you still need income in addition to your social security, then a part time-job with less physical strain or less stress might be in line. Just make sure that you have prayed about your decision before you make it.

Health Is Another Factor

If your job is jeopardizing your health, you need to consider retiring or changing employment. It is said that stress can cause health difficulties. If you have a sedentary job, you need to make sure that you get exercise. I learned this the hard way. As a Christian school administrator I had little time for exercise. At least, I thought that I had little time. At age fifty-four I had some chest pains and found out that my right artery was 97 percent blocked. After having angioplasty, I was sent home with a new outlook on two things. First, I realized that I needed to take time to exercise. I started running at least three days a week. I also went on a limited fat diet. Sixteen years later, after having my right kidney taken out because of a cancerous tumor on it, I had a blood clot go into my heart and I had a massive heart attack. The same artery at that time was 70 percent open.

On the other hand if you have good health and enjoy what you are doing, you may want to keep working until you are older. Someone has said that you are only as old as you feel. If your employment is enjoyable, you might not think of it as work but fun.

Money Needed to Retire

You need to decide how much money you need to live on after retirement by taking into account inflation. Are you anticipating the same life-style after retirement as before you retired? If your home is paid for, that is one less expense you are going to have. However, it is likely that you will be paying more for health insurance in the future. It would be wise to sit down and make out a spending plan as to what you think you will need to live on after retirement.

How long you think you are going to live should be another factor to consider when you retire. No one knows how long they are going to live. However, you can look at your ancestors and see how long they lived. My mother was five when her mother died from cancer; her father died in his sixties from cancer; her sisters died in their late sixties and her two brothers died in their early eighties. However, she lived to be ninety-seven. Only God knows the answer as to how long one will live. Ideally you can look at the age of your parents. My father died at eighty-two. There is a good chance I will live to be that age. When considering how much money you need to live on during retirement, you may want to add a few years to your parents' life span. To be on the safe side, you might want to consider at least ten years. Again, there is no formula that you can use to determine how long you are going to live, but you need to prepare for a long life.

It is very likely that most people cannot live on social security alone. Therefore, it is imperative that you determine how much fixed income you are going to have when you retire. If you have social security, that is a start. If you are married and one of the spouses has a retirement program to draw from, you can add that to your fixed income at retirement. I would highly suggest that this retirement account be put in both spouses' name, so that if one dies before the other that the other will continue to receive the benefits. The amount that you will receive is less if the benefit goes to both spouses. This adds income security to both marriage partners. These are fixed incomes that you should have the remainder of your lives. Once you add those retirement benefits up you need to look at your retirement spending plan and see if you can live on that amount. Don't forget to add some for inflation. If you cannot, then you might look at drawing from your 401(k) account. The rule is that if you want this fund to continue to last, you should take less than 4 to 6 percent of it each year. If you cannot live on social security, a retirement pension, and what you can take out of a 401(K) savings, you might want to consider at least working part-time for several years after you retire from your full-time job. You do not want your money to run out ten years before you leave this world.

When a person has a full retirement pension coming to him from his employer, should he or she retire at that time? A lot of people do retire when they have full retirement from their employer, and some of those people take on different employment. Age needs to play a factor. At the time of this writing you can draw on your social security when you turn 62. However, each year after age 62 you get a little more. You may want to wait until you are 65 or older to be able to draw more social security. Check with your local Social Security Office to find out what the amount will be at different ages. You may want to find another source of full-time or part-time employment until you can draw your social security.

When I retired from Christian education after twenty-five years in that profession, I decided that I still needed to keep on working; at least until when my wife, Donna, retired. Therefore, I took training to become a Realtor. As a Realtor I sold homes as a self-employed person. I could take time off when I wanted to and work as hard as I wanted to work. However, my income was based on my work effort.

How Do We Save for Retirement?

The earlier that you start saving for retirement, the better off you will be. Compound interest is the secret to seeing your retirement account grow. If your employer has a 401(k) matching account, you cannot afford not to take advantage of it. For example, if your employer will match every dollar you put in a 401(k) account up to $2,000; your account will grow by $4,000. You only have to put in $2,000. If at all possible, take advantage of this opportunity.

Sometimes people say they cannot afford to put money into a matching fund. Work on your spending plan and see if you can. It may even mean sacrificing now for your future. Donna started working, as a District Sales Manager for Avon when the oldest of our three children was starting college. We had both been working in Christian education prior to that time. We had prayed about one of the two of us getting a better-paying job because we wanted to help our children with their college expenses. The Lord opened up a job for Donna with Avon shortly thereafter. When she started with Avon, she took advantage of Avon's matching fund and continued until she retired. When our children got out of college, we upped the amount, by putting twenty percent of her income into her retirement account. We also lived on Donna's salary and started putting my income into a retirement account. However, we made sure that we tithed and gave gifts to the Lord's work.

The earlier you start saving, the more income you will have at the time of retirement. Donna and I do financial counseling as a ministry. We do not charge for our counseling. So many young couples today are credit-card poor. They get hung up on not living within their means. It is so easy to use a credit card today. If you want one, you have one. It is a lot like setting candy in front of a child, and then telling him that he cannot have any. Donna and I use a credit card all the time, but we make sure that we pay it fully at the end of the month. When we were both working in Christian education, and not making much money; however, we never spent more than what we had coming in at any one time. All through the New Testament we are encouraged to sacrifice now for the rewards that we will get when we get to Heaven. We cannot out-give God. It is also prudent to sacrifice now by saving for our retirement years. Dave Ramsey says, "Live like no one else now, so later you can live like no one else and also give like no one else."

Often when you invest in a 401(k) with your employer, the company gives you an option to invest within a mutual fund, either into an aggressive account or conservative funds. Sometimes you need to know what is going on in the stock market so you know whether to keep your money in aggressive funds or in conservative funds. If you are in retirement or close to retirement, most financial advisors will recommend that you invest in conservative funds. God has entrusted you with His money, and you have a responsibility not to throw it away. He also expects us to be accountable for what we are investing our money into whether it is considered "clean" funds or "dirty" funds which do not honor God or support Godly activities.

Knowing God's Will in Retirement Is a Major Factor

As Christians we need to make sure that we retire when we believe that is what God wants for us. We are God's children and we need to accomplish in our lifetime what He wants us to accomplish. A Christian who retires from working for a living should never retire from working for God. We are in His workforce and He wants us to continue to use our talents and abilities to do His work. Therefore, as children of God, we are never to retire from doing His work if we are going to finish strong.

When Christians terminate their employment to retire, it should mean to them that they then have more time to give to their Creator, their Savior, the One who is preparing a home for them in Heaven. It is also when we can give more time to church ministries and spend more time in His Word.

So What Can Christians Do When They Retire?

Every Christian can pray. This is something we can do when we can do nothing physically. Christians need to be praying for the unsaved. God does not want anyone to spend eternity in Hell. If we have unsaved loved ones, we need to be praying for them daily. If we have friends who are unsaved, we need to pray for them. We need to pray for our neighbors. Often missionaries will list people they are seeking to reach for the Lord in their prayer letters for whom you can pray. If your church has an outreach ministry, you need to be praying for those they are seeking to reach. Make a list of those that you are going to pray for and pray for them daily.

There are things in our local churches that almost any retired person can get involved in if he or she is willing. You can ask your pastor or another leader in your church what you might be able to do. Mentoring new Christians is a needed ministry in most churches. Visiting the sick, visiting those in nursing homes, and serving on committees are all areas of service in which senior adults can become involved. Some retired people write the missionaries whom the church supports. Missionaries love to know what is going on in your church and your life. Some missionaries love to hear what is going on in the sports field and what is going on with our government from a Christian's perspective? You can ask them what they would like to hear about. During the two years that Donna and I spent on the mission field in Brazil with our three children, mail was very important to us. It was great to know what was going on in our family's lives, our friends' lives, our church, and in the lives of anyone else who took the time to write us. Today you can e-mail or skype your missionaries.

Working in the nursery of your church, children's ministry, and Vacation Bible School are some of the areas where you can work. Volunteering to help out in your church's Christian school, if it has one, is another area of potential service. Do repair work for others in your church family if you have that type of ability.

When Donna and I were teaching in Brazil, there was also a retired couple who were there as volunteers. She worked as an art teacher in the elementary school, and he did odd jobs such as taking a bus downtown to pick up missionaries' mail for them. There are many opportunities to spend time helping in different mission fields for a short period of time.

152

We have a number of men in our church who are retired but are busy serving in ministry. There are a number of them who help others with special needs doing things like remodeling homes, helping people move, and putting on a new roof. Ladies can prepare meals for the ill or for the men working on the above projects or maybe clean a home for a person who is not able.

Retiring from employment to make a living has to come sometime in most of our lives, but retiring from God's work is not optional. Note when Joshua was between 85-100 years old: *"Now Joshua was old and advanced in years. And the Lord said unto him: 'You are old, advanced in years, and there remains very much land yet to be possessed'"* (Joshua 13:1). God still had work for him to do. Older people are filled with the wisdom that comes from experience. That wisdom needs to be utilized within our churches. Therefore, Christians need to continue to use those abilities they have to serve Him until He takes them home. We need to do this if we want to finish strong. Moses did his most fruitful ministry from the age of eighty to one hundred and twenty. Keep trucking for Jesus until He calls you home; there will be joy in your life if you do, and you will finish strong.

Lesson Nine

No Assurance of What Tomorrow Will Bring

"*W*hereas ye know not what will happen tomorrow. For what is your life? It is even a vapor that appears for a little time and then vanishes away" (James 4:14). When things are going well in our lives, we don't think about death. This verse is a reminder that our lives are for only a short time and then we die. You wake up in the morning and you look out your bedroom window and there is a heavy fog. It is so foggy that you cannot see your neighbor's home. You go downstairs, eat your breakfast and walk out the door to go to work, and the fog is gone. The fog evaporates sometimes so quickly we don't even realize where it has gone. Likewise, we have no guarantee when our lives will come to an end.

Things were going well for Donna and me when we returned to Michigan in March of 2008. I did not know what was in store for me in the days ahead. We have no assurance of tomorrow, but if we are children of God, we know who holds our future. That is all that is important. That truth gives us the satisfaction that He is with us and will never leave us.

When we become the older generation, and see our grandchildren growing up, then we have great-grandchildren, we begin to realize that our lives are passing by quickly. We have to rest in knowing that God is in control.

My whole family was with me on my first "outing" since entering the hospital 18 days previously. I was given permission to go up to the atrium on top of the hospital for one hour. Family and fresh air—oh what a blessing!

Chapter XVII

Grandparenting God's Way

Respecting Their Parents

I have said often that it is great to have grandchildren because you can "Love them, spoil them and send them home." It sounds nice from a grandparent's standpoint but not from a parent's perspective. When grandparents do that, they discourage parents from letting their children visit again. For example, your grandchildren's parents may not want their children to have a lot of sweets because it makes them hyper. You give the children sweets and then send them home on a sugar high. The parents have to deal with the consequences. You know that is not going to set well with them.

As grandparents we need to respect our grandchildren's parents. We may not agree with everything they ask us to do on behalf of their children, but we need to fulfill their desires. If we have our grandchildren for a weekend and they have homework to do and we don't help them get it done, that is a no-no. If their parents want them to have eight to nine hours of sleep and we allow them to stay up late and get up early, we are neglecting their desires and that is wrong. If we allow them to watch TV programs that their parents do not allow them to watch at home, that is wrong. We can enjoy our grandchildren, but at the same time we have to respect the parents' guidelines.

Parenting Grandchildren

We need to respect how our children parent their children. We should never criticize our children in front of our grandchildren. You might ask what to do when you think that their parents are too strict or too lax. We know of a set of parents, who did not discipline their children, and today they have spoiled, grown-up children who give them many headaches. You can point out a family like this to your child. Show the weaknesses of how this family's children turned out. Use some discretion.

We have set up guidelines in our home for our grandchildren. We are parenting by helping them to live within the boundaries that have been set for them. When our grandchildren were toddlers, we did not take things off our coffee table; we taught them that they could look, even touch, but not pick up. We have never had anything broken. They learned at a young age what the guidelines were for them.

Be an Encourager

Grandparents need to be encouragers for their grandchildren. This can be done in many different ways. Making sure that you watch some of their ball games or other special activities that they are involved in can be a real encouragement to them. They need to be cheered on to do their best. Let them know that not winning is OK and just having fun is more important. I get very upset with parents or grandparents when they are watching their children or grandchildren and yell at the referee or umpire over a call that has been made. Even lower yet is yelling at their coach. Or even worse is when they get all over their own child when he or she makes a mistake.

Grandparents can encourage their grandchildren to get good grades. You can offer the "B" student some money for each "A" he or she gets. The "C" student you can offer a monetary reward for each "B" he or she receives. Money is not the only motivator so maybe a camping or shopping trip would be appropriate. Your goal is to get them to work up to capacity. With their parents' permission, you can offer to take them out of school for a day or two to have a long weekend to do something they enjoy doing. This would be a reward for working up to their ability in school. You can also come up with some other incentives. Our oldest grandchild was told that if he were to get a "B" average or better the first semester in college, we would give him tuition money. We had to give him the tuition money.

I have two grandchildren who were having a little difficulty in reading up to their grade level. As grandparents we would have them read to one of us when they came to visit for a couple days. I would tell them when they were not excited about reading to Grandpa that the more they read, the better they would get. Then I would encourage them whenever I saw any improvement. Since I have worked in education most of my life, I have a real concern for students who are not reading up to their grade level. I have experienced firsthand how difficult it is for students to excel when they are having difficulty reading.

Encouraging our grandchildren in their spiritual walks is very important. Having a relationship where your grandchild can talk to you about his or her spiritual walk, is an area that will be an encouragement to him or her to continue in their walks with the Lord. It is not easy today for young people to walk with the Lord.

We have had our grandchildren visit during the week of VBS at our church. This is an opportunity to help them receive some spiritual input in their lives. I had the opportunity to talk with one of my granddaughters when she came forward at Bible school to make sure that she was saved. It is a real blessing when you can be involved with a grandchild that way. A different year I had the opportunity to lead one of my grandsons to the Lord. It doesn't get any better than that.

Praying for Them

There is nothing more important that we can do for our grandchildren than to pray for them. They should be in our prayers every day. The most important thing that we can pray for is their salvation. I prayed for my last two grandchildren that they would become Christians while they were still in their mother's womb. The thinking here is that I don't want any family member coming into this world without accepting Christ as their personal Savior. We need to pray that they will grow spiritually. We, as grandparents, need to be praying that all our descendants who follow us will become Christians. Could there be a greater joy than to think that all those who follow in your family line would be Christians. I don't think so! The only assurance that we will have is praying that all those in our family line will become Christians. "Dear God, please save all those who follow me because I do not want any of my descendants to come into this world and not come to know you as their personal Savior."

As our grandchildren grow older we need to pray that they will make right decisions. Peer pressure is very strong and making the right friends is important. We can encourage them along the way, but we definitely need to be praying for them. The influence that we have on our grandchildren tapers off as they get older. Our praying for them becomes even more important. We need to continue to let them know that they are important to us. We need to make sure that the doors of communication are open. Hopefully, they will know that the door is always open for them to talk with us.

We as grandparents need to let our grandchildren know that we are praying for them, and if they have some special things that they want us to pray for, that we will do so. When talking with us about the concerns that they have, we need to make sure that we let them know that we will pray for their concerns. For example, if they talk to us about where they want to go to college, we need to make sure that they know that we will pray that they make the right decision. We need to make sure that we follow up by asking them if our prayer has been answered.

We need to pray that they will be people who will bring honor and glory to God. We need to pray that they will choose the college that God wants them to attend and the career that God has for them, or even that they will know if they should go to college. We need to pray, pray and pray continually for them!

Making Memories

Donna likes to play games with our grandchildren. Once in a while one or the other gets upset because one of their siblings beats them. Donna tells them that when we do our best it doesn't matter if we win or lose. She tells them that they "are making memories." It is very important that we do make memories. That has become our mantra when playing games together.

Our two sons have great memories of going up into the Upper Peninsula of Michigan and to Canada with Donna's parents. They even got out of school for a week to do so. (As teachers we once frowned on students being absent, but soon learned the value of students being gone when the homework was properly done ahead or turned in upon return.) These are memories that they will never forget.

Years later, Donna and I, along with our two sons and their grandmother, started going back to the Upper Peninsula to the same lakes to fish with them because they had such good memories of being there with their grandparents. This last year our daughter and her family went with us. Again, we are making memories.

One of the things that my younger grandchildren enjoy having me do with them is to tell them a story when they go to bed. Usually I will ask them what they want the story to be about, and then I make up a story as I tell it to them. It is customary that I start each story with, "A long, long time ago, far, far away…". I don't tell great stories, but they look forward to the next time I tell them a story. I try to end the story with some type of character development principle.

During the time we spend in Tucson, Arizona, Donna has been scrapbooking. She has made albums with a lot of pictures of our grandchildren and their grandparents that someday can be passed on to our grandchildren. These will be memories that they will have to remember the good times we had together.

I can still remember my grandfather letting me drive his car when I was fifteen years old. We lived in a country area. He and I would get a haircut in town, five miles away, and he would let me drive home. That has been a great memory for me. My eight-year-old grandson was sitting in the front seat with me coming home from our fishing trip, and I let him steer the car. He thought that was big stuff. Of course Grandpa had his hand resting on the bottom of the steering wheel.

Again, doing things with our grandchildren that will have lasting memories for them is important. May each of your grandchildren have a memory of you as being a loving and fun grandparent.

Being a Spiritual Example

"O God, You have taught me from my youth; And to this day I declare Your wondrous works. Now also when I am old and grayheaded, O God, do not forsake me, until I declare Your strength to this generation..." (Psalm 71:17-18).

What role should we play as grandparents in our grandchildren's spiritual growth? How do our grandchildren see us in our Christian walk? Do they see us being faithful to the Word of God? We need to be walking the Christian walk in a way that we are being a model (example) to our grandchildren. "*...when I call to remembrance the genuine faith that is in you, which dwelt first in your grandmother Lois and your mother Eunice...*" (2 Timothy 1:5). As Lois did, we Christian grandparents have open doors to inspire our grandchildren to faith in God. We need to live up to the challenge that is set before us. We must not fail. The stakes are too high. Satan is mounting an all-out attack on young people today. Our grandchildren are encountering drugs, alcohol, promiscuity, suicide, humanism, pornography, and much more. You are not the first line of defense. That is the parent's job, but the front line needs support and that is you, the grandparent.

Our grandchildren need to see that we are faithful to God, that we put Him first in our lives. Our prayers that we pray at the supper table can reflect our closeness to Him. When we praise the Lord, when we acknowledge Him as our Lord and Savior, when we thank Him for the blessings that He has given us and ask Him to guide us in our walk, our grandchildren will see what is important in our lives.

When our grandchildren are with us and we witness to someone, they get the idea that witnessing is important. When they see us going to church regularly, they know that church is important to us. When they go to church with us and we ask them what they learned, they know that what we learn at church is important to us. Often we can expand on what they learned in Sunday school or junior church so they again know spiritual things are important to us.

When our grandchildren witness us reading our Bible and praying, we are setting that example for them that having devotions is important. Displaying the fruit of the Spirit in our daily conduct is vital to our testimony. *"But the fruit of the Spirit is love, joy, peace, longsuffering, kindness, goodness, faithfulness, gentleness, self-control."* (Galatians 5:22). When they see these character traits in our lives, we are being a spiritual example to them.

We need to leave a spiritual legacy for our grandchildren, a legacy that has a real impact on their lives. We are going to leave our grandchildren a legacy, and we want it to be a good legacy. We want to leave a legacy that will illuminate Christ and set a standard for decency. We can do this by living out the fruit of the Spirit in our lives. May each of your grandchildren have a memory of you as being a spiritual example.

Worthy of Respect

> *"That the older men be sober, reverent, temperate, sound in faith, in love and patience; the older women likewise, that they be reverent in behavior, not slanderers, not given to much wine, teachers of good things"* (Titus 2:2-3).

The word "temperate" means to be moderate. Grandparents need to be moderate in giving advice, which means to give sparingly and be sensitive to the right timing. They need to be moderate in their gift-giving to their grandchildren, not to overindulge in giving Christmas and birthday gifts. Overindulging can teach wrong values.

Grandparents need to be worthy of respect by setting a positive moral example. They need to hold to a high, positive moral walk. Grandparenting should display a life style of discernment, discretion and judgment that comes from a close walk with the Lord over the years.

Grandparents need to show a consistency in trusting their God. They need to demonstrate that they have no doubt in the sufficiency of His Word. If a grandchild who is not living for the Lord and comes to your home, you need to let him or her know that they are not to use unacceptable language while there. If a grandchild brings his girlfriend to your home to spend the night, and you have heard that they have been living together, you need to let them know that in your home they will sleep in separate bedrooms.

Your grandchildren need to see you as an example in a godly marriage. Even though you are up in years they need to see that there is "love" displayed between the two of you. Donna and I have been married for fifty-one years, but we show affection to one another in front of them. They sometimes act a little embarrassed when we kiss each other in front of them, but they know there is a love relationship between us.

"In all things showing yourself to be a pattern of good works; in doctrine showing integrity, reverence, incorruptibility…" (Titus 2:7) Grandchildren need to see their grandparents involved in ministry.

Can your grandchildren see Christ in your life? Do they see things in your life that will draw them to Christ? Are we worthy of their respect?

Sharing Your Influence

Grandparents need to seize opportunities to share a positive influence with their grandchildren. This needs to be done with discretion and balance. If you are too aggressive, it can be counterproductive; and if you are too passive, you will not have any influence. If you disagree with a parent's discipline you need to keep quiet. You should never say to a grandchild that he or she doesn't have to eat any beans because his or her dad didn't eat them even when the child's mother wants the child to eat them.

"Don't you think that he is old enough to take the garbage out? He's lazy!" or "Why didn't you discipline him for talking back to you?" or "We disciplined you with a bar of soap in your mouth." You may be right, but negativity will agitate your children, and it undermines your credibility with your grandchildren. There will be inconsistency in their lives. Don't make critical comments or subtle hints. Your parents gave you some slack to raise your children, and you need to do likewise with your children.

The opportunity will come when our children will ask us for input in areas of dealing with different situations with their children. This is when they will accept your advice that you give in love. We need to treat our children as grown-up adults, and they will respect us for it.

You need to make every effort possible to support your grandchildren's parents. You need to be that positive support when you can. You need to let your grandchildren know that God put their parents in charge of them and that they have a responsibility to obey their parents. They need to know that when they are at Grandma's and Grandpa's, the boundaries will be the same as they are at home.

As grandparents we need to be there for our grandchildren when they face a crisis in their lives. If our grandchildren's parents get a divorce, we need to be there to support our grandchildren. We can be very upset with one or both of our grandchildren's parents, but we need to be there for our grandchildren.

We need to have an open ear to our grandchildren. When we are out in Tucson, Arizona, for the winter months, Donna and I call our grandchildren. We don't talk about ourselves unless they ask, but we do listen to them. We will ask questions about what they are doing. We want them to know that we are interested in them. It is easy to bore your grandchildren with our "good ole day" talk. It doesn't mean that your grandchildren wouldn't benefit from knowing about you when you were growing up. But I have heard so many times from relatives, "When I was a boy I had to do this and that." When you hear the same story over and over again it is boring at best.

As grandparents we need to be good listeners. We need to be available with an open ear if they have a situation in their lives that they want to share with us. Letting them know that it is safe to talk with us is important. They need to know that we will display unconditional love for them.

"A good man leaves an inheritance to his children's children..." (Proverbs 13:22). We need to share our faith with our grandchildren. We need to let them know that living the Christian life is important to us. We need to let them know that we are praying that they too will want to live the Christian life. We want them to know that the most important thing we want for them is to know Jesus

as their personal Savior, and to live their lives to bring glory to Him. There is nothing more important than leaving our grandchildren a spiritual heritage. It is nice if we can leave them a monetary gift, but a spiritual heritage will have eternal dividends. If you do not have grandchildren, it would be great to adopt a grandchild. There are single parents most likely in your church or extended family who could benefit from your getting involved with their children. Some do not have parental support or grandparents there to give them help when needed.

Enjoy your grandchildren, for they have been given to you as a heritage. May God bless you in your ministry as grandparents. Love them when they are with you and send them home being better grandchildren than when they came. Just don't spoil them. May they be a blessing to you. May you do your very best in your role as a grandparent, that you might give the praise and glory to God.

No grandparents have ever been sorry that they had godly input in their grandchildren's lives. We have a responsibility to pray for our grandchildren, be there for them, encourage them, and be the example that God would have us be for them.

Be thankful to God for giving you grandchildren. Ask Him and thank Him for helping you to carry out your responsibility as a grandparent so they will see Jesus in and through your life. May God help and bless you in this awesome responsibility. Might each of your grandchildren live for something bigger than themselves; might they live for the Lord Jesus Christ. Let's pray for a strong finish to that end.

Lesson Ten

Being Content

Philippians 4:11 *"… for I have learned in whatever state I am, to be content."* Lying in a hospital bed after a cancer operation, a massive heart attack, and other complications doesn't make it easy to be content. Again, I have to say it was because people were praying for me that God gave me contentment and peace in the situation that I found myself.

When difficult things come our way, we need to accept them as part of God's plan for our lives. We either trust God that He is doing what is best for us or not trust in God at all. God's way for us is always best. God often brings things our way because He wants to strengthen our faith and trust in Him. He wants us to grow closer to Him as we experience each event throughout our life.

Chapter XVIII

Making Marriage Last a Lifetime

If marriages are going to last a lifetime, there has to be contentment within the marriage. If a couple have prayed and asked God to direct them to the right person to marry, and they have peace that they are going to love this person for a lifetime, there should be contentment in their marriage. There may be a lot of adjustments that have to be made, but there should be that contentment that this is the person who God wants me to spend my lifetime.

Keeping your marriage intact until "death draws you apart" is a good way to finish strong. So what is the recipe that keeps a marriage together until you or your spouse passes away? One couple stated, "Our marriage is a triangle: God, husband and wife." When God is first, it makes the marriage go better. Another couple that we will call Kevin and Bev have been married for fifty-seven years. Bev was seventeen and just out of high school when they got married. Kevin was twenty and going to college. They indicated that they never got upset enough over a disagreement in which they were not able to work things out. They never took a disagreement to someone else; they worked things out, forgot it and did not bring it back up. Kevin said, "We were faithful and loyal to each other." They were both Christians before they got married but were not living for the Lord. When they gave their lives over to the Lord, their marriage was strengthened.

My mother and dad were married over 56 years when my father passed away. In asking my mother what kept their marriage together, she said, "A deep love for each other, a respect for each other and giving 110 percent." My mother looks back and she has no regrets. Mother and Dad never had a fight in front of us kids that I can recall. They were a great example to us, their children. They always showed affection to each other in front of us.

One lady told me that she was married twice. She said that she was an accountant and took care of the bills and finances. Her first husband was deaf, and they talked a great deal through sign language. She thought that they had a close relationship because they communicated much more than the average couple.

In talking to a lady who had celebrated her sixtieth wedding anniversary, she stated that their marriage stayed together because that was what was expected of them when they got married. It was a commitment for a lifetime. She moved away from her parents when she got married and built a home for her family.

I talked with Mack, and he told me that he had been married for sixty-eight years and that his wife had passed away four years prior. Mack told me that their marriage lasted for sixty-eight years because they continually did things for each other. Doing nice things and taking care of each other through health and sickness was all part of it. In asking Mack what was the most difficult thing for him was after his wife passed away, he stated, "loneliness." I could tell it was very difficult for him. Can you imagine living with someone for sixty-eight years – someone who has been part of your life for so long? We talked about the many good memories that he had with her and that because they were both Christians, that they would see each other again.

A friend of mine who had been married for sixty-seven years stated, "For me the longevity of marriage must be based on being completely committed to your wife. Then you must take your marriage vows seriously, 'For better or for worse, for richer or poorer, in sickness or in health.' You must love your wife unconditionally. Provide times when you can be alone to share your dreams, your concerns, and especially your heartfelt love for your marriage partner. Be willing to give and forgive and always have your spouse's best interest at heart. Pray together every day – it always draws you closer together!"

His wife, also a friend of ours, stated that, "There is a need for a true commitment to your husband." A separation or divorce never enters your mind; because of this, my love for my husband grew and grew. I have always respected who he is and appreciated all he has done for me and our children. If love prevails, your marriage will be strong – just as ours is. I believe for certain that God chose my husband for me! Pray, live, laugh, cry and love together – that pretty much covers it all."

The best thing that a couple who is getting married has going for them when they get married is having parents that are a good example for them to follow. When parents are a good example in their marriage before their children, it gives them a guide as to how to strengthen their own marriage.

What does the Bible have to say about making a marriage last? *"For the woman who has a husband is bound by the law to her husband as long as he lives. But if the husband dies, she is released from the law of her husband"* (Romans 7:2). According to God's Word, they are "bound" until one of them passes away. When one of them dies, the bond is then broken. God commanded that they stay together. The American Psychological Association reported that from forty to fifty percent of first-time marriages in the U.S. end up breaking their marriage vow, "Till death do us part." Christian marriages are breaking up as fast as non-Christians ones. If Christian marriages are going to last, there needs to be obedience to the Word of God. A believer should not have a close relationship with an unbeliever. *"Do not be unequally yoked together with unbelievers. For what fellowship has righteousness with lawlessness? And what communion has light with darkness"* (2 Corinthians 6:14). A lot of suffering and heartache would be saved if this principle were followed.

Husbands who follow the principles laid out in Ephesians 5:25-31 will protect the longevity of a marriage.

> *"Husbands, love your wives, just as Christ also loved the church and gave Himself for her, that He might sanctify and cleanse her with the washing of water by the word, that He might present her to Himself a glorious church, not having spot or wrinkle or any such thing, but that she should be holy and without blemish. So husbands ought to love their own wives as their own bodies; he who loves his wife loves himself. For no one ever hated his own flesh, but nourishes and cherishes it, just as the Lord does the church for we are members of His body, of His flesh and of His bones. 'For this reason a man shall leave his father and mother and be joined to his wife, and the two shall become one flesh.'"*

The husband's authority has been established in (verses 22-24); now the emphasis is moved to the supreme responsibility of husbands in regard to their wives, which is to love them with the same selfless, unreserved, and sacrificial love that Christ has for His church. Christ gave His life for His church and leaves a standard of sacrificial love for the husband to follow in loving his wife.

Likewise the wife needs to obey God and be submissive to her husband. *"Wives, submit to your own husbands, as to the Lord" (Ephesians* 5:23). The submission is not for the man to demand, but for the wife to willingly and lovingly offer to her husband. When the husband and wife are submissive to God, it becomes easier for the wife to be submissive to her husband. She can then lovingly submit because her husband submitted to the Lord.

The Spirit-filled wife recognizes that her husband's role in giving leadership is not only God-ordained, but is also a reflection of Christ's own loving authoritative headship to His church. (1)

The picture of the marriage between a man and woman is a picture of the relationship between Christ and the church. This is stated in Revelation 19:7-9.

"Let us be glad and rejoice and give Him glory, for the marriage of the Lamb has come, and His wife has made herself ready. And to her it was granted to be arrayed in fine linen, clean and bright, for the fine linen is the righteous acts of the saints. Then he said to me, 'Write: Blessed are those who are called to the marriage supper of the Lamb!' And he said to me, 'These are the true sayings of God."

When God saw that it was not good for man to live alone, the first marriage took place as described in Genesis 2:20, 23-24:

"And the LORD God caused a deep sleep to fall on Adam, and he slept; and He took one of his ribs, and closed up the flesh in its place. And Adam said: 'This is now bone of my bones and flesh of my flesh; she shall be called Woman, because she was taken out of Man. Therefore a man shall leave his father and mother and be joined to his wife, and they shall become one.' She was made from his 'flesh and bone' and they then became one flesh."

We have here more than a physical union; we have the meeting of the mind and soul to form one unit. This new relationship goes beyond emotional and sensual attraction but into the realm of spiritual "oneness" which can only be found when both partners are surrendered to God and to each other. This relationship is centered on "us and our," and not on "me and my." This is a main ingredient to a lasting marriage. Both partners have to make their marriage top priority, to make the marriage last until death. When a married couple has a vertical relationship with God, it makes it possible for a horizontal relationship between the husband and his wife to be a lasting relationship. The marriage then can be a God-honoring marriage.

When a couple has a commitment to God, they are willing to follow the guidelines laid out in the Bible. The couple who have made a commitment to love Christ will find it easier to love their mate. When you love Christ and seek to follow Him, it becomes natural to love your spouse. When we are committed to God we then can begin to love by His standards, not our own. It is when a couple has become accountable to God for their behavior (their actions); that they will then become aware of their accountability to each other.

When we experience the love of God and His forgiveness, it is easier to forgive our spouse. When the love of God is in each of the couple's lives, they will stay together and accept their mate for who he or she is.

When our hearts are right with God we will realize that often the problem is with ourselves. I will see that, many of the times, I am the one who needs to change to be able to love my mate.

Marriage after Retirement

Marriages go through different stages. The first stage is before children. This is the time that a couple gets to know each other and make the adjustments of living together. The second stage is when children are born into the family. The wife and husband both take on new roles and less time is devoted to each other. The third stage is the "empty nest" stage when all the children have moved out of the home. This is the stage when grandchildren come into their lives. It is a time that the grandparents can have their grandchildren for a weekend, love them, spoil them with extra love and be satisfied when they go home. This is when you realize why God gave children to young adults. You are happy to send them home because they have worn you out.

The next stage is after retirement. If both spouses have been working and they retire, there is a void in their lives. Work occupied a great deal of their time and energy. Some retirees seem to make the adjustment quite well, while others have a hard time. I know of one husband who retired and has become a "couch potato." All he does is sit on the couch, watch television, and do crossword puzzles all day. His wife keeps on working outside the home and also does all the yard work and the chores inside as well. She just accepts this and continues on each day.

When I retired from my full-time job as administrator of a Christian school, I sold real estate for several years until I had my heart attack. Donna worked full-time for about five years after I retired. Since both of us have retired, we have become more involved in Christian work. Donna took on the Christmas Basket program for our community, a big job. She serves on the board of Christian Neighbors, which provides assistance to families in need and teaches classes and mentors individuals who need financial help. She has also headed up the women's ministry in our church, speaks to outside groups, teaches classes in budgeting and teaches a ladies' class, and is co-chairwoman of our church's hospitality committee. I have served on our deacon board and have headed up our calling program. I try to go calling once a week with Pastor Jones as he has mentored me in my desire to win others to the Lord. Donna and I serve as greeters in our church. Likewise, we have headed up our Friendship Festival, an event that draws over a thousand people to our church grounds.

Do we have time for each other? Yes, we do. Each winter, we are out in Tucson, Arizona, for three months. When we are out in Tucson, we enjoy walking together. Donna brought scrapbooking supplies with her, and I brought material to write. We bowl with a group from our church each Tuesday and go out to eat Sunday night after church with a group. I spend a great deal of my time writing this book. I can do this because I am away from my other responsibilities.

We are basically doing things that we enjoy doing but serving the Lord at the same time. When you retire you may need to take up a hobby or two to help occupy your time. Since my heart attack, it takes me a lot longer to do anything physically. But Donna and I enjoy gardening. We do financial counseling together when a couple is involved.

Making an adjustment from full-time work to retirement may not be easy for you, but make sure that your spouse makes the adjustment with you. It is a time when you can do more things together. When you retire you will have more time to serve in your church.

God has commanded us to be witnesses for Him. Retirement is an ideal time for us to build relationships with the unsaved for the purpose of leading them to a saving knowledge of the Lord Jesus. Let's use our time wisely and seek to win others to Christ. Set a goal of talking to the unsaved as often as you can.

The retirement phase of your life should be an enjoyable time. It can also be a challenging time of your life. It is the time of life when you probably will have more doctor appointments and aches and pains. Someone has well said that "you have to be tough to get old."

Retirement is the time when one spouse may have to take care of the other spouse. A friend of ours got married about a year ago. She had been a caregiver to her husband for a long time before he passed away. The man she married had also been a caregiver to his wife for a period of time before his wife passed away. Being content in our circumstances is part of growing old. God never promised us a "rose garden," but He did promise that He will never leave us or forsake us.

When we love our spouse as Christ loves us, we will be able to care for our loved one when the time comes. Growing old together may not always be easy, but it is commanded by God that we do so. If we do our part to keep our marriage strong to the end, God will do His part by helping us through all the ups and downs. Let's finish strong by keeping our marriage strong. Remember it takes work, forgiveness, unity, and the love of God expressed through our actions to keep a marriage strong to the finish line.

Chapter XIX

Living After the Loss of a Loved One

When God puts a couple together in marriage for a life-time it is likely one of those spouses will pass away before the other. I've asked a number of individuals who have lost a loved one, "What were the most difficult things that you faced after the loss of your spouse?" Here are some of their responses: When couples live together for over a half century there is a big void in their life when they are left by themselves for the first time. A lady who had been married for fifty-nine years before her husband passed away stated that the most difficult thing that she faced was "learning to take care of all the responsibility that he had done." She indicated, "It helped me in remembering that God would guide me through the difficult days. I am so thankful to know God has His hand on me and will lead me through the difficult times."

A lady I will call "Jill" stated that, "I was married twice and I did not grieve when I lost each husband. It wasn't that I did not love them. Her first husband was sick for a very long period of time. As I watched life being taken away from him over a period of time, I experienced losing him each day a little bit. When he finally passed away it was a relief that he no longer had to suffer but was in a much better place, Heaven."

Mary (not her real name) was married for forty-six years, and her husband had passed away seven years prior to asking her, "What were the most difficult things that you had to face after your husband passed away?" She stated, "lack of motivation, loneliness, dealing with legal things, getting insurance in my name, and learning to live on one income. Where to find help with repair work without always asking my children was another challenge. Then the big question that I faced was, 'Why, God?' Having lots of friends that were still married, who did not understand some of the decisions that I had to make, made it difficult for me."

A 95 year old friend who lost his wife about a year earlier responded to my question by saying: "My wife had Alzheimer's for several years before she died, and not having someone to communicate with was very difficult. Then when she did pass away, it was a time of loneliness. Having a life partner with whom you shared your dreams, and the joy of family for most of your life was hard to give up."

Several responded that loneliness and quietness in the home made it difficult. Another lady who had been married for thirty-eight years and had lost her husband eight years prior, stated, "Living by myself and not being able to do things which my husband did, such as things that have to be fixed. If he could not fix something, he saw to it that someone else took care of it. I miss him each and every day." Another lady who was married for forty-one years stated that she had financial difficulties after her husband passed away. They both had worked for the State of Michigan. It took six months before she finally started receiving her retirement benefits again. Meanwhile, she almost lost her home and everything they had worked for, for forty-one years. She was very thankful for her church family that helped her through this time.

In asking these same spouses who lost their loved one, "What recommendations do you have for others that will lose a spouse?" One lady responded by saying, "First ask God to be your go-to Person. He is always there ready and willing. Try to get involved with a small Bible study group. Volunteer someplace, if your health permits. Keep God always first!"

Another lady stated, "Make sure you have God in your life, and make sure you are saved so when you die you know where you are going. Without God you have nothing."

After being married sixty-six years another lady's recommendation was, "Keep busy. Get more involved in church. I visit the sick in our church. Keep in close touch with grandkids. Volunteer where needed in your community. Join a Bible study. Read your Bible and pray. I am going on eighty-seven years old and still maintain many rental properties and use the computer. Keep active! If you play an instrument, get a small group and 'jam' together. I learned hammered dulcimer after eighty and have three others who play with me. We go to nursing homes, etc."

One lady recommended, "Do not lose your faith. Lean on others in your church for support and prayer. I would not have made it (well, maybe I would have) but for their support. It was my fellow church members and my Bible study group praying for me which helped a lot."

The hardest thing for my mother after Dad died was "just him not being here. I did not like going places alone. Just hearing his footsteps coming into the house was missed." Mother had a dog in her home after Dad died who kept Mother company and also provided her security. The dog also helped her with loneliness. Mother looked forward to each of her five children calling her at least once a week. Those phone calls were always at least a half-hour long. One of my sisters called mother every day. Mother always said that she appreciated our calls, and she always ended her call with, "Thanks for calling, and I love you all."

Loneliness seems to be a big challenge for many who have lost a loved one. The local church needs to step up and help those who have lost their spouses. Every widow and widower needs someone of the same sex to come alongside them from their church. They need someone who will just be there for them; someone that they can just lean on in time of need. Ideally this person would be someone who has previously lost a spouse. They may need help in learning how to do things that their spouse had previously done. They may need help in getting involved in new activities to fill a void in their lives.

A few months after my mother had passed away I traveled back to her home alone to attend the funeral of a high school classmate. His home was just down the street from my mother and I often stopped at his home to visit him. I sat in my mother's chair and got a little sense of the loneliness that she must have had when she was living alone after my dad died. There was no TV, no radio, just me. Wow! I don't think most of us who do not live by ourselves understand loneliness.

We in the church need to reach out to help meet the needs of our widows and widowers. Let's come alongside them, befriend them, visit them and help them in the areas in which they struggle. We can ask them to go with us to events, invite them out to eat with us or invite them to our homes for a home cooked dinner. Let's be there for others who have special needs. Let us finish strong by helping others finish strong alongside us.

Part IV

Finishing the Last Lap Strong

Lesson 11

Humility

*"...God resists the proud, but gives grace
to the humble."* (1 Peter 5:5)

Being in ICU and in the hospital for twenty-one days can present you with many humbling situations. Maybe it is a macho thing, but having someone put a bedpan under you and then helping you is a little humiliating to say the least. Then there was the experience of just having to rely on others for all your needs like being given a bath, being fed food and drink (when they would let me have something) and depending upon someone else for all my other needs was humbling. There were a number of times Donna and I would have to call a nurse to help us straighten out all the lines and cords, so I could get back in bed after sitting in my chair.

It was also humbling to know that Donna or one of our two sons, Mark or Matt, was with me continuously during my stay in the hospital helping to watch over my care and assist me with any of my needs. Our daughter Kendra was there often to support them, but she had a new baby and was nursing her.

Also, it was very humbling to know that people were praying for me. God's grace was sufficient!

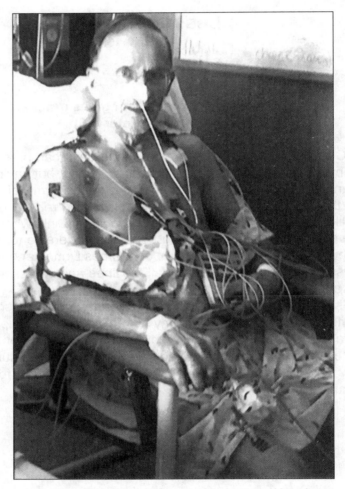

I was hooked to cords from top to bottom. Keeping
them untangled was a monumental task.

Chapter XX

Obeying to the End

What does God want the most from us in our daily walks with Him? Obedience is a very high priority. Does God take things away from us because of our lack of total obedience to His Word? Do we lose blessings from God because we do things for God, but we really do them to bring glory to ourselves and not to God? Let's take a look at Saul and David, the first two kings of Israel. Why did God reject Saul as king, while David became "a man after God's own heart"?

Samuel, the prophet, told Saul what God wanted him to do in 1Sameul 15:1-3.

> "Samuel also said to Saul, 'The Lord sent me to anoint you king over His people, over Israel. Now therefore, heed the voice of the words of the LORD. Thus says the LORD of hosts: 'I will punish Amalek for what he did to Israel, how he ambushed him on the way when he came up from Egypt. Now go and attack Amalek, and utterly destroy all that they have, and do not spare them. But kill both man and woman, infant and nursing child, ox and sheep, camel and donkey.'"

Saul was obedient in the fact that he went down and killed all the Amalekites. That is, he killed all of them except their king, Agag. It seems he should have been the first one to have been killed. Not only did he spare the life of Agag, he also kept the best of the sheep, the oxen, the fatlings and the lambs. God tells Samuel, "*I greatly regret that I have set up Saul as king, for he has turned back from following Me, and has not performed my commandments*" (1 Samuel 15:11). When Samuel confronts Saul (verses 13 & 14),

> *"Saul said to him, 'Blessed are you of the LORD! I have per-formed the commandment of the Jehovah.' But Samuel said, 'What then is this bleating of sheep in my ears, and lowing of the oxen which I hear?'"*

Then in verse 15 Saul puts the blame on the people by telling Samuel that they brought the best back to sacrifice to the LORD your God. In verse 16 Samuel has to tell Saul to, *"Be quiet!"*

How often do we try to justify our own actions when we know that we have not completely obeyed the Word of God? Does God sometimes have to stop us in our tracks and say to us, "Be quiet!" and listen to My Word?

In verse 17 Samuel reminds Saul that he was not even heard of when God made him king over Israel, and that he had been a humble person. In verse 19 Samuel questions Saul as to why he did not obey the command of the LORD. Then in verse 20, Saul again says that he obeyed the command of the LORD. Note verse 21 where he blames the people for taking the plunder. Saul, instead of repenting, continues to try to justify himself. In verse 22 Samuel lets Saul know that God desires heart obedience over the ritual sacrifice of animals. Then in verse 23 (KJV) we read the following summary of Saul's attitude: *"For rebellion is as the sin of witchcraft, and stubbornness is as iniquity and idol-atry. Because you have rejected the word of the LORD, He also has rejected you from being king."* Saul pays a real price for his partial obedience to God's command and lack of full repentance.

The second king of Israel, David, also sinned against God. What made him different from Saul? David had a couple opportunities to take Saul's life when Saul was pursuing him, but David spares Saul's life because he knows that God anointed Saul king and God would take the throne away from Saul at the appropriate time.

We pick up on David's major sins in 2 Samuel 11:1-5:

> *"It happened in the spring of the year, at the time when kings go out to battle, that David sent Joab and his servants with him, and all Israel; and they destroyed the people of the Ammon and besieged Rabbah. But David remained at Jerusalem. Then it happened one evening that David arose from his bed and walked on the roof of the king's house. And from the roof he saw a woman bathing, and the woman was very beautiful to behold. So David sent and inquired about the woman. And someone said, 'Is this not Bathsheba the daughter of Eliam, the wife of Uriah the Hittite?' Then David sent messengers, and took her; and she came to him, and he lay with her, for she was cleansed from her impurity; and she returned to her house. And*

*the woman conceived; so she sent and told David, and said. 'I
am with child.'"*

In verses 6-7 David calls Bathsheba's husband, Uriah, to come home from battle and sleep with his wife so that it would appear that Uriah had fathered the child. Then in verses 8-9, David tells Uriah to go home and be with his wife for the evening, but Uriah being a loyal example to his soldiers does not take advantage of the king's less-than-honorable offer and slept at the door of the king's house. David tries a second time (verse 13) by getting him drunk, but he still did not go home. The next morning David sent a letter with Uriah (verses 14-17) to Joab which tells Joab to have Uriah placed in the front line, where he will battle to his death.

Nathan, the prophet, confronts David as he confronted Saul. We find this in 2 Samuel 12:1-4,

> *"And the LORD sent Nathan to David. And he came to him, and
> said to him: 'There were two men in one city, one rich and the
> other poor. The rich man had exceedingly many flocks and
> herds. But the poor man had nothing, except one little ewe lamb
> which he had bought and nourished; and it grew up together
> with him and with his children. It ate of his own food and drank
> from his own cup and lay in his bosom; and it was like a daughter
> to him. And a traveler came to the rich man, who refused to take
> from his own flock and from his own herd to prepare a meal for
> the wayfaring man who had come to him; but he took the poor
> man's lamb and prepared it for the man who had come to him.'"*

In verses 5-6 David expresses anger and tells Nathan that this man should die for this act. *"Then Nathan said to David, 'you are the man! Thus says the LORD God of Israel...'"* (2 Samuel 12:7)

Then in verses 9-12, Nathan tells David that his life will be spared, but there will be major consequences because of his sin. He is told that the sword will never depart from his house and that there will be adversity from his house; (i.e., the rape of his daughter Tamar, as well as Absalom's murder of Amnon, and Absalom's rebellion against David) all proved Nathan's statement to be true.

In verse 13 we find David's response, *"So David said to Nathan, 'I have sinned against the LORD.' And Nathan said to David, 'The LORD also has put away your sin; you shall not die.'"* Then in verse 14 Nathan tells David that Bathsheba's baby son will die.

David paid a huge price for his sins, but David repented of his sins. Read some of David's Psalms and you will realize the pain that David had to endure.

181

Saul partially obeyed God and did not confess his sin. God had raised him up from a "nobody" to become king, but he took pride in himself.

If we are going to finish strong God's way we need to be obedient to His Word. We need to do completely what He wants us to do. We sometimes want to take credit for what we do ourselves and not give God the credit that He deserves. Our goal needs to be to bring glory to Him, not ourselves.

Obeying His Word

I believe that God takes blessings away from us and sometimes gives us heartaches in our lives because we do not obey Him completely. When we are faithful to God in the little things, He will bless us with bigger things.

"Jesus answered and said to him, 'If anyone loves Me, he will keep My word; and My Father will love him, and We will come to him and make Our home with him'" (John 14:23). By nature we are self-centered. But if we love God, we will obey Him as a servant obeys his master. A servant is not self-centered. He seeks to please his master. It is rebellion when a servant does not obey his master, and it is rebellion when the Christian does not obey God's Word. If we are going to be obedient to God's will in our lives, it starts when we obey His Word. When God wants us to start out flipping hamburgers and we want to go right to upper management, we are being very self-centered. God will often give us little responsibilities to test our faithfulness before He gives us a bigger assignment.

Obedience is when you outwardly express your love for God. God will make Himself known to you as a reward for being obedient. You will obey Him if you love Him. When you do not obey Him, you have a love problem. (1) Jesus tells us, *"I will be a Father to you, and you shall be My sons and daughters, says the Lord Almighty"* (2 Corinthians 6:18).

Obedience Can Be Costly

Being obedient to God can be costly to some Christians. If you live in an Islamic country, when you accept Christ your family will likely disown you. That is very costly. When Donna and I left my good-paying job in Michigan and went to teach missionary children in Fortaleza, Brazil, we had to leave our families and completely depend on others for our support. I will never forget taking Donna's grandparents' to their home after a going-away get-together with her family. Her grandpa's last words to me were, "Why do you have to go?" Within a year's time he passed away. We can rejoice that her grandfather accepted the Lord a few years before his death. We look forward to the day that we will see him again.

As we look back at the two years that we spent in Brazil, we can rejoice also that we were obedient to His leading in our lives. Those were the two most memorable years of our lives. The calling to Brazil was also a calling for us to work in Christian education. When I left college, I remember thinking about Christian school ministry. I knew of only one Christian school which was in Miami, Florida, where an upperclassman had found a job. When Donna and I came back from Brazil there was a big movement in starting Christian schools across the United States. God gave us a burden for Christian education, not just to be involved in it as a career, but also to have our children enrolled in the Christian school.

In knowing the will of God, you will have to make necessary adjustments. Counting the cost is a major adjustment that you will have to make. Many of Christ's disciples turned back when they counted the cost (note John 6:66).

When Saul had his encounter with Christ on the Damascus Road, he had to count the cost of making an about-face in his life. His decision to obey Christ was very costly. Paul changed from a persecutor to being persecuted himself.

Jesus counted the cost when He was obedient to His Father by being willing to be crucified on the cross for us. Jesus' disciples paid the cost of serving Him. Likewise, we need to realize that the time may come when we will have to pay a high price to serve the Lord here in the United States. (2) Obedience may be costly in this lifetime, but it pays eternal rewards.

Major Adjustments May Be Necessary

If you are going to be obedient to God's leading in your life; you may have to make major adjustments. Saul did what God wanted Him to do, but not completely. Your obedience or your lack of obedience will reveal what you really believe about God. It likewise will determine whether you will experience His mighty work in and through you. Then it will determine whether you will know or not know Him more intimately. You have to trust God to obey Him. Likewise, you trust Him because you love Him. As you grow in your faith and you are obeying Him in each step you take, you will be developing a personal relationship with Jesus Christ.

It is the Holy Spirit who indwells you who is your teacher, guide, and helper in being obedient. However, you are the one who needs to respond in obedience. Note what 1 John 1:3-5 says to the reader:

> *"That which we have seen and heard we declare to you, that you also may have fellowship with us; and truly our fellowship is with the Father and with His Son Jesus Christ. And these things we write to you that your joy may be full. This is the message which we have heard from Him and declare to you, that God is light and in Him is no darkness at all."* (3)

When we are faithful in obeying God in small things, He then can trust us with bigger things in our lives. When a church takes on new missionaries by faith, they often are blessed in two ways: One, they can see God supply their needs and two, when a missionary reports back that they have started a new church and they are seeing souls saved, there is a blessing of knowing that you had a part in those who have come to Christ.

When you step out of your comfort zone because the Holy Spirit is speaking to you to witness to a friend and that person gets saved, you receive a special blessing. There is great joy that overcomes the heart when a soul is saved from going to Hell.

The price to be obedient to God may seem high, but usually the cost of not obeying God is much higher. Look back at Saul's life if you do not think so. Those major adjustments of obedience have to come before you can experience God's presence and His power. Finishing strong requires making major adjustments, adjustments in obedience.

Chapter XXI

Leaving a Legacy

A legacy is something handed down from the past, as from an ancestor. It is a gift that is left to someone. Legacy is the character of the person, the example that they leave others to follow.

So what is your legacy? Have you ever taken the time to think of the kind of legacy you are leaving the next generation to follow? If you are going to finish the race strong, you should be leaving a spiritual legacy to your children, grandchildren, those who know you, and those who will know of you.

"Therefore we also, since we are surrounded by so great a cloud of witnesses, let us lay aside every weight, and the sin which so easily ensnares us, and let us run with endurance the race that is set before us" (Hebrews 12:1). (1) In chapter eleven of Hebrews we have the saints who left a legacy of faith. These faithful servants gave witness to the value and blessing of living by faith. Their example of faith should inspire us to run the race. The great cloud here is not composed of spectators, but it is rather comprised of those whose past lives of faith are an encouragement to others to live as they did, by faith. The reference to the Hebrews here is to those who had made a profession of faith in Christ but had some growing to do to go all the way to full faith. The race starts with salvation, and they had just begun the race. (2)

Taking off every weight refers to sin, which was their unbelief. The illustration that is used here is of the Greek foot races in the games that took place throughout the Roman Empire, which included Palestine. The writer here is saying to us to run with patience the race which God has set before us. Run the Christian race with steadfast perseverance.

The apostle Paul is an example of one who finished strong. *"I have fought the good fight, I have finished the race, I have kept the faith"* (2 Timothy 4:7). Paul's legacy is expressed here as he pondered his life as it was coming to an end. He had "fought the good fight." He was standing firm as a spiritual warrior, he was clothed in the armor of God, and he was defending the truth of the gospel faithfully. Paul was not disheartened in his marathon of ministry and life, because he had "finished the race." He had "kept the faith." He had remained true to the end, loyal and committed to his Savior, who had rescued him from sin.

Paul does not talk about his education, his travels, the letters he wrote, the people he had witnessed to, or the churches he had started. He wanted his legacy to be labeled as "faithful." Let us be like Paul. *"...forgetting those things which are behind and reaching forward to those things which are ahead, I press toward the goal for the prize of the upward call of God in Christ Jesus"* (Philippians 3:13-14). Paul's goal was to become more Christlike.

The nation of Israel had just completed a spiritual high when they crossed the Red Sea to escape from Egypt. They spent years wandering in the wilderness, and they were now closing in on the land that God had promised them. Moses had chosen twelve men, probably the most capable men within Israel. He sent them on an important mission to go into enemy territory, check out the land and those who dwelt there, and determine if they could conquer the land. When they returned Moses was informed. Ten of the twelve stated the "Promised Land Operation" was impossible. They were right in the fact that it was impossible without the intervention of God. They apparently forgot the "Red Sea Operation." Do you remember the names of those ten? Do you know of anyone who has named their children after them (Shammua, Shaphat, Igal)? We do remember the two who came back and reported that, with God, "The Promised Land Operation" was possible. They both left us a legacy to follow. Caleb and Joshua both trusted God completely. They knew God intimately and believed that He would be faithful to keep His promise. They had the courage and the faith to know that God would go before them and be with them. This is why Caleb could say, "Give me this mountain." These two men we remember; we name our children after them. When we follow God wholeheartedly and trust Him to do for us what we cannot do for ourselves, we will leave a legacy that can be followed. (3)

We often hear our presidents speak of leaving a "legacy" when their term is completed. They are now saying that President Ronald Reagan will go down in history as one of our greatest presidents. President Abraham Lincoln, our sixteenth president, has been described as one of our best presidents. However, he had many failures, though not in character. He was a failure in a business, and he ran for office a number of times and lost; yet he left a legacy of being one of the greatest of our presidents because he was a man of character.

When we speak of a spiritual legacy, we are speaking of a legacy whose impact outlasts our life span. If we want to leave a spiritual legacy, there are biblical principles that we need to follow. It is a spiritual legacy that has eternal values. This is much more important than any temporal inheritance of property or money. *"A good man leaves an inheritance to his children's children"* (Proverbs 13:22). Our children should be our top priority for our legacy. Our children are the ones who see us as we are. We can put on a good face Sunday morning, but our children see us every day. They know if we have devotions; they know if we put God first in our lives. When we instill the truths of God's Word within our children through our lifestyle, our living the truths of God's Word in front of them, and our teaching them God's Word; it is then, we will be leaving them a beneficial legacy. When we see our children living for God it shows we are passing on a legacy to them. *"For bodily exercise profits a little, but godliness is profitable for all things, having promise of the life that now is and of that which is to come"* (I Timothy 4:8). Godly living has eternal values; it has an impact on the life to come. Likewise, ungodliness will have an impact beyond this life.

There is a way to reach beyond our families and leave a legacy to others. We can do this by having the light of our Christian faith shine forth in the good deeds that we perform.

> *"Nor do they light a lamp and put it under a basket, but on a lampstand, and it gives light to all who are in the house. Let your light so shine before men, that they may see your good works and glorify your Father in heaven"* (Matthew 5:15-16).

The unsaved are watching us as Christians. Our lifestyle needs to show forth God's love. When we show acts of kindness such as bringing cookies across the street to our unsaved neighbors, we are leaving a legacy of kindness. When we verbally witness to someone we are showing an act of kindness, because we want them to be able to spend eternity in Heaven with us. We can leave a legacy of good deeds, acts of kindness and loving service wherever we go.

"And he who wins souls is wise" (Proverbs 11:30). *"And those who turn many to righteousness like the stars forever and ever"* (Daniel 12:3). When you have influence in leading someone to a saving faith in Jesus Christ, there is an immediate and eternal legacy for that person. When you accepted Christ as your personal Savior, you inherited eternal life. We need to offer that legacy to others. (4)

While wintering in Tucson, Arizona, I had the opportunity to witness to a man named Frank while I was at McDonald's. Donna and I had gone there to get on the Internet. We were sitting at a counter and two men came in and sat across from us. I began a conversation with one of the guys and finally asked him if he went to church. He did not. I was able to share the gospel with him and made arrangements to meet with him. I visited Frank's home and found out that he had a Catholic background. He was not ready to make a decision, so I left the book *Done*. (5) This book points out that salvation is not by works, but by faith in Jesus Christ. He has already paid for our sins on the cross. I told him when he finished the book I would meet with him again and bring him a Bible since he did not have one. We need to do everything we can to witness to those that come into contact with us.

The book of Judges paints a picture that could be prophetic of the state of the church today. *"When all that generation had been gathered to their fathers, another generation arose after them who did not know the LORD nor the work which He had done for Israel"* (Judges 2:10). The character of the children of tomorrow will depend on what is put into their hearts today. If we want the younger generation to grow spiritually, then we who are older have to pass on that which we possess.

Those who have already run the Christian race ahead of us have shaped and molded our lives for good or bad. The baton has been handed on to us, and it is now our responsibility to safeguard it, to not drop it, and pass it on to the next generation. My dad spent his first forty-two years living a worldly life. Then he accepted Jesus as his personal Savior, and his life was changed. He left his tobacco on his dresser and never used it again. He became a student of God's Word. He became a faithful servant in his church. His legacy to me was his completely changed life when he became a Christian. I will never forget his love for God. He died at eighty-two, and he finished the race strong.

When my dad passed away, my younger brother (who was four years of age when my dad was saved) said to me, "Dad left us a real legacy." My answer to him was, "You grew up in a Christian home, but those of us who were older did not have the same Christian influence. When we live our lives in obedience to Christ, some may see it as extreme, but it should be normal for the Christian. We as Christians need to understand that we are under observation. Others are watching us. The way we live our lives now, whether we like it or not, will be remembered by others. So what kind of legacy are you leaving for others? When we speak of leaving a legacy we are here referring to the character of the person, the example he or she will leave for others to follow. Mother Teresa left a legacy for others to follow. She left a legacy which was simply, "Give your life to those in need." She had no financial wealth, yet her legacy was much greater than giving wealth. When Mother Teresa's name is brought up, she is recognized as a humble, yet strong, little woman who had compassion for the destitute. *"The memory of the righteous is blessed, but the name of the wicked will rot"* (Proverbs 10:7). Let's make sure that memories of us will not rot. (6)

Two young men started out as great evangelists, Charles Templeton and Billy Graham, and both held crusades with Youth for Christ. Charles was drawing larger crowds than Billy. They became good friends. Together they had envisioned plans to win the world for Christ. Charles lost his faith, left the ministry, and became an atheist. Billy's faith was challenged at the time Charles left the ministry, but he kept his faith. Both left a legacy, one for righteousness and the other for unrighteousness.

On February 1, 2009, George Beverly Shea celebrated his 100th birthday with an intimate gathering of friends, family, and loved ones. He continued to speak and sing of the good news of salvation through his Lord Jesus Christ. He spoke enthusiastically about his plans for the future as he greeted those who were present and shared one of his favorite hymns. He was a sweet man who finished strong. He passed away at the age of 104.

The outstanding German composer, Johann Sebastian Bach, wrote courageously of the Christian faith in his classic hymns "How Joyful Is My Heart," "God Alone Should Have My Heart," "Joy of Man's Desiring" and many more. He lived a long time ago, but his music and his legacy still live on. They are still inspiring the adoration and worship of Jesus Christ.

John Wesley finished strong. An English evangelist and the founder of Methodism endured many things such as bad press for preaching the gospel. He was known for saying that when he got a little money, he got rid of it quickly, so it would not find a place in his heart.

In the late 1800s Booker T. Washington founded the Tuskegee Institute in Alabama with a faculty of 200 and a student body of 1,500. He changed the prejudice and perspective of thousands of Americans when they read his book *Up From Slavery.* He finished strong by leaving an outstanding legacy.

Jesus leaves us the greatest legacy of all. Our calendar is based on the date of Jesus' birth. The period before His birth is referred to as "B.C." and after His birth as "A.D." A.D. is the abbreviation for the Latin term Anno Domini, meaning "in the year of our Lord." Look at a coin and see the date imprinted on it with the number of years after His birth. Jesus is the one about whom unlimited songs have been composed. He made an everlasting impression during the thirty-three years that He lived on this earth. During the time of His ministry here on earth, everybody knew about Him. When He left this earth, everyone knew where He went. Now many are waiting for His return. He left a legacy because of His holiness while here on earth. He left a legacy of love as the one who gave His life for us. He is the one who laid down His life, so that by believing in Him we can have eternal life. (7)

How will you be remembered? As a lukewarm Christian or as a person who lived a righteous life? As one who is not ashamed to witness of your love for Christ or as one who is ashamed to witness? Are you a Sunday morning hypocrite? A hypocrite is one who comes to church on Sunday morning and lives for himself and the world throughout the week. We have a choice. Every day we make choices, choices that will help us finish strong or weak. Let's make the right decisions so that we can finish strong. What type of an example are you leaving for those who will follow you? If your life were a picture, what would you portray to those who come behind you? What type of legacy will you leave for others to follow? Only what is done for God now will have eternal value.

Chapter XXII

Writing Your Last Chapter

Your oncology doctor tells you that you have sixty days left. You know you have cancer, but the short time span comes as a shock. Your doctor says, "You need to get your life in order." So what does it mean to get your life in order? For a Christian, it certainly means we need to make sure we have taken care of any unfinished business. If we have someone that we have a difference with, we need to make sure that we have those fences mended. However, this should be done before we get to this point in our lives, for our lives can end unexpectedly.

Saying Goodbye

Saying goodbye to loved ones is important. Make sure, if at all possible, you do this before you are placed on heavy medication so you are not incoherent and can still communicate. We all have to realize that we may not have time to mend fences and say our goodbyes. None of us knows the time that God is going to take us out of this world. Therefore, we need to be ready at all times. However, if we have the time, we need to take the opportunity to do so.

My mother and dad had time to say goodbye to each other. My dad was dying of cancer and he knew that this disease was going to take his life. There was a lot of love that was shown between the two of them during their 50 plus years of marriage. They were much more in love with each other when Dad died then they were when they got married. They were a testimony to us five children and those who knew them. They had time to reminisce with each other about their long history together. They spent time letting each other know that they loved each other. Some of the last words that my dad said to me were, "It is going to be hard to leave Jo," his nickname for my mother.

Planning for Your Departure

My father passed away at the age of eighty-two, and my mother passed away at ninety-seven. Several years before Mother passed away, she sent a letter to all of her five children letting us know what songs she wanted at her funeral, what special number she wanted and who she wanted to sing, who she wanted to preside over her funeral, and asking us to let her know if we had any suggestions. We made some suggestions, such as having her son and grandson, who are both pastors; preside over her funeral in place of former pastors. She decided to make the changes. My older brother told her that it was a good start, but there were other things she should do also.

If you really want to be a help to your family, you will want to consider the following:

1. Do you want your funeral at a church or at a funeral home? If you have a home church, you probably will want your funeral at your church.
2. Do you want to be cremated or be buried the traditional way? It is more economical to be cremated if finances are an issue. I don't think there is anything unscriptural about cremation.
3. You can pick out your own casket. When you do this, those who would have to do it for you do not have to make that difficult decision. Donna and I have picked out our caskets. Donna's is green, her favorite color. Mine is blue.
4. You can prepay for your funeral. Make sure you're guaranteed the service you specify at the contracted price. If you move, make sure that the contract can go to a different funeral home.
5. If you are going to be buried, picking out your cemetery lot and having it paid for doesn't leave any questions as to where you want to be buried.
6. You could also pick out your own stone, have it inscribed with what you want and placed on your cemetery lot.
7. Write your obituary. You know a whole lot better what you would like in your obituary than anyone else would. If you are not up to writing it, dictate it to someone else.
8. If you have a will or a trust it spells out who your estate goes to, but it usually does not spell out who gets personal possessions. If you have various possessions you want to go to a particular heir, you need to have these listed with your will or in your trust with your signature and, if possible, a witness signature. Ideally, they should be listed in your will or trust. You want to try to be fair to all of your heirs. I have read where a couple invited all their children to spend a day with them. The day was to be set aside for the children to determine who would get what possessions, when the parents passed away. They were all given an equal amount of play money. Then they began to bid on each possession that would be theirs when their parents passed away. As it was reported,

it was a fine day. Each got the things that were most valued by them. It sure makes it a lot easier when possessions need to be divided up.

Thanking God for Your Life

When we think of the last chapter of our lives here on earth, we need to thank the Lord for being with us and providing for us. We need to praise Him for being with us, for the good things that He has given us, and for the good memories that we have. We need to praise Him for whom He is. We need to thank Him for our salvation. We need to thank Him for what He has saved us from. We need to look forward to the days when we will spend eternity with our Savior.

When I was lying on my hospital bed after my surgery and heart attack, Donna and I had a heart-to-heart talk in which we told each other how much we loved each other. If God would have taken me home, we had assured each other that we had a deep love for each other. I would not have wanted to have left this earth any other way.

Pray

We need to pray that God will guide us in our last days. He wants to hear from us. In a short time, we will be spending eternity with Him, and He wants that transition to be delightful. When my father knew that he was dying from cancer, he asked God for two things: First that he would not have pain, and second, that God would give him a sound mind until the day he died. God granted him both of these requests. There is no guarantee that He will answer every request for which you ask, but I do know that the Bible says: *"you have not, because you do not ask"* (James 4:3).

Pray for peace, contentment, hope, joy and fulfillment. Pray that God will give you a sweet testimony for Him regardless of your circumstances in your last days. *"Be anxious for nothing, but in everything by prayer and supplication, with thanksgiving, let your requests be made known to God"* (Philippians 4:6).

Promises of Comfort

When those last weeks and days come, cling to the promises of God. The day I thought I was going to die after my heart attack, God brought this verse to my mind: *"Yea, though I walk through the valley of the shadow of death, I will fear no evil; for You are with me: Your rod and Your staff, they comfort me"* (Psalm 23:4). That verse brought real comfort to me. Read all of Psalm 23; it will give you comfort.

Think about what you have to look forward to in Heaven. Think upon your final victory.

"Now this I say, brethren, that flesh and blood cannot inherit the kingdom of God; nor does corruption inherit incorruption. Behold, I tell you a mystery: We shall not all sleep, but we shall all be changed – in a moment, in the twinkling of an eye, at the last trumpet. For the trumpet will sound, and the dead will be changed. For this corruptible must put on immortality. So when this corruptible has put on incorruption, and this mortal has put on immortality, then shall be brought to pass the saying that is written:

"Death is swallowed up in victory,
O Death where is your sting?
O Hades, where is your victory?

The sting of death is sin, and the strength of sin is the law. But thanks be to God, who gives us the victory through our Lord Jesus Christ" (1 Corinthians 15:51-57).

We do have victory in Jesus, and we can cling on to this victory.

"For our citizenship is in heaven, from which we also eagerly wait for the Savior, the Lord Jesus Christ, who will transform our lowly body that it may be conformed to His glorious body, according to the working by which He is able even to subdue all things to Himself" (Philippians 3:20-21).

Our citizenship is in heaven. This is where God dwells and where Christ is present. *"Giving thanks to the Father who has qualified us to be partakers of the inheritance of the saints in the light"* (Colossians 1:12).

Take a hymnal and read or sing some of the songs that give us promise for our future. God's Word and the old hymnbooks will give you much comfort. My friend who knew he was going to die sang a song in church a short time before his death which stated the following: "Some call it Heaven, some call it pie in the sky, but I call it home." There wasn't a dry eye in the auditorium after he sang that song with sincerity. When my father was on his deathbed, we five children were called home. We were all around his bed in the living room, when my younger brother began to sing "I'll Fly Away." My father at that time was in a coma, and I am not sure he could hear the words of that song; but it was only minutes after my brother had sung that song that my father was "flying away to Heaven." Donna's mother passed away at home alone, minutes between when a neighbor was there and her daughter stopped in. At the close of her burial, each grandchild held a red balloon and as they released them the family burst into song singing "I'll Fly Away". Music soothes the soul.

Hope

I have two different friends who are dying of cancer. They both are trusting that they will be cured from this deadly disease. One has hope that the chemo and radiation will put his cancer in remission. He is planning on bowling again and is thinking about buying some new golf clubs. He is very upbeat that he is going to be around for some time. The doctor has told the other friend that he only has a few months to live. He rode his motorcycle up until his death. His attitude was, "I know Heaven is going to be great, and if God wants to take me, I know that I am ready." These guys both had the hope of eternal life which God, who cannot lie, promised before time began (Titus 1:2). They both knew that they were going to Heaven. Both of these men could have given into the temptation of despair. Hope gave both of these gentlemen the courage to confront their circumstances. This hope that we have is an anchor of the soul (Hebrews 6:19). We can have hope in God's Word (Psalm 119:147). We can have hope in God (Acts 24:15). As a result of hope we can have inner peace, joy and contentment that God will never leave us or forsake us.

Peace

I have talked with a lot of people who do not know for sure that they are going to Heaven. They just hope they will be going to Heaven but do not have any assurance from God's Word. When we take a close look at Scripture we can have that assurance that we are going to Heaven. If you have accepted Jesus Christ as your Lord and Savior, you know that you are going to Heaven.

> *"That if you confess with your mouth the Lord Jesus and believe in your heart that God has raised Him from the dead, you will be saved. For with the heart one believes unto righteousness, and with the mouth confession is made unto salvation. 'For who- ever calls on the name of the LORD shall be saved'* "(Romans 10:9-10, 13). *"Most assuredly, I say to you, he who hears My word and believes in Him who sent Me has everlasting life, and shall not come into judgment, but has passed from death into life"* (John 5:24).

These passages of Scripture let us know that when we accept Christ as our Lord and Savior, we will have eternal life. He will never leave us or forsake us. What a comfort to know–*"...absent from the body, present with the Lord"* (II Corinthians 5:8). I don't know of any greater joy. God has appointed a time that each of us is to die, and when that happens we can have the peace of mind to know that we will spend eternity with Him.

Make sure, at the end of the last chapter of your life, that you know that you have eternal life. You can pray the following sinner's prayer and accept Christ as your personal Savior: "Dear God, I know I am a sinner, and I deserve to spend eternity in Hell. I am asking that You will forgive me of my sins. I acknowledge (accept) you as my Lord and Savior. I thank you for accepting me as one of Your children. Amen."

I trust your "last chapter" will show that you are part of the family of God. That you have accepted Him as your personal Savior and that you are closing "your chapter" living for Him. Might your last chapter be a chapter of peace, joy and contentment knowing that you are living for Him and looking forward to eternity with Him.

Chapter XXIII

Keeping Your Eyes on Heaven

As Christians get closer to the finish line, they often long to cross the finish line to enter into the Promised Land – Heaven. When a spouse or a close loved one leaves us, and we know that he or she is going to Heaven, there is a longing to be with that person again. The better grasp we have as to what Heaven is like, the more we will desire to be there.

My mother was longing for the day that she would be escorted up to Heaven. She said in her last days that she couldn't do anything but sleep, eat and sit in her chair. I told her a number of times that she would live to be at least a hundred, but that was not her desire. My dad left her over a decade and a half prior to her death, and all her brothers and sisters were gone. Her mother passed away when she was only five years old. She was longing to cross that finish line. My mother was still praying for her family, and God was still using her to intercede for us until the end. What a blessing for us as her family. God had His purpose in keeping my mother here on earth for a long time, but at the same time she wanted to step over that finish line and take her first step into Heaven. She wanted to be reunited with loved ones who had gone before her. Can you imagine what it must have been like for her to meet her mother, whom she hardly knew when she left this world?

Heaven Is a Real Place

"Let not your heart be troubled; you believe in God, believe also in Me. In My Father's house are many mansions; If it were not so, I would have told you. I go to prepare a place for you. And if I go and prepare a place for you, I will come again and receive

*you to Myself; that where I am there you may be also. And
where I go you know, and the way you know"* (John 14:1-3).

John twice calls it a place. In the upper room, just prior to His death, Jesus took His disciples aside by themselves and taught them. He was preparing them for the fact that He would soon be leaving them. In a short time, He was to be crucified. It would be a very dark hour for each of them. It was then that Jesus uttered these words of hope and comfort about Heaven. He told them that He would be preparing a place for them. It would be in the Father's house. Heaven is real; it is a place as literal and concrete as the house you live in here on earth. Mansions literally mean dwelling places. Likewise, Heaven is a permanent place.

> *"Blessed be the God and Father of our Lord Jesus Christ, who
> according to His abundant mercy has begotten us again to a
> living hope through the resurrection of Jesus Christ from the
> dead, to an inheritance incorruptible and undefiled and that
> does not fade away, reserved in heaven for you"* (1 Peter 1:3-4).

Peter is telling those persecuted Christians that they needed to look past their troubles to their eternal inheritance in Heaven. Their heavenly inheritance will be eternal life, righteousness, peace, joy, perfection, Christ's glorious companionship, rewards, and much more that God has planned for them. That should make us all excited about crossing the finish line. (1)

Are you longing for Heaven? We need to realize that this world is not our home, and we are just passing through. *"...For what is your life? It is even a vapor that appears for a little time and then vanishes away"* (James 4:14).

Heaven Is a Beautiful Place

God has placed much beauty on this earth for us to enjoy. The changing of leaves in the fall, the snow-covered mountains peeking through the clouds, waves splashing on the lakes and ocean shores, the stars in the sky on a warm evening, winding rivers through the forests: all of these do not compare to Heaven's beauty. Heaven will have perfection of beauty along with sounds that we here on earth cannot comprehend.

John writes in Revelation 21:18-21 about the New Jerusalem:

> *"The construction of its wall was of jasper; and the city was pure
> gold, like clear glass. The foundations of the wall of the city
> were adorned with all kinds of precious stones: the first foun-
> dation was jasper, the second sapphire, the third chalcedony,
> the fourth emerald, the fifth sardonyx, the sixth sardius, the*

> *seventh chrysolite, the eighth beryl, the ninth topaz, the tenth chrysoprase, the eleventh jacinth, and the twelfth amethyst. The twelve gates were twelve pearls: each individual gate was one pearl. And the street of the city was pure gold, like transparent glass."*

Sardius has a color range from orange-red to brownish-red to blood-red. Chrysolite is a gem of transparent gold or yellowish tone. Beryl, which is a mineral, has several varieties of color, ranging from golden-yellow to green emerald to light blue-aquamarine. Topaz is a softer stone with a yellow or yellow-green color. (2) We cannot comprehend how beautiful Heaven is, and there is nothing on earth which can compare to its beauty.

Those Who Will Be in Heaven

Jesus will be there. God will be there. Those who have died in the Lord before us are there, and those who will die in the Lord after us will be there. John writes in Revelation 21 that the bride of Christ will be in Heaven, which is made up of those who have been saved during the age of grace. Then there will be those saints of the Old Testament. There will be Moses and Elijah, who were taken up into Heaven by a chariot. Abraham, David, and many other well-known Old Testament patriarchs will be in Heaven. We will meet some of the outstanding saints who lived during the dispensation of grace. There will also be angels in Heaven.

> *"I say to you that likewise there will be more joy in Heaven over one sinner who repents…Likewise, I say to you, there is joy in the presence of the angels of God over one sinner who repents"* (Luke 15:7, 10).

When you cross the finish line here on earth and arrive in Heaven you will meet your loved ones. Wow! A grandpa whom I never met who died a year before I was born, my father and mother and a whole lot of relatives and friends will greet me. It will be a great reunion. The best is that we will see Jesus face-to-face and will be able to thank Him personally for what He did for us. Stephen, the first martyr, said, *"… Look! I see the heavens opened and the Son of Man standing at the right hand of God'"* (Acts 7:56)! Paul lets us know that being with Jesus was one of the most attractive thoughts that he had about heaven. *"For to me, to live is Christ, and to die is gain"* (Philippians 1:21). God will be there to meet us, as the father waited for his prodigal son (Luke 15:11-24). We will experience exhilaration of joy when we see Him for the first time. As the father had a celebration for his prodigal son, there will be a robe that will be put on our shoulders, a family ring placed on our finger and sandals on our feet (Luke

15:21-22). (3) What a celebration that will be! Are you longing for Heaven? Are you looking forward to being in your eternal Home?

A New Body

When we accept Jesus Christ as our Savior, we are adopted into the family of God. The true benefits of the Christian's adoption into God's family will not come until we get to Heaven. When we get to Heaven we will have new bodies, ones that do not wear out, ones that have no pain, ones that are not aging, and ones that look better than the ones we have now.

After having cancer twice, along with two operations to remove the cancer, and a massive heart attack, I'm looking forward to a new body, a total body makeover. I recently asked my cardiologist why I do not have a lot of energy. Knowing that a lot of my heart was destroyed, he said to me, "You have a four-cylinder heart, where as I have a six-cylinder heart." After seven decades of use, it is wearing out. It will be at the resurrection of the redeemed that we will get amazing new bodies, but we will still be recognized by others who knew us on earth. He has assured us of our new bodies at the resurrection (1 Corinthians 15:14-20). In Heaven we will have glorious bodies. *"Then the righteous will shine forth as the sun in the kingdom of their Father. He who has ears to hear, let him hear"* (Matthew 13:43)! Scripture gives us insight on what to expect when Jesus appears for us at the resurrection. *"Beloved, now we are children of God; and it has not yet been revealed what we shall be, we know that when He is revealed, we shall be like Him, for we shall see Him as He is"* (1 John 3:2). Our bodies will be like the body the disciples saw after Jesus rose from the dead. Jesus was able to defy gravity and rise up into the clouds (Act 1:9). (4)

Just think, there will be no saying good-bye to loved ones in Heaven, no funeral services, nor cemeteries. Our new bodies will never die; death will forever be left behind. (5)

> *"For this corruptible must put on incorruption, and this mortal must put on immortality. So when this corruptible has put on incorruption, and this mortal has put on immortality, then shall be brought to pass the saying that is written: 'O Death is swallowed up in victory.' 'O Death, where is your sting? O Hades, where is your victory?' The sting of death is sin, and the strength of sin is the law. But thanks be to God, who gives us the victory through our Lord Jesus Christ"* (1 Corinthians 15:53-57).

Heaven Will Be a Holy Place

"And God will wipe away every tear from their eyes; there shall be no more death, nor sorrow, nor crying. There shall be no more pain, for the former things have passed away" (Revelation 21:4). *"Do you not know that the unrighteous will not inherit the kingdom of God? Do not be deceived. Neither fornicators, nor idolaters, nor adulterers, nor homosexuals, nor sodomites, nor thieves, nor covetous, nor drunkards, nor revilers, nor extortioners will inherit the kingdom of God"* (1 Corinthians 6:9-10).

Heaven will be a holy place, a place where there is no fear and no loneliness. There will be neither sickness nor pain. There will be no poverty. God's inexhaustible wealth will be at everyone's disposal. (6)

A Perfect Place

Faith will be swallowed up in sight. Those perplexing problems of man, of time and eternity, will be solved. There will be no doubts, nor questions or uncertainties, nor errors that will trouble us. In Heaven those with little education will fathom the truths of the universe. It is a place where there will be joy continually, happiness, satisfaction, contentment, and peace. (7)

It is okay to get excited about our arrival in Heaven, where we will see Jesus face to face. As the hymn "When We All Get to Heaven", says "What a day of rejoicing that will be." (Written by J.G. Wilson) Are you ready to cross the finish line when He calls your name?

Heaven is a place of love. God is love, and we shall be like our God. *"He who does not love does not know God, for God is love"* (1 John 4:8). What a place Heaven will be, where love is perfect. We will all love each other. It will be a happy home where love will triumph. Love will be pure, unbounded, unchanging, unfaltering, and it will be Christlike. (8)

Heaven is a place of praise as we see in Revelation 7:9-12.

"After these things I looked, and behold, a great multitude which no one could number, of all nations, tribes, people, and tongues, standing before the throne and before the Lamb, clothed with white robes, with palm branches in their hands, and crying out with a loud voice, saying, 'Salvation belongs to our God who sits on the throne, and to the Lamb!' All the angels stood around the throne and the elders and the four living creatures, and fell on their faces before the throne and worshiped God, saying: 'Amen! Blessing and glory and wisdom, thanksgiving and honor and power and might, be to our God forever and ever, Amen.'"

All the earth's people groups together will worship God. Salvation will be the theme of their worship, as they recognize that it comes solely from Him. (9)

Judgments

Each person who has lived on earth will face a judgment after death. Those who are not part of the family of God because they have not accepted Jesus Christ as their personal Savior will meet their judge at the Great White Throne Judgment as explained in Revelation 20:11-13.

> *"Then I saw a great white throne and Him who sat on it, from whose face the earth and the heaven fled away. And there was found no place for them. And I saw the dead, small and great, standing before God, and books were opened. And another book was opened, which is the Book of Life. And the dead were judged according to their works, by the things which were written in the books. The sea gave up the dead who were in it, and Death and Hades delivered up the dead who were in them. And they were judged, each one according to his works."*

This punishment for the unsaved will be unbearable! Hell is a place where judgment will last forever. There will be nothing to look forward to except eternal misery in a lake of fire. When you think about those who are on their way to eternity without Christ, I trust that you will do everything in your power to show them the way to Jesus so that they will not go to hell.

Those who have accepted Jesus Christ as their personal Savior will meet Christ at the judgment seat of Christ. *"For we must all appear before the judgment seat of Christ, that each one may receive the things done in the body, according to what he had done, whether good or bad"* (2 Corinthians 5:10). This could be considered an outstanding awards banquet. It will be a positive event where awards will be given out. '*"And behold, I am coming quickly, and My reward is with Me, to give to every one according to his work."*' (Revelation 22:12).

Jesus is the perfect judge because over two thousand years ago He came to earth from Heaven as a full participant. His was a humble birth in a stable. He grew up like each of us, learned to walk, learned to talk and was a teenager. He had friends and enemies, was tempted, and was hungry and thirsty; and He became tired like we do. Likewise, He died. He can empathize with the things we face, yet He lived a sinless life. Therefore, that makes Him the perfect judge. He knows everything about you, all your secrets. He will not miss any of the good things that you have done either. He will be your only judge. Paul's description of the judgment seat of Christ is an examination by fire in 1 Corinthians 3:11-15.

201

> *"For no other foundation can anyone lay than that which is laid, which is Jesus Christ. Now if anyone builds on this foundation with gold, silver, precious stones, wood, hay, straw, each one's work will become clear, for the Day will declare it, because it will be revealed by fire; and the fire will test each one's work, of what sort it is. If anyone's work which he has built on it endures, he will receive a reward. If anyone's work is burned, he will suffer loss; but he himself will be saved, yet so as through fire."*
> (1 Corinthians 3:11-15).

The sinful things that were done which are described as wood, hay and straw, will be burned up. Those good things that have been done, described as gold, silver and precious stones, will be refined and become more beautiful, and crowns will be given out. The purpose of a crown is not for self, but the opposite. They are soul-winning crowns that can be cast at Jesus' feet. It is a perfect way to let Jesus know we recognize the reason that we received the crown in the first place. It is because of all He has done for us. It will be a great big "thank you!" (10)

Heaven is a place that we need to be longing for, but meanwhile we need to see that the lost become God's children. We do not know what the future holds for us here on earth, but we do know who holds the future. We need to realize that where we live now is our temporary home; our permanent home is in Heaven. Let's use our time that we have here on earth to bring glory to His name, so that when we get to Heaven we can give glory back to Him as we lay our crowns at His feet. Keep your eyes on the finish line...Heaven!

Chapter XXIV

Living and Dying for Crowns of Priceless Worth

H ave you ever stopped to think that what you do in this lifetime will affect your lifetime for eternity? If you are unsaved, you will spend eternity in Hell. For the Christian, the crowns you will receive in Heaven must be earned here on earth. Our goal should be to do our best in this lifetime because we want to bring glory to God, and He has promised to award us accordingly.

Some people save money for retirement and others don't. Those who save do it so their needs will be met during retirement. They are prudent. Therefore, they don't have to be concerned about not having enough money to live on when retirement comes. There are those who are only concerned about today, enjoying themselves and spending their money as if there would be no tomorrow. Because they get almost weekly opportunities to purchase a new credit card, some spend beyond their means without any thought of what it will cost them to pay it back. They paralyze themselves from saving and giving to God. There is a parallel in investing for eternity. We have to realize that only what is done for Christ will have eternal value. What we do with the time that God has given us becomes very important if we are going to invest in eternal things. Our time in prayer, our time in His Word, time that we spend at church, the time and financial support we give to ministry and our love that we show toward others all have eternal values.

God has promised us crown rewards when we get to Heaven if we do certain things. Do we get these crowns so we can let others know what we have achieved? No! We get these crowns so that we can place them at Jesus' feet when we get to Heaven. That will be a great privilege and great joy when we will be able to give them back to Jesus. We will want to give our crowns back to Him in appreciation of all that He has done for us. (Revelation 22:12). God is going to give rewards. Only those works which meet God's testing by fire will have eternal value. Do we give our tithes and offering out of duty or out of love for the blessings that God has given us?

Moses made a choice to be part of the family of God rather than the royal family of Pharaoh.

> *"By faith Moses, when he became of age, refused to be called the son of Pharaoh's daughter, choosing rather to suffer afflic- tion with the people of God than to enjoy the passing pleasures of sin, esteeming the reproach of Christ greater riches than the treasures in Egypt; for he looked to the reward"* (Hebrews 11:24-25).

When you read the rest of the account of Moses' life, you know that he made the right decision and God rewarded him for his decision.

"Now he who plants and he who waters are one, and each one will receive his own reward according to his own labor" (1 Corinthians 3:8). There can be a number of different people who play a part in the salvation of another person but are equally considered and rewarded for their willingness to be used by God. However, all the glory goes to Him; He who is the only one who can save them. You may pray for a lost person. Several people may witness to that person, and another may help that person in the sinner's prayer. Each person will be rewarded for his or her efforts.

When we love our enemies, when we do good things for others and when we lend things to others, God is going to reward us for our actions. *"But love your enemies, do good, and lend, hoping for nothing in return; and your reward will be great"* (Luke 6:35).

In the New Testament there are five different crowns that can be given to Christians as recognition and special honor for a life of Christian service. In the Greek Olympic Games a winning athlete was given a crown. The Greek word for crown is "stephanos." The stephanos was an adornment that was worn around the head of the athlete, representing a crown of victory in those Olympic games. This crown was placed around the head of the runner who crossed the finish line first. The Christian's crowns are symbolic of something of inexpressible value.

The Crown of Rejoicing (Soul-Winner's Crown)

The crown of rejoicing is also referred to as the "soul-winner's crown." *"For what is our hope, or joy, or crown of rejoicing? Is it not even you in the pres- ence of our Lord Jesus Christ at His coming? For you are our glory and joy"* (1 Thessalonians 2:19). Paul also referred to the Philippian believers who he had won to the Lord as his hope, and joy, and crown of rejoicing—his glory. They were the cause of his hope, that they would be saved. They would be his joy because of their conversion by his ministry and his crown of rejoicing in Christ's presence at His coming.(1) Those who sow and those who reap shall rejoice together in the presence of our Lord Jesus Christ at His coming. (2) This crown is going to be given to those who played a part in winning souls to Christ. Some college teams are awarded with a star or some other emblem on their football helmets for good plays they make. Maybe God will have a gold star on the crown of rejoicing for each soul that a Christian has been instrumental in winning to the Lord. This is a crown that the Bible commands us to work for. What a joy to lay that crown before His feet to have Him say to you, *"...Well done, good and faithful servant..."* (Matthew 25:21).

The Incorruptible Crown

> *"Do you not know that those who run in a race all run, but one receives the prize? Run in such a way that you may obtain it. And everyone who competes for the prize is temperate in all things. Now they do it to obtain a perishable crown, but we for an imperishable crown"* (1 Corinthians 9:24-25).

Paul's topic in chapter 9 is mostly about the preaching of the gospel. He is using terminology that is very familiar to the Corinthians to teach spiritual truths.(3) In the Greek games the athlete was kept on a set diet and discipline. Those who won in these races were crowned with withering leaves, boughs of trees, or olive laurels. But the Christian has an incorruptible crown in view. In the Christian race, we all can win. The Christian needs to keep his body under subjection to the Holy Spirit. If he is going to win, he needs to have a diet of spiritual food. Paul is drilling home spiritual truths by using Greek games terminology when he tells the Corinthians that physical training is important for training in their games. Such training as exercising self-control, keeping their minds and bodies in subjection to the will of God, was done for the purpose of winning the most people to the Lord. The incorruptible crown is for those who keep running the Christian race and have not been rejected from the competition. (4) The Christian's race is a spiritual race; it is not strengthening of legs and lungs, but of faith and patience. Other races involve natural abilities; the spiritual race is accomplished through supernatural power and strength. Every step in our race brings us closer to the goal, and it implies perseverance if the Christian racer is going to finish the race strong.

In Matthew 25:14-29, we read the parable of the talents. A man is traveling to a far country, and he gives his servants different talents and instructs them to invest these talents. To one he gave five talents, to another two and to another one talent. Each doubled their talents except for the one who only had one talent. In verse. 23, we read that to the first two men, their lord said,

'*"Well done, good and faithful servant; you have been faithful over a few things, I will make you ruler over many things. Enter into the joy of your lord."'*

In today's church, the man with one talent just sits in the pew on Sunday mornings and never uses his ability for anything. He could have been a music leader but just didn't want to. In other words, he was lazy and did not see the value of using his ability for the Lord. Another man, who sits in the pew, has the potential of a ten-talent servant. But when a missionary needs gifts to build a new church, in an area of a foreign country, where the gospel has not been preached at all, yet he does not give even though he could well afford to give. There cannot be any greater joy than to finish our race here on earth and meet our Maker and have Him say to us, "Well done, my faithful servant." What joy it will be to hear those words. The man with the five talents and the man with only two received the exact same reward, which indicates the reward is based on faithfulness and not results.

The Crown of Righteousness

"Finally, there is laid up for me the crown of righteousness, which the Lord, the righteous Judge, will give to me on that Day, and not to me only but also to all who have loved His appearing" (2 Timothy 4:8). The previous verse states that Paul had fought the good fight, had finished the race, and had kept the faith. This reward is given to those who have finished the race strong with integrity, with their eyes fixed on the finish line and looking forward to meeting their coming Lord. This is a reward that is given to those who have fulfilled the ministry that was entrusted to them. Paul is looking forward to the life after death. He is encouraging Timothy and those that read these words to endure hardship as good soldiers of Jesus Christ, realizing that there is a crown waiting for the faithful. It is called the "crown of righteousness" because our righteousness and holiness will there be perfected and therefore will be our crown. This crown is for all those who love His appearing. It is for those who look forward to His second appearing and long for it. (5) This crown is for those who really believe and anticipate that at any moment Christ may return. Therefore, they are more prone to live a more "righteous" life (1 John 3:3).

Paul is letting the reader know that this crown is for those who fight the good fight, for those who keep the faith, and for those that love His appearing. In the Grecian games only one could obtain the prize. The righteous crown can be won by all who sincerely desire the return of the Savior, and they will welcome His appearing in the clouds of Heaven. (6)

This crown represents eternal righteousness. Believers receive this imputed righteousness of Christ (justification) at salvation. It is the Holy Spirit who works practical righteousness (sanctification) during the believer's lifetime of struggle with sin. It is when the struggle is completed that the Christian will receive Christ's righteousness perfected in the righteous Judge. (7)

Crown of Life

Revelation 2:10 says that, *"Be faithful until death, and I will give you the crown of life."* This crown is sometimes called the "Martyr's Crown" because they "endured" to the end.

"Blessed is the man who endures temptation; for when he has been approved, he will receive the crown of life which the Lord has promised to those who love Him" (James 1:12). James makes it very clear in James chapter one that God's people will be besieged with temptations. *"For this reason, when I could no longer endure it, I sent to know your faith, lest by some means the tempter had tempted you, and our labor might be in vain"* (1 Thessalonians 3:5). There is a blessing that is pronounced on those who endure trials and temptations in their lives. The Christian who endures trials is a happy Christian. The word temptation can be translated "trials." "Approved" here means that the "test has been passed." Like Job, the believer's faith has endured, and the believer has successfully and victoriously gone through his trials, indicating that he is genuine. (8)

The tried Christian shall receive a crown of life. We only have to bear the cross for a short time. When we endure the temptations, we must do so from a principle of love of God and our Lord Jesus Christ. The crown of life is awarded to all those who have the love of God within their hearts and have persevered and resisted temptations.

The Crown of Glory

"...when the Chief Shepherd appears, you will receive the crown of glory that does not fade away." (1 Peter 5:4). Jesus Christ is the Chief Shepherd and when He returns, those under-shepherds will receive a crown that will never wither or fade, a crown of glory.

This crown is for those pastors who faithfully minister to their flock to the end. The receiver of this crown is the one who feeds his flock, not for monetary gain and not to lord over his flock; but he is one who leads by example, one who employs body, soul, spirit, talents and time in endeavoring to save souls from an eternal fire. He is one who does all he can to bring his flock to a loving relationship with Christ. The pastor also builds his church up for the glory of God and not self. He is a man who is heavenly-minded. The minister who finishes strong God's way will receive the crown of glory. (9) *"And behold, I am coming quickly, and My reward is with Me, to give to everyone according to his work"* (Revelation 22:12).

In the Greek Olympic Games there was one winner. All Christians are eligible for the crowns that will be given out to those Christians who have successfully crossed the finish line. If we want to look forward to at least one crown, we need to finish our race strong. Those sitting on the sidelines will not be winning any crowns. 1 Corinthians 3:15 tells us, *"If anyone's work is burned, he will suffer loss; but he himself will be saved; yet so as by fire."* As Christians we need to help each other finish strong so that together we can lay down our crowns at Jesus' feet. What a day of rejoicing that will be!

Chapter XXV

Bringing Glory to God

If we are going to finish strong, it is imperative that we set a primary goal to glorify our God and our Savior Jesus Christ in all that we do. The word "glory" means brightness, splendor and radiance. It means majesty, sublimity and the might and power of our God. It should be our goal, our motive, our theme, our reason and our purpose to glorify our God and our Savior Jesus Christ. He is the creator of our vast universe and the minuteness of the universe. We can only begin to scratch the surface in trying to describe the glory of God. *"You are God, and I will praise You; You are my God, I will exalt You"* (Psalms 118:28).

When a child makes an achievement in life, he or she is often given honor and glorified in that accomplishment. The parents are glorified in the child's achievement. Likewise, God is pleased and glorified when His children live a righteous and faithful life. *"...being filled with the fruits of righteousness which are by Jesus Christ, to the glory and the praise of God"* (Philippians 1:11). It is the righteous life that produces fruit, which in turn glorifies God.

On the other hand, a parent is dishonored and shamed when his or her child behaves badly. Bad deeds of children have left mothers and fathers with heartache and shame and often cause them to cry themselves to sleep. Parents want the best for their children who they have worked so hard for and have sacrificed to bring them up the best they can. When a child shows contempt by living an evil and immoral life, it brings dishonor and shame to the parent. The honor and glory of a parent is in the satisfaction of seeing their children walking with the Lord. The same is true with the Lord; He is honored by our obedient behavior in achieving His will for our lives. (1)

The majority of mankind does not bring honor to or glorify God. They are rebellious and sinful and show no glory for their Creator. At therapy on my broken thumb, I witnessed to a man who was sitting next to me, and he did not know if there even was a God. I left him with a tract and a *Gospel of John* booklet with the plan of salvation. This man, along with all the other unsaved, cannot bring glory to God until they accept Christ as their personal Savior.

God created mankind for the purpose of reflecting His glory. We are to display Him in our walk bringing honor and glory to Him. God deserves our glory because of who He is in all His majesty, greatness and power. *"To see Your power and Your glory."* (Psalms 63:2) *"With God is awesome majesty"* (Job 37:22).

It is wonderful that God loves the rebellious man as shown in 1Thessaloninas 1:9,12.

> *"These shall be punished with everlasting destruction from the presence of the Lord and from the glory of His power, when He comes, in that Day to be glorified in His saints and to be admired among all those who believe, because our testimony among you was believed. Therefore we also pray always for you that our God would count you worthy of this calling, and fulfill all the good pleasure of His goodness and the work of faith with power, that the name of our Lord Jesus may be glorified in you, and you in Him, according to the grace of God and the Lord Jesus Christ."* (2)

Note verse 9: *"...everlasting destruction from the presence of the Lord."* What Paul described here is Hell, which is the place of eternal separation from God. Those who reject Christ will be forever confined to Hell and will be excluded from the presence of the Lord and all His glory. Verse 10 lets us know that those who trust Him as Savior and accept Him as their Lord and God will be glorified. They will be witnesses to the glory of God and His greatness. In verses 11 and 12 we find God's purpose is to make us more Christlike. The Christian's calling is to become more Christlike and filled with *"His goodness."* As our faith grows in God, God increases the power available to us to do what is right. As the Christian grows, God will be glorified in his or her life.

As a child of God, the Scripture clearly teaches that you are to live your life to show forth the glory of God. When a person rejects the grace of God and the mercy of God, they defame Him. Because God is righteous and holy, when mankind refuses God's free gift of forgiveness, they slander Him.

Satan wants man to be fooled into thinking that his works and rituals will give him a free ticket to Heaven. This is far from the truth. God sent His Son to save mankind from their sins. It is what God has done through His Son, not something that man does to earn salvation. The true born-again Christian is going to be faithful in overcoming sin in his life. It is contrary to God's righteousness and holiness when the child of God receives the grace of God and still lives in sin as he or she did before.

> *"And you have forgotten the exhortation which speaks to you as to sons. 'My son do not despise the chastening of the LORD, nor be discouraged when you are rebuked by Him; for whom the LORD loves He chastens, and scourges every son whom He receives.' If you endure chastening, God deals with you as with sons; for what son is there whom a father does not chasten? But if you are without chastening, of which all have become partakers, then you are illegitimate and not sons"* (Hebrew 12:5-8).

Does a father love his child when he allows that child to do something that will harm him or her? The father who correctly trains and even punishes the child to teach the child what is right is the one who loves his child. God's discipline of His children is a sign that He has a deep love for them. It is proof that God loves you when He disciplines you. When He disciplines you, you need to ask Him what He is trying to teach you. 1 John 5:16-17 and 1 Corinthians 11:29-30 teach us that God will punish His children. He may even take the lives of His children who do not repent. It is not one particular sin but whatever sin that is the final one in God's tolerance.

Philippians 2:9-11 tells us that all mankind will bow and confess that Jesus Christ is Lord. This is a real event that is going to happen in due time. It will be done to glorify God. (3) Those who believe and accept God's grace and salvation will do it when this transpires in their lives. It is very sad to say that others will bow their knees before the Lord Jesus Christ at the Great White Throne Judgment. At this judgment they will justly be judged for not accepting Christ as their Savior and then will be cast alive into the eternal lake of fire. See Revelation 20:11-15.

> *"Then I saw a great white throne and Him who sat on it, from whose face the earth and the heaven fled away. And there was found no place for them. And I saw the dead, small and great, standing before God, and books were opened. And another book was opened, which is the Book of Life. And the dead were judged according to their works, by the things which were written in the books. The sea gave up the dead who were in it, and Death and Hades delivered up the dead who were in them. And they were judged each one according to his works. Then Death and Hades were cast into the lake of fire. This is the second death. And anyone not found written in the Book of Life was cast into the lake of fire."*

Can we read this passage of Scripture and not have a burden for those who are going to spend eternity in the Lake of Fire? Should we not have tears in our eyes knowing that we have family members, friends, and neighbors who are on the road to this horrible place for eternity?

- Would you ask God to give you a compassion for the lost?
- Would you pray for those who are unsaved?
- Would you become a verbal witness to them?

We can bring glory to God by having compassion for the lost. We are all commissioned to witness to the lost. (Matthew 28:19-20)

Why are there so many Christians today who have very little commitment to live a Christ-centered life? Many who profess to be Christians today are not living as if it were important to be faithful and obedient to the Word of God. It seems that they can receive God's grace for salvation, but after that everything is optional for them. *"...not forsaking the assembling of ourselves together, as is the manner of some, but exhorting one another, and so much the more as you see the Day approaching"* (Hebrews 10:25). Many do not think that attending church regularly is important when other events come up. Some think that attending church once a week on Sunday morning is all they need. The question that they need to ask is, are they bringing glory to God when they take attending church so lightly? God has a purpose for us attending church regularly where we can feed on His Word and encourage each other through Christian fellowship.

Today we have a small percentage of the church family doing most of the work which needs to be done within the church.

> *"And He Himself gave some to be apostles, some prophets, some evangelists, and some pastors and teachers, for the equipping of the saints for the work of ministry, for edifying of the body of Christ"* (Ephesians 4:11-12).

When we take a look at the human body, we know that all of the parts need to work together. Each part of the body is inter-dependent with the other parts and they all have to be functioning properly. When one or more parts of one's body are not functioning properly, the body malfunctions, and we call it a sickness. If the church is going to successfully bring glory to our Lord, each member needs to be faithfully working together. (4)

As Christians our primary goal is to bring glory to God. We are to glorify God in all things. *"...in all things God be glorified through Jesus Christ, to whom belongs the glory...."* (1 Peter 4:11). The glory of God should be woven through all that we do. *"Therefore, whether you eat or drink, or whatever you do, do all to the glory of God"* (1 Corinthians 10:31). *"For you were bought at a price; therefore glorify God in your body and in your spirit which are God's"* (1 Corinthians 6:20).

Four Different Ways to Glorify God

There are four different ways in which we can glorify God: adoration, appreciation, affection and subjection. Adoration or worship is a way that we can glorify God. *"Give unto the LORD the glory due to His name; worship the LORD in the beauty of holiness"* (Psalms 29:2).

God must be highest in our thoughts and be esteemed as the Most High if we are going to show Him just appreciation. *"For You, LORD, are most high above all the earth"* (Psalms 97:9). We glorify God when we admire His attributes.

Our affection is part of the glory that we give to God. He counts Himself glorified when we show Him our love. *"You shall love the LORD with all your heart"* (Deuteronomy 6:5).

Subjection is yielding to His will and to His service. It is a submission to God's will and law. When we are willing to receive the Lord's chastening, we will have a richer and more abundant life. *"Furthermore, we have had human fathers who corrected us and we paid them respect. Shall we not much more readily be in subjection to the Father of spirits and live"* (Hebrews 12:9)?

We have an obligation to glorify God because He gave us our lives. *"It is He who made us"* (Psalms 100:3). All that we have is from the kindness of God. Our health, the supplying of our needs, our families, and all that we have comes from Him. It is by His grace that we have eternal life. How can we not glorify Him for all that we have? (5) Our hope hinges upon Him; therefore, we should bring glory to God. *"My hope is in You."* (Psalms 39:7).

When we sincerely confess our sins, we bring glory to Him. *"...My son, I beg you, give glory to the LORD God of Israel, and make confession to Him..."* (Joshua 7:19). When we have a humble confession, it exalts God. Adam did not have a full confession when he ate the forbidden fruit... *'"The woman whom You gave to be with me, she gave me of the tree, and I ate'"* (Genesis 3:12). Our complete confession glorifies God; it therefore acknowledges His holiness and His righteousness. *'"Father I have sinned against heaven and before you'"* (Luke 15:18). The prodigal son had a sincere confession to his father.

We glorify God with our faith. *"He did not waver at the promise of God through unbelief, but was strengthened in faith, giving glory to God"* (Romans 4:20). Abraham had a strong faith in God when he left his homeland to go to a promised land.

We likewise can glorify God by our fruitfulness.

> *"By this My Father is glorified, that you bear much fruit"* (John 15:8). *"Let your light so shine before men, that they may see your good works and glorify your Father in heaven"* (Matthew 5:16). *"...being filled with the fruits of righteousness which are by Jesus Christ to the glory and praise of God"* (Philippians 1:11).

213

When we bear fruit we bring glory to God. However, when we do not bear fruit in our lives, we bring dishonor to Him. It is important that we bring forth fruits of good works in love.

God is glorified when we are content in the situation where God places us. We do not know what the future holds for our lives, but we do know who holds the future. The apostle Paul endured many dramatic situations in his life, but he still gave glory to God. *"Three times I was beaten with rods; once I was stoned; three times I was shipwrecked…"* (2 Corinthians 11:25). Paul still could say that he was content in bearing fruit for God as he shows in Philippians 4:11-13

> *"I have learned, in whatever state I am, therein to be content: I know how to be abased, and I know how to be abound. Everywhere and in everything and in all things I have learned both to be full and to be hungry, both to abound and to suffer need. I can do all things through Christ who strengthen me."*

Paul was content whether he was in jail or when he was preaching.God is glorified when we do not live for self, but for Him.

> *"And He died for all, that those who live should live no longer for themselves, but for Him who died for them and rose again"* (2 Corinthians 5:15). *"For if we live, we live to the Lord; and if we die, we die to the Lord"* (Romans 14:8).

The unsaved usually live for themselves; we as God's children need to live for Him. (6)

We glorify God when we see life from an eternal perspective. For those who do not believe in God, life on this earth is all there is; so many strive for money, popularity, power and prestige. Paul's perspective was to focus on developing eternal values and telling others about Christ. *"… so now also Christ will be magnified in my body, whether by life or by death. For to me, to live is Christ, and to die is gain"* (Philippians 1:20 -21).

We glorify God when we serve Him with cheerfulness. *"Serve the Lord with gladness"* (Psalms 100:2). Unless we serve the Lord with gladness, we don't bring glory to Him. There are those who do jobs within a church because no one else will do it. They don't enjoy doing it, and it shows. Some employees work reluctantly, always complaining. Their employer cuts their health benefits, and they complain. The employer had to do it or else cut some of his employees. We are to be like the faithful employees who work with gladness. We need to have gratitude that we have a job when there are those who are unemployed. When we have a cheerful disposition, it glorifies God.

God is glorified when we stand up for His truths. *"…I found it necessary to write to you exhorting you to contend earnestly for the faith"* (Jude 3). Jude is emphasizing the important relationship between correct doctrine and true faith. The truth of the Bible gives us the real facts about Jesus and salvation and therefore should not be compromised. Much of God's glory lies in His truth. We need to be advocates for His truth so we can glorify God.

Another way that we can glorify God is by praising Him. *"Whoever offers praise glorifies Me"* (Psalms 50:23). *"I will praise You, O Lord my God with all my heart, and I will glorify Your Name forevermore"* (Psalms 86:12). When we give praise to God in the eyes of others, we are displaying the trophies of His excellence. Our hearts should be full of praise all the time for what He is doing for us and the promises that He has given us.

We glorify God through our eating and drinking and all that we do. *"Therefore, whether you eat or drink, or whatever you do, do all to the glory of God."* (I Corinthians 10:31). God's love must direct our motives in all that we do so we bring glory to Him. A couple good questions that will help guide us in our quest for God's glory should be: "Will this action bring glory to God?" or "How can I bring honor to God through this action?" (7)

When a person becomes a born-again Christian through our witness and we help him or her to mature, it glorifies God. *"My little children, for whom I labor in birth again until Christ is formed in you…"* (Galatians 4:19).

When we give God the glory for all that we do, it glorifies Him. *"Will a man rob God"* (Malachi 3:8)? We rob God when we take the glory due to God. We bring glory to God when our walks are holy walks. *"He who says he abides in Him ought himself also to walk just as He walked"* (1 John 2:6). Jesus' walk of obedience is a pattern for Christians to follow. We bring glory to Him when we walk as He walked. A sinful life brings dishonor to God.

Our desire should be to bring glory to God because His Word instructs us to do so. It brings joy to our hearts when we glorify Him, the one who created us, who died for us and gave us eternal life when we put our faith in Him. It will be a great comfort in your dying days to know that you have glorified God in your life. Let's finish the race by bringing glory to God in our lives now.

When our race is over and we stand before God, we will want to hear the words, "Well done, thou good and faithful child." When you hear those words, you will know that you have finished strong. I trust that God's Word and the words you have read in this book will encourage you to **finish strong God's way** so that you will glorify Him, the one who has done everything for you.

Endnotes

Chapter 1 – Finishing Strong
1. Gary Bruland, *Christian Life: Running Well, Finishing Strong, 2 Timothy 4:6-8,* (www.preaching.com).
2. Dr. Jim Feeney, *Crossing the Finish Line, Finishing Strong, (The Race is Not to the Swift)*, (www.jimfeeney.org/finishstrong.html).
3. Gary Bruland, *Christian Life: Running Well, Finishing Strong,* 2 Timothy 4:6-8.
4. The MacArthur Study Bible, footnotes on 2 Timothy 4:6-8, (Nashville: Thomas Nelson, Inc., 1982).
5. Ibid.
6. Ibid.

Chapter 2 – Knowing That You Are a Bible-Believing Christian
1. Pastor Merlyn Jones, "Can a Christian Be Saved & Backslide?" sermon preached at First Baptist Church, Otsego, Michigan, January 10, 2010.
2. Ibid.
3. Ibid.
4. Ibid.
5. The MacArthur Study Bible, footnotes on 1 John 2:19, (Nashville: Thomas Nelson, Inc., 1982).
6. Pastor Merlyn Jones, *"Can a Christian Be Saved & Backslide?"*
7. Pastor Merlyn Jones, "Can a Person Who is Saved Choose Not to Follow Christ?" sermon preached at First Baptist Church, Otsego, Michigan, January 17, 2010.
8. Ibid.
9. The MacArthur Study Bible, footnotes on Romans 8:14-16.

Chapter 3 – Knowing Your True Identity
1. J.L. Packer, *Knowing God*, (Intervarsity Press, June 24, 1993), page 228.
2. Ibid, page 201.
3. Ibid, page 205.

4. Myles Munroe, *Rediscovering the Kingdom*, pp172-174, (www.youtube.com/watch?v=j9XB5ntqITo).
5. J.L. Packer, *Knowing God*, p 213.
6. Ibid, pp 219-220.
7. Ibid, p 238.

Chapter 4 – Learning From Bible Heroes
1. Max Lucado, *Cast of Characters*, (Thomas Nelson Publishing Inc., 2008), pp 138-139.
2. John L. Kachelman, Jr., *Nehemiah – Great Duty Cannot Be Shirked*, www.churchesofchrist.net/authors/John_L_Kachelman_Jr/.../nehemiah.ht...[
3. The MacArthur Study Bible, footnotes on Daniel 1:8. (Nashville: Thomas Nelson Publishing Inc., 1982).
4. J.L. Packer, *Knowing God*, (Intervarsity Press, June 24, 1993), pp 30-31.
5. Gene Taylor, (www.expositorysermonoutlines.com).
6. Author Unknown.

Chapter 5–Utilizing the Power of Prayer
1. Life Application Bible, footnote on Psalm 51:10, (Wheaton: Tyndale House Publishers Inc., 1989).
2. Ibid, footnotes on 1 John 3:21.
3. The MacArthur Study Bible footnotes on John 14:23-24. (Nashville: Thomas Nelson Publishing Inc., 1982).
4. R.A. Torrey, *How to Pray*, (Whitaker House, 1983), page 46.
5. The MacArthur Study Bible, notes on 1 John 14:23-24.
6. R.A. Torrey, *How to Pray*, page 36.
7. Life Application Bible, footnotes on John 1:7.
8. Charles Stanley, *Handle with Prayer*, (Victory Books 1982), pages 57-58.
9. Fred R. Brock, Jr., *The Power of Prayer*, (Regular Baptist Press, 1975), page 2.
10. Henry T. & Richard Blackaby, *Experiencing God Day-By-Day*, (Broadman & Holman Publishing, 1997), page 9.
11. Charles Stanley, *Handle with Prayer*, page 75.
12. MacArthur Study Bible, footnotes on John 14:13-14.
13. Frederick W. Faber, *My God, How Wonderful You Art*, 1848.
14. Henry T. & Richard Blackaby, *Experiencing God Day-By-Day*, page 257.
15. Ibid, page 191.
16. Life Application Bible, footnotes on Romans 8:26-27.
17. Charles Stanley, *Handle with Prayer*, pages 71-72.
18. R. A. Torrey, *How to Pray*, pages 59-60.
19. Ibid, pages 59-60.

Chapter 6–Allowing the Holy Spirit to Control Your Life
1. John Piper, *Holy Spirit*, Galatians 5:25, (desiringGod.org).
2. Ibid.
3. Life Application Bible, footnotes on Galatians 5:22-23, (Wheaton: Tyndale House Publisher Inc., 1989).
4. John Piper, *Holy Spirit*, Galatians 5:25, (desiringGod,org).

5.   Ibid.
6.   Matthew Henry's Commentary on the Whole Bible, notes on Romans 15:13.

Chapter 7 – Living by Faith
1.   Matthew J. Slick, message on *Faith*, Christian Apologetics & Research Ministry @ Matthew J Slick, 1995-2010, (Carm.org).
2.   The MacArthur Study Bible, footnotes on Romans 1:17, (Nashville: Thomas Nelson Publishing Inc., 1982).
3.   Ibid, Galatians 5:5.
4.   Matthew J. Slick, message on *Faith*, (carm.org/matt-slick0).
5.   Ibid.
6.   The MacArthur Study Bible, footnotes on Hebrews 11:7.
7.   Life Application Bible, footnotes on Hebrews 1:7, (Wheaton: Thomas Nelson Publishing, 1982).
8.   Ibid, footnotes on Genesis 22:1-19.

Chapter 8 – Putting on the Whole Armor of God
1.   The MacArthur Study Bible, footnotes on Ephesians 6:10. (Nashville: Thomas Nelson Publishing Inc., 1982).
2.   Albert Barnes' N.T. Commentary notes on Ephesians 6:10.
3.   Matthew Henry's Commentary notes on Ephesians 6:12.
4.   The MacArthur Study Bible, footnotes on Ephesians 6:13.
5.   Matthew Henry Commentary notes on Ephesians 6:13.
6.   Albert Barnes' N.T. *Commentary* notes on Ephesians 6:14.
7.   The MacArthur Study Bible, footnotes on Ephesians 6:14.
8.   Albert Barnes' Commentary notes on Ephesians 6:14.
9.   The MacArthur Study Bible, footnotes on Ephesians 6:14.
10. Charles Stanley, *Handbook with Prayer*, (Victory Books, 1977), page 114.
11. The MacArthur Study Bible, footnotes on Ephesians 6:15.
12. Albert Barnes' *N.T. Commentary* notes on Ephesians 6:15.
13. Charles Stanley, *Handle with Prayer*, pages 114-115.
14. The MacArthur Study Bible, footnotes on Ephesians 6:15.
15. Albert Barnes' Commentary notes on Ephesians 6:15.
16. Matthew Henry *N.T. Commentary* notes on Ephesians 6:15.
17. David Ben Yakov, *The Armor of God*, (www.delusionresistance.org/christian/armor.html).
18. Ibid.
19. Albert Barnes' Commentary notes on Ephesians 6:16.
20. Matthew Henry's Commentary notes on Ephesians 6:17.
21. The MacArthur Study Bible, footnotes on Ephesians 6:17.
22. David Ben Yakov, *The Armor of God*.
23. Charles Stanley, *Handle with Prayer*, pages 116-117.
24. David Ben Yakov, *The Armor of God*.
25. The MacArthur Study Bible, footnotes on Ephesians 6:17.
26. John Wesley's *O & N Commentary*, notes on Ephesians 6:17.
27. Ibid.
28. David Ben Yakov, *The Armor of God*.

29. Albert Barnes' *N.T. Commentary* notes on Ephesians 5:18.
30. Albert Barnes' *N.T. Commentary* notes on Ephesians 6:15.

Chapter 9 – Living a Life of Joy
1. Stephan Brown, *Christian Joy*, (www.sermoncentral.com/christian-joy-stephan).
2. Ibid.
3. The MacArthur Study Bible, footnotes on Hebrews 12:2, (Nashville: Thomas Nelson Publishing Inc., 1982).
4. Ibid.
5. Albert Barnes' *New Testament Commentary* notes on Galatians 5:22.
6. Adam Clark's Commentaries, notes on Romans 14:17.
7. Robertson's *NT Word Pictures Commentary*, notes on Luke 10:21.
8. Stephan Brown, Christian Joy, (www.sermomcentral.com/christian-joy-stephan).
9. John Maxwell, *Partner in Prayer*, Thomas Nelson Publishers, 1906, page 73.

Chapter 10 – Becoming More Christlike
1. Dr. John Stott's Final Sermon: *The Model Becoming More Like Christ*, August 17, 2007, www.christiantoday.com/article/john.stott.final.sermon.
2. The MacArthur Study Bible, footnotes on Ephesians 5:18, (Nashville: Thomas Nelson Publishing Inc., 1982).
3. "Dr. John Stott's Final Sermon: The Model Becoming More Like Christ." www.christiantoday.com/article/john.stott.final.sermon.
4. The MacArthur Study Bible, footnotes on John 13:4-6.
5. Ibid, John 13:4-6.
6. Life Application Bible, footnotes on Ephesians 5:2, (Wheaton: Tyndale House Inc., 1989).
7. Ibid, 1 Peter 2:18-21.
8. Albert Barnes' *N.T. Commentary*, notes on Revelation 3:11.
9. Brian Pepper, *Walking with Jesus*, bibleinsong.com/Sermons/ChristianlifeWalking.

Chapter 11 – Building Christian Character
1. Pastor Terry Vaughan, *Christian Character*,
2. www.sermoncentral.com/sermons/christian-characters-terry. Life Application Bible footnotes on Luke 9:62, (Wheaton: Tyndale House Publishers Inc., 1989).
3. The MacArthur Study Bible, footnotes on John 8:32-33, (Nashville: Thomas Nelson Publishing Inc., 1982).
4. 4. Ibid.
5. Pastor Terry Vaughan, *Christian Character*.
6. Life Application Bible, footnotes on Timothy 3:15
7. 7. The MacArthur Study Bible, footnotes on Titus 2:2.
8. 8Life Application Bible, footnotes on Titus 2:3.
9. 9Pastor Terry Vaughan, *Christian Character*.
10. Ibid.
11. Life Application Bible, footnotes on Luke 9:62.
12. The MacArthur Study Bible, footnotes on John 8:32-33.
13. Ibid.

14. Pastor Terry Vaughan, *Christian Character*.
15. Life Application Bible, footnotes on 1Timothy 3:15.
16. The MacArthur Study Bible, footnotes on Titus 2:2.   17
17. Life Application Bible, footnotes on Titus 2:3.
18. Pastor Terry Vaughan, *Christian Character*.
19. The MacArthur Study Bible, footnotes on I Corinthians 9:27
20. Ibid, Ephesians 4:29.
21. Pastor Terry Vaughan, *Christian Character*.
22. Ibid.
23. Life Application Bible, footnotes on Luke 9:62.
24. The MacArthur Study Bible, footnotes on John 8:32-33.
25. Ibid
26. Pastor Terry Vaughan, *Christian Character*.
27. Life Application Bible, footnotes on Timothy 3:15.
28. The MacArthur Study Bible, footnotes on Titus 2:2.
29. Life Application Bible, footnotes on Titus 2:3
30. Pastor Terry Vaughan, *Christian Character*.
31. The MacArthur Study Bible, footnotes on 1 Corinthians 9:27.
32. Ibid, Ephesians 4:29.

Chapter 12–Developing a Compassion for the Lost
1. "More Than 9 in 10 Americans Continue to Believe in God"–Gallup, www.gallup.com/poll/.../americans-continue-believe-god.aspx.

Chapter 13 – Giving God's Way
1. The MacArthur Study Bible, footnotes on 2 Corinthians 8:2, (Nashville: Thomas Nelson Publishing Inc., 1982).
2. Randy L. Alcorn, *The Treasure Principle*, (Multnomah Books, A division of Random House, Inc. 2001), page 25.
3. Ibid, pages 17-18.
4. Dr. Kregg Hood, *Take God at His Word,* kregghood.com/2011/03/19/mini-campaigns-take-at-his-word/ March 19, 2011.
5. Randy L. Alcorn, *The Treasure Principle,* Pages 17-18.
6. Ibid, pp 52-53.
7. Ibid. Page 36.

Chapter 15 – Being There for the Younger Generation
1. Dr. Howard G. Hendricks, "A Mandate for Mentoring in Seven Promises of a Promise Keeper." youtube.com/watch?v=14DhLlt_Umo&feature=related.
2. Bill Brian, *Mentoring Men*, Sermoncentral.com.
3. Ibid.

Chapter 18 – Making Marriages Last a Life Time
1. The MacArthur Study Bible, footnotes on Ephesians 5:23, (Nashville: Thomas Nelson Publishing Inc., 1982).

Chapter 20 – Obeying to the End

1. Henry & Richard Blackaby & Claude King, *Experiencing God*, (Nashville: B & H Publishing Group, 2008), page 240.
2. Ibid, pages 244-243.
3. Ibid, page 243.

Chapter 21 – Leaving a Legacy

1. The MacArthur Study Bible, footnotes on Hebrews 12:1, (Nashville: Thomas Nelson Publishing Inc., 1982).
2. *People's New Testament Commentary*, notes on Hebrews 12:1.
3. Joe Stowell, *Leaving a Legacy,* www.sermoncentral.com/sermons/leaving-a-legacy-sermon.
4. Andy Knight, *Leaving a Legacy of Courage & Faith*, www.andyknight.com/article/leavingalegacyofcourageandfaith.
5. Cary Schmidt, *Done,* Lancaster: Striving Together Publication, 2005.
6. Jim Feeney, *Leaving a Spiritual Legacy*, www.jimfeeney.org/leaving-legacy-inheritance.html.
7. Ibid.
8. Ibid.

Chapter 23 – Keeping Your Eyes on Heaven

1. The MacArthur Study Bible, footnotes on 1 Peter 1:4, (Nashville: Thomas Publishing Inc., 1982).
2. Ibid, Revelation 21:18-21.
3. Dave Earley, *Truth about Heaven*, (Hal Higdon, Marathon, Rodale Press, 1993), page 52.
4. Ibid, page 94.
5. Ibid, page 95.
6. R.R. Torrey, *Heaven & Hell*, (Whitaker House, 2000), page 73.
7. Ibid. page 78.
8. Ibid. page 81.
9. The MacArthur Study Bible, footnotes on Revelation 12:7-9.
10. RA. Torrey, *Heaven & Hell*, page 120.

Chapter 24 – Living and Dying for Crowns of Priceless Worth

1. William Burkitt's *New Testament Commentary*, notes on 1 Thessalonians 2:19.
2. Matthew Henry's Commentary, notes on 1 Thessalonians 2:19-21.
3. Peter Miller, *Five Crowns of Christian Service*, www.faithclopart.com/guide/Christian-principles/new.
4. Ibid.
5. Matthew Henry's Commentary notes on 2 Timothy 4:8.
6. Albert Barnes' *N. T. Commentary* notes on 2 Timothy 4:8.
7. The MacArthur Study Bible, footnotes on 1 Peter 5:4. (Nashville: Thomas Publishing Inc., 1982).
8. Ibid, notes on 1 Thessalonians 3:5.
9. Adam Clark's Commentary notes on 1 Peter 5:4.

Chapter 25 – Bringing Glory to God

1. Abram Cooper, "Bring Glory to our Savior," hhp://www.bible-truth.org/msg2.html.
2. *Ibid.*
3. Ibid.
4. Ibid.
5. Thomas Watson, *"Man's Chief End is to Glorify God"*—Puritan and Reformed Writings, www.puritansermons.com/watson/watson5.htm.
6. Ibid.
7. Ibid.